THE NOT-SO-SPECIAL INTERESTS

THE NOT-SO-SPECIAL INTERESTS

Interest Groups, Public Representation, and American Governance

Matt Grossmann

Stanford University Press
Stanford, California

Stanford University Press
Stanford, California

Library of Congress Cataloging-in-Publication Data

Grossmann, Matthew, author.
  The not-so-special interests : interest groups, public representation, and American governance / Matt Grossmann.
    pages cm
  Includes bibliographical references and index.
    ISBN 978-0-8047-8115-2 (cloth : alk. paper)—ISBN 978-0-8047-8116-9 (pbk. : alk. paper)
    1. Pressure groups—United States. 2. Lobbying—United States. 3. Representative government and representation—United States. 4. United States—Politics and government. I. Title.

JK1118.G76 2012
324'.40973—dc23

                                                              2011044277

Typeset by Thompson Type in 10/14 Minion

In memory of Nelson W. Polsby

Contents

Acknowledgments

I could not have completed this book without the helpful contributions of my family, friends, and colleagues. The book is dedicated to my mentor, the late Nelson W. Polsby. Nelson offered witty counsel and big-picture analysis and created a scholarly community that I relied on. At Berkeley, I also benefited from great ideas and challenging feedback from Laura Stoker, Chris Ansell, Todd LaPorte, and Neil Fligstein. The project was advanced through conversations with Margaret Weir, Paul Pierson, Henry Brady, Jack Citrin, Rui De Figueiredo, Taeku Lee, Merrill Shanks, Steve Vogel, Nick Ziegler, Christine Trost, Mike Hout, Eric Shickler, Terri Bimes, Deirdre Mulligan, Bruce Cain, Pradeep Chhibber, David Karol, Dave Hopkins, Brendan Doherty, Jill Greenlee, Rachel VanSickle-Ward, Rachel Sullivan, Peter Hanson, Lee Drutman, Danielle Lussier, Amy Lerman, Rebecca Hamlin, Alison Gash, Mike Murakami, and Angelo Gonzales. Jill Hammberbeck and Scott Janczyk helped collect data.

At Michigan State, I benefited from the support and criticism of Steve Kautz, Paul Abramson, Chuck Ostrom, Dan Lee, Ryan Black, Carlos Pereira, Cristina Bodea, Eric Chang, Mike Colaresi, Josh Sapotichne, Ani Sarkissian, Jeff Conroy-Krutz, Tom Hammond, Ric Hula, Cory Smidt, Bill Jacoby, Sandy Schneider, and Eric Juenke. At other institutions, I received important feedback from McGee Young, Kristin Goss, Amy McKay, Allan Cigler, Kevin Esterling, Kay Schlozman, Kristina Miller, Michael Heaney, Ken Wald, Andrew McFarland, Mary Katzenstein, Elizabeth Sanders, Suzanne Mettler, Richard

Boyd, Gary King, Allan Brandt, Charles Shipan, John Aldrich, Scott Page, John Sides, Ray La Raja, Keena Lipsitz, Dorie Appollonio, and Rick Hall. During the publication process, I received assistance from Stacy Wagner, Jessica Walsh, and several anonymous reviewers.

My family has also been remarkably supportive. Thanks to my mother and father, Jan and Larry, as well as Mindy, Sandy, and Valerie, for their love and patience. Sarah Reckhow, my wife and colleague, deserves more credit than anyone else for encouraging me as I wrote this book, providing constant support and feedback for the last eight years.

THE NOT-SO-SPECIAL INTERESTS

Introduction

Public Factions and Organized Interests

Depending on one's perspective, Washington, DC, either is overrun by special interest groups or features the world's most active civil society. Today, more than 1,600 organizations in Washington claim to speak on behalf of public groups or issue perspectives in national politics.[1] Some of these nongovernmental advocacy organizations are household names, such as the National Rifle Association (NRA) and the Sierra Club, but most represent small constituencies and are only peripheral participants in policymaking. Beyond the familiar faces at the NAACP[2] and the Christian Coalition, for example, more than 150 organizations represent ethnic and religious groups in the nation's capital. The advocacy community has been expanding dramatically for several decades (Berry 1989; Walker 1991).

The burgeoning of advocacy raises two fundamental questions of democratic politics that this book hopes to answer. First, what types of public groups generate extensive organized representation to speak on their behalf?[3] Second, how and why do some advocacy organizations become the most prominent in public debate and the most involved in policymaking?[4] In short, who is represented, and whose voice is heard?

Commentators frequently raise more sensationalized versions of these questions. For instance, the possibility that some Indian tribes bought their way to political influence through the disgraced lobbyist Jack Abramoff was a prominent concern of 2006. The alternative story, that Abramoff extorted millions of dollars without delivering the promised favors in return, seemed just as abhorrent. If American Indians can have their voice heard in Washington only by hiring a lobbying firm and making campaign contributions, democracy seems worthy of indictment. In addition to worrying that some public groups and organizations lack a route to influence, Americans fear that powerful constituencies and organizations can wield a veto over government action. John Mearsheimer and Steven Walt (2007), for example, feign incredulity over the disproportionate influence of Washington organizations that seek to align American and Israeli foreign policy. Because these organizations seek to represent Jews in policy discussions, the authors were met with charges of anti-Semitism. The suspicion that some groups use interest groups to gain advantage over others stimulates robust and often vitriolic commentary, but these public debates also reflect the two important concerns that this book raises: How do some constituencies become better represented by interest groups than others, and why are some organizations much more successful in advocating on behalf of these groups?

Detached investigations of the implications of Washington's system of organized advocacy are not common. Both public intellectuals and political elites find it preferable to cry out against the unearned clout of the underspecified groups that they oppose. In each of the last ten sessions of Congress, for example, members have denounced the influence of "the special interests" in floor speeches at least fifty times. Opposition to these villains seems just as profitable for political candidates. In each of the last six presidential elections, candidates have vowed to oppose "the special interests" during nationally televised debates. Bills reforming lobbying, ethics, and campaign finance designed to cure undue interest-group influence are introduced in every session of Congress; reforms were passed in 1995, 2002, and 2006. On taking office, President Obama also implemented new restrictions on lobbyist participation in his administration. Each time, policymakers explain that they are finally putting an end to the poor practices of their predecessors, reducing the influence of interest groups. Meanwhile, the Washington interest-group community continues to expand, along with the amount of money spent to influence national policy.

Campaigning against interest groups and their lobbyists in Washington remains a winning political strategy, especially compared to parsing which interests are and should be well represented. During the campaign for the 2008 presidential primaries, for example, Hillary Clinton earned derision by suggesting that some lobbyists represent "real Americans," including nurses and social workers.[5] Throughout the primary process, both John Edwards and Barack Obama distinguished themselves from Clinton by stressing that they did not take money from special-interest political action committees (PACs) or lobbyists.

Popular commentators tend to position interest groups in opposition to an imagined public interest. Yet much organized advocacy is, at least in the view of the advocates, designed to advance public interests and ideas. Clinton was correct to claim that many organized advocates and lobbyists represent public groups, including broad occupations. Claims to represent public constituencies are now commonplace among professional activists. Organizations ostensibly acting on behalf of such broad social movements as environmentalism and feminism have taken up permanent residence in downtown Washington office buildings. They see themselves as exercising countervailing power against established interests.

These pretentions seem quaint in a city where billionaires fund networks of public-interest advocacy organizations, including some that have been active in policymaking for decades. Each new organization designed to plug a hole in the advocacy system seems less imaginative than the last; each new tactic deployed to bring a silent majority from the grassroots to the Capitol appears less innovative. Even the Tea Party protests of 2009 and 2010, touted as a new form of political mobilization against special-interest politics, were organized with support from Americans for Tax Reform and FreedomWorks, two of the nation's most established conservative advocacy organizations.

Social scientists usually study advocacy organizations as nongovernmental civil society actors. Nevertheless, they are now an important component of national political institutions rather than outsiders to American governance. As such, they raise important concerns for public representation and American democracy. Behind the fearmongering about the Israel lobby, for example, is a legitimate concern that some constituencies may use interest groups to become substantially more influential than their opponents. Likewise, the Abramoff affair was scandalous because it raised the concern that constituencies such as American Indians may have to resort to sordid methods of buying influence due to their lack of representation. Despite the heightened public rhetoric, most assertions of undue influence involve unproven assumptions and shaky empirical foundations. To move past polemics and toward credible evaluations of democratic government, Americans must return to fundamental empirical questions about political representation and governance.

The Big Questions

In seeking to understand the types of public groups that generate extensive organized representation to speak on their behalf, I ask whether the characteristics of the individuals in a public group are related to how well that group is represented by political organizations. For example, how do the attributes of doctors and Jews in the American population relate to the extent to which these groups have organizations representing their interests in Washington? Answering this question helps citizens understand one important aspect of the broader question of who is represented in the political system.

In seeking to understand how and why some advocacy organizations become the most prominent in public debate and the most involved in policymaking, I ask how the characteristics of organizations affect their ability to draw attention from the media and gain a hearing in the branches of the federal government. For example, why are organizations like the NAACP and the NRA successful? How do their organizational attributes affect their prominence in print, television, and online news as well as their involvement in congressional, administrative, and judicial politics? Answering this question should illuminate an important facet of the wider question of whose voice is heard in American governance.

These two research questions relate to the perennial questions of political science: Whose interests and ideas are represented by political leaders, articulated in political debate, and incorporated in policymaking? These questions, although formulated in distinct terms, have long been at the heart of the discipline.[6] Harold Lasswell (1958) famously asked: "Who gets what, when, and how?" He saw politics as a competition over goods obtained from government. Some interests were more equipped to win these battles, and the results would likely reveal evidence of their disproportionate influence. E. E. Schattschneider (1960) was similarly interested in the "mobilization of bias" in the political system. He believed that all political institutions advanced some interests at the expense of others and sought to explain the interests that gain from each stage in the process of mobilization and influence. Robert Dahl (1961) asked simply: "Who governs?" He was not convinced that the beneficiaries of government action were always its proponents; he directed attention to the processes of decision making and the visible actions and stated motivations of decision makers. In theory and in practice, political scientists have long endeavored to find out why some political factions succeed whereas others fail and in what way public groups are represented in political institutions.

Advocacy organizations are now central actors in both processes. The organization of factions takes place in the advocacy system. Public political interests and ideas are articulated by sectors of advocacy organizations. These organizations are included in public debate and policymaking as the presumed representatives of public constituencies. Understanding "who governs" requires an investigation of which groups are best represented in the advocacy system and which organizations are included in the policymaking process. Not every route to policy influence runs through the advocacy system; politicians also represent public ideas and interests. Yet we cannot understand "who gets what" without considering the "mobilization of bias" in this important arena.

Two large tasks are involved in this consideration. First, to find out who develops the most representation in the advocacy system, this study connects organized leaders to their claimed public constituencies. Different ethnic, religious, occupational, and ideological groups have generated dramatically different levels of organized representation. The differential mobilization of some public groups over others in the advocacy system likely affects who wins and loses in the American political system. Asking the question of which constituencies are represented by advocacy organizations will answer several important related questions: Do only small and financially affluent groups develop extensive representation? Do groups with extreme views generate more organized representation than groups with ideological moderates? Do public groups need to be interested in politics and attentive to current events to generate and support organized leaders? Are some categories of groups inherently excluded from political representation by advocacy organizations? Each of these questions can be assessed with a broader investigation of which public constituencies are best represented by advocacy organizations.

Scholars already know much about the most obvious bias in the interest-mobilization process: the overrepresentation of business interests and government entities (Salisbury 1984). According to some scholars, representation of public constituencies by advocacy groups is an important countervailing force against the strength of business representation (Berry 1999). Nevertheless, one cannot assume that every public group benefits equally from the mobilization of advocacy organizations. Why, for example, do gun-control opponents have better representation than proponents? Why are Jews better represented than Catholics?[7] Substantial differences among groups are apparent in their levels of organizational mobilization, their participation in public political debate, and their involvement in the policymaking process. To examine the reasons particular public groups benefit from interest-group representation, this study identifies groups in American society and asks how their characteristics affect the extent of their organized representation and its inclusion in media debates and policymaking institutions.

People may naturally disagree about what constitutes "better" representation of one group over another. Representation, in its fullest sense, incorporates the content of advocacy as well as the pretense to stand in for others. Jews have many organizations claiming to represent them but may still be dissatisfied with the actions of their leaders. This study assesses which groups have organizations claiming to represent them and the way these organizations act in the political arena. One can view the prominence of Jewish organizations in Washington as evidence that Jews as a public group have mobilized in the advocacy community. The study does not imply, however, that every organization claiming to represent a constituency does so effectively or even honestly. Organizations refine constituent complaints, aggregate their demands, and relate them to the policy agenda (Hansen 1991, 229). Whatever the content of their advocacy, however, organized representatives may be dependent on the character of the public constituencies they claim to represent.

The second key question moves from the public groups to the organizations: How and why do some advocacy organizations become prominent voices in the news media and frequent participants in policymaking institutions? It is not obvious why any nongovernmental leaders should be brought into the policymaking process or why Washington organizations should be sought to speak on behalf of whole categories of people or widely held issue positions. Their involvement raises several questions: Why do the official public servants, policymakers, bring advocacy organizations into governing for this purpose? Why do journalists call someone in Washington to find out what social groups like evangelicals or doctors think about policy proposals? How do some organizations gain representative status? An organization like the NAACP, for example, can become so prominently associated with representation of African Americans that observers view political candidates' decisions to skip its convention as an affront to an entire racial group. Similarly, an organization like the American Bar Association (ABA) is so deeply associated with the representation of lawyers that it has obtained an official role in evaluating federal court nominees.

Even if some organizations are invited to be regular participants in policymaking, it is not clear who will be sought after. Given the ubiquity of organized representation in Washington, relatively few of the more than 1,600 advocacy organizations become prominent players in national politics. AARP and the American Medical Association (AMA), to use two successful examples, are unquestionably important actors in national politics. To quantify their prominence and involvement, this study observes that both organizations frequently appear at public congressional hearings, in Washington newspapers, in behind-the-scenes administrative rulemaking procedures, and in televised newscasts. Many other organizations, however, make the same representative claims, derive their support from similar constituencies, and compete for attention from the same set of policymakers. Yet reporters and policymakers do not regularly seek out their views. Advocacy groups are available to speak on many different sides of most policy issues, but not all gain a hearing. Scholars have only limited knowledge of the determinants of their success or failure. By asking which factors determine advocacy organization prominence and involvement, one can reach conclusions about related questions: Do organizations need to mobilize public supporters to succeed? Do they need to hire lobbyists and provide campaign contributions? Do they need to specialize in only a few issue areas? To understand the influence of each of these factors, this study characterizes advocacy organizations and investigates why a select few become the most prominent and involved.

The Argument

Advocates for many different types of social groups and political perspectives have mobilized in organizations designed to influence national political decisions, but some groups and perspectives are much better represented than others, and some organizations are much more prominent and involved than others. To explain the relative representation of public groups, this book uses a new theory called Behavioral Pluralism. To explain why some organizations representing these groups are more successful than others, it uses a new theory called Institutionalized Pluralism. Table I.1 outlines the concepts used in each theory and their components.

Independent   *Depends*

TABLE I.1. Concepts in the analysis.

	Units of interest	Significant characteristics	Relevant process	Important outcome
Behavioral Pluralism	Public groups (constituencies of advocacy organizations)	Civic and political capacity (community involvement, political interest, efficacy)	Development of organized representation	Better representation (more organizations and staff representing interests in D.C.)
Institutionalized Pluralism	Advocacy organizations (representatives of social groups and issue perspectives)	Structural attributes (size, longevity, membership, issue agenda)	Institutionalization as public representatives and policy debate participants	Success (prominence in media and involvement in policymaking)

Behavioral Pluralism suggests that advocacy organizations represent the distinct interests and ideas of public groups in proportion to the civic and political capacity of those groups. Certain public groups, such as Jews, lawyers, and gun owners, develop substantially more representation than others; more spokespersons for these groups appear in the advocacy community. The development of sectors of organized representatives that claim to speak for these public groups is dependent on the characteristics of their public constituencies. In other words, groups in the American public consisting of civically and politically engaged constituents are more likely to develop an extensive organized leadership to speak on their behalf. The average characteristics of public constituencies influence their level of organized political mobilization through multiple mechanisms: Constituencies with more civic and political capacity are more likely to produce stronger leaders, more extensive support networks, and a group-level reputation for political interest and involvement. As a result, the advantages of extensive organized representation accrue to those public groups that are involved in their communities, interested in politics, and efficacious about their participation.[10]

To explain the reasons some advocacy organizations representing these groups succeed, Institutionalized Pluralism suggests that certain organizations become the presumed representatives of public groups in all types of media and all branches of government. Some advocacy organizations are taken for granted as surrogates for public groups and perspectives. Their structural attributes enable them to play these legitimized roles in public representation and policy deliberation. Advocacy organizations succeed if they possess attributes that match these roles: They mobilize members, create a lasting and large presence in Washington, and articulate many policy positions. Organizations with these features become prominent in public debate and involved in policymaking institutions because reporters and policymakers see them as public representatives and expert policy proponents. As government officials and the media take the roles of these organizations as public spokespersons and issue advocates for granted, the groups become institutionalized participants in political debate and policymaking. As a result, policymakers see the same advocacy organizations repeatedly, and Americans find the usual suspects in all media outlets and policy venues.[11]

These theories are meant to provide the context for understanding public group representation and advocacy organization involvement in American governance, but they do not attempt to exhaust all of the factors that influence the success of individual constituencies and organizations. Like studies of electoral politics, interest-group research should strive to explain the big picture determinants of who wins and loses while investigating the strategies and histories of individual organizations. Electoral politics research has successfully shown that election outcomes are predictable based on economic conditions, party strength, and basic candidate attributes like experience, even though some candidates underperform and outperform their expectations based on strategic decisions and historical contingencies. In comparison, interest-group research is far too concentrated on the microlevel concerns of organizational history and strategy, without fully exploring the macrolevel context that makes some political factions and organizations much more likely to succeed. Just as the United States produces many more candidates than elected officials, it has a broad array of interest groups but a smaller subset of regular participants in governance. Just as only a few of the many potential electoral constituencies can swing election outcomes, a minority of political factions produces substantial organized representation. The key hindrance to macrolevel understanding has been the insistence on using rational choice models of microlevel exchanges designed to predict organizational mobilization and influence. Neither of this book's theories relies predominantly on exchange. Instead, both return to the original pluralist formulation of interest-group theory, adding ideas from the literatures on mass political behavior and organizational sociology to produce a macrolevel view of how public factions organize and succeed in political advocacy.

The American advocacy system empowers a few unelected leaders to speak repeatedly on behalf of some public constituencies. The advocacy system is premised on the democratic expectations of bringing everyone into the process and giving all views a fair hearing. The vague allegiance to these political values is widespread in the political system, giving advocacy-organization leaders an important space to fill in the political process. The system establishes some organizations as intermediaries between public groups and policymakers, serving as permanent surrogates for public subpopulations. It also gives some societal groups a louder voice in national politics by allowing their leadership a more prominent role in policy debate. Reliance on advocacy organizations by the American government thus advances some ideas and interests much more than others.

Returning to the Problem of Factions

The proliferation of advocacy organizations in Washington may be relatively new, but the questions raised by their activities are not. Questions about which interests benefit from the political process and which actors gain positions of power in governance are at least as old as the American system of government. Empirical observations of the relative influence of some groups over others can be retraced to the founding era. Normative criticisms leveled at inequalities among citizens have typically accompanied these observations of disproportionate influence. Americans' shared faith in the functioning of democracy and popular governance seems to depend, in part, on the way they see group influence operating in government. As a result, the answers to narrower questions about public group representation by advocacy organizations and their role in government have important implications for some long-standing empirical and normative concerns about democratic government.

In the most famous text written in support of the American constitution, James Madison articulated an empirical theory of politics to justify his analysis of the purpose of government. The cause of political conflict, he argued, is the human tendency to form factions; the proper role of government is to channel factional mobilization into competition within public institutions:

> The latent causes of faction are thus sown in the nature of man; and we see them everywhere brought into different degrees of activity, according to the different circumstances of civil society. A zeal for different opinions concerning religion, concerning government, and many other points, as well of speculation as of practice; an attachment to different leaders ambitiously contending for pre-eminence and power; or to persons of other descriptions whose fortunes

have been interesting to the human passions, have, in turn, divided mankind into parties, inflamed them with mutual animosity, and rendered them much more disposed to vex and oppress each other than to co-operate for their common good . . . The regulation of these various and interfering interests forms the principal task of modern legislation, and involves the spirit of party and faction in the necessary and ordinary operations of the government. (*Federalist 10*)

Madison's characterization of the political process remains pertinent; he identifies several basic features of democratic politics. First, differences of interest, social allegiance, and opinion in a society produce multiple and conflicting groups to compete over collective decision making. Second, new interests and new conflicts among groups arise as a society matures. Third, the operation of government necessarily involves cooperation and competition among these groups. This conception of politics as factional competition has been an enduring foundation of the popular and scholarly understanding of government. In the group theory of politics, Bentley (1935) and Truman (1951) later extended these ideas and explored their implications for the governing process.

Madison's normative concerns have also continued to play an important role in attitudes toward the limitations and potential of American government. A recurrent debate addresses whether the constitutional system succeeds in controlling the effects of faction. Distress about the differential influence of some interests over others has been a chief mark of political critique in every period. This concern about interest groups, for example, served as the underpinning for many of the reforms of the Progressive Era, including moves toward direct democracy. A similar concern continues to animate modern movements for reform of political campaigns and the legislative process.

Nevertheless, political factions do not always garner such an adverse name. In the most cited analysis of American democracy, Alexis de Tocqueville (1835) celebrated the tendency of Americans to form associations to advance their interests. The process of developing shared ideas and the motivation to combine actions to achieve collective goals is, for de Tocqueville, the essence of democracy in practice. Many contemporary critics agree that, for democracy to succeed, citizens must actively engage in political decision making through associations (Putnam 2000; Skocpol 2003). In contemporary parlance, the impulse to form factions also produces "civic engagement."

Scholars and public intellectuals all seem to resist accepting the basic trade-off involved in political mobilization: People generally cooperate in order to compete. They mobilize to pursue shared interests and ideas when those interests or ideas are thought to be different from those of other groups. The organization of civil society that Americans admire is dependent on the impulse to mobilize into interest groups that Americans detest. Citizens, scholars, and popular commentators often insist that some qualitative difference separates interest groups that they admire from those they detest. In practice, these normative distinctions among groups rarely conform to actual groups' formation or behavior (James 2004; Mathiowetz 2008). Groups of all kinds, for example, involve fluid boundaries among members, combinations of motivations involving both ideas and interests, and particularistic claims that conflict with the ideas and interests of others (Mansbridge 1992; Post and Rosenblum 2002). Even in cases where popular participation and influence expand dramatically across constituencies, people are often dissatisfied with the results (Fiorina 1999).

The problem of factions, including their inevitability and consequences, constitutes a foundational dilemma of democracy. Interest mobilization, the process by which factions come to be represented in the political system, is a fundamental element of democratic participation. Interest aggregation, the process by which the ideas and concerns of factions are integrated in political institutions and policies, is a basic feature of democratic governance. The description of these processes and the explanation of why they unfold as they do should be a primary curiosity for all observers of democracy.

What's New Here?

This book revisits the problem of factions with a fresh theoretical perspective and new empirical data. The focus is on national advocacy organizations and the constituencies they represent. Rather than merely isolating and analyzing one set of actors, however, the study of these organizations is designed to be a lens for understanding the means by which public factions involve themselves in political decision making. As a result, the book blends the analysis of political competition within institutions with the analysis of public political behavior. The analysis centers on the intermediaries, the organizations that stand between public groups and government, and connects their behavior to the characteristics of the public subpopulations that they represent, as well as the many targets of their advocacy.

A New Approach

The book's focus on the role of the advocacy system in interest aggregation is inspired by a recent turn in political science literature that emphasizes the connections among group mobilization, interest representation, and governance. Scholars of legislative politics (Sulkin 2005; Bishin 2009) now contend that policymaker actions are impossible to understand without connecting investigations of government institutions and public political behavior. They seek macropolitical theories, accounting for congressional behavior by incorporating the ideas and interests of public constituencies. Scholars studying interest groups have likewise argued that their subfield can return to high status in political science by updating its foundations in pluralist theory. Virginia Gray and David Lowery (2004) and Andrew McFarland (2004) label this suggested reformulation "neopluralism." This book extends the neopluralist perspective by introducing two theories with the marks of both traditional pluralist assumptions and recent scholarly innovations. First, Behavioral Pluralism combines the original ideas of group theory with contemporary analysis of individual political behavior to predict which public groups will be best represented in Washington. Second, Institutionalized Pluralism combines pluralist ideas about the way interest groups serve as intermediaries in democratic politics with contemporary ideas borrowed from organizational theory to predict which organized leaders' voices will be heard in national political debates.[12]

These macropolitical theories are used to understand how public political factions organize for involvement in American national politics. Scholars of particular social groups, policy areas, and political institutions could all benefit from a better understanding of the way public constituencies are represented by organized advocates in political debates. If interest-group research regains this breadth, it can become useful to scholars throughout the discipline.

New Evidence

The research program here begins with original data on the activities and characteristics of organizations that claim to speak for public constituencies along with data on the characteristics of public groups they claim to represent. First, the study identifies more than 1,600 advocacy organizations with a presence in Washington and categorizes them based on the people or perspective they claim to represent. Second, it identifies hundreds of public constituencies that have generated some level of organized representation in

Washington. Third, it measures the prominence of each organization and each sector of representative organizations in the print, television, and online media and the involvement of each organization and sector in congressional testimony, presidential directives, administrative rulemaking, and federal litigation. Fourth, the study compiles aggregate public-opinion-survey data to measure the characteristics of public constituencies (such as Jews, physicians, and environmentalists) that may influence the extent of their organized representation, including their demographic traits and levels of public engagement, civic involvement, and political participation. Fifth, the study uses new data on dozens of factors that might influence each organization's prominence or involvement, including measures of its structure and issue agenda and its ties to public membership, financial contributions, and issue expertise. Sixth, qualitative material from interviews with policymakers and organizational leaders helps flesh out the mechanisms by which some advocacy organizations become institutionalized participants in policymaking.

New Implications

Beyond the specific results of this analysis, the findings point toward an important new perspective on the advocacy system in American government. The underlying processes of public-group mobilization and interest representation appear to be uniform across the political spectrum. Organizational leaders are unable to succeed independently of the characteristics of their constituency and their organization, regardless of their political views or tactics. Similarly, public groups do not generate extensive representation unless they have the civic and political capacity, no matter the ideas or group interests they share.

To understand the way some groups or perspectives gain advantage in political debate, scholars often examine the biases of policymakers or media outlets. This study, however, finds few differences in which voices are heard across media outlets or policy venues and few differences in success between conservative and liberal advocacy groups. Rather than assume that who gets a seat at the table is a function of the political biases of the news media or the differences in policymaking across the branches of government, scholars should acknowledge an alternative: The relative mobilization of different public groups in the advocacy system may be reflected in all arenas. The same groups gain advantage in all outlets and venues for the same underlying reasons.

The analysis also has important implications for public representation. It suggests that Americans have created a system that relies on organizations seen as public representatives to serve as surrogates for important constituencies and perspectives in political discussions. When political elites speak of the opinions of the "black community" for example, they often refer to the expressed opinions of organized leaders. This mode of public-group representation through organizational sectors may be as important to the political process as the traditional idea that policymakers respond to public opinion as a whole or the notion that public opinion influences government through its expression in elections. Group opinions may find their way into the governing process through organized advocates as often as aggregate public opinion influences policy decisions and as often as individual opinions influence election results.

From a normative standpoint, the analysis suggests that recent anxieties about special-interest politics are mere restatements of old concerns about the role of factions in democratic government. Americans remain uneasy about whether organized leaders can properly represent public groups and whether the conflicting ideas and interests of the public can be incorporated into policymaking. The role of the organizations that claim to speak on behalf of public groups or perspectives reinforces these two concerns. Advocacy organizations are taken as surrogates for broad constituencies, even though they may have only tenuous connections to their supporters. Policymakers and media elites take it for granted that they incorporate multiple public ideas and interests by listening to competing voices from this set of organizations, which represent heavily mobilized groups. The organization of factions predictably reinforces inequalities among public groups and among their presumed leaders.

The Structure of the Book

This analysis proceeds in two parts. Part I investigates who is represented; it analyzes the public constituencies of national advocacy organizations. It begins by cataloging the breadth of interest representation in Washington in Chapter 1. A wide range of public groups associated with a great diversity of interests and ideas mobilize to influence national politics. This public-group representation does not necessarily involve membership organizations; many organizations claim to represent public groups without having members. Although hundreds of public groups have some representatives, enormous differences appear in levels of representation. Some public groups generate substantially more organizations, staff, and lobbyists to speak on their behalf. The most highly represented groups do not fall easily into any one category; a few ideological, occupational, and ethnic groups have a great deal of political representation, but most public groups in each of these categories have minimal representation.

Chapter 2 explains differences in representation across public groups by articulating and testing a theory called "Behavioral Pluralism." To explain why some groups generate more representation than others, it aggregates the analysis of individual political participation to the group level. From this perspective, socially engaged, politically efficacious, and civically involved constituencies are likely to generate the most extensive representation to speak on their behalf, no matter the size of the group and no matter the views they espouse. The explanation for which groups are best represented relies on describing the social and political behavior of constituencies in the mass public, rather than by categorizing types of interests. To test these ideas, the study merges data on the prominence of over 100 sectors of organizations with data on the aggregate demographics, levels of social and political engagement, and political views of their constituencies. The chapter offers some of the first tests of whether larger constituencies, those of higher socioeconomic status, or those with extreme views generate more organized representation in Washington. The evidence suggests that political attentiveness and civic involvement among constituencies explain more than any of these factors.

Chapter 3 moves the focus to the characteristics of the organizations that claim to represent public groups in national politics. It demonstrates that the organizations representing these constituencies differ dramatically in their scale, scope, and behavior, even among those representing the same constituency. The findings consistently illustrate skewed distributions of resources, prominence, and involvement that imply that a small number of organizations achieve disproportionate success. Among the resourceful and successful subset, however, there is a stunning diversity of types of interests.

Part II of the book focuses on the factors that influence the success of advocacy organizations. Chapter 4 begins by introducing a theory of how and why particular advocacy organizations succeed, called "Institutionalized Pluralism." Organizations with specified structural features manage to be seen by political elites as representatives of public constituencies and spokespersons for issue perspectives. Organizations that become institutionalized into these two roles become the obvious sources in media coverage and the obvious participants in policymaking arenas. AARP serves as a case study; the chapter concludes that AARP succeeds by serving as the assumed representative of older Americans.

Chapter 5 demonstrates that the media amplify the voices of advocacy organizations that become recognized constituency representatives. The structural characteristics of organizations, rather than their ideological orientations, determine whether they gain attention from the Washington print media, the television news media, and World Wide Web publishers. Differences in the supply of organized spokespersons, not internal biases in the news media, explain the pattern of interest group source usage.

Chapter 6 demonstrates that policymakers respond to the same types of institutionalized leaders. Using data on organizational involvement in legislative hearings, regulatory agency rulemaking, federal court cases, and presidential announcements, the chapter reveals that the same organizational characteristics predict which organizations are most involved in all venues. One can explain whose voices are heard in political institutions by noting the structural characteristics of organizations rather than the particular strategies of policymakers or organized leaders. The community of participants in policymaking in Congress and the White House, however, is more representative of the broad range of interests mobilized in Washington than the same communities in administrative agencies and courts because Congress and the president act as seekers of an assembly of different advocates, rather than passive receivers of advocacy.

The conclusion explores the implications of the research for scholars' general understanding of interest mobilization and aggregation in American democracy. The tendency of all branches of government and the media to empower organized representatives to speak on behalf of public constituencies opens most policy arenas to similar casts of participants. These tendencies suggest that most normative critiques of democratic decision making are subsumed within the fundamental problems associated with political factions: whether leaders can represent broad collective interests and whether conflicting ideas and interests can be incorporated into political outcomes.

The analysis offers a revised perspective on these recurring questions, focusing on the organized representation afforded to different public groups. The book describes and analyzes a key aspect of interest mobilization and aggregation: the organization of public constituency representation in the advocacy system. This approach can focus attention on the way political factions are reflected in contemporary civil society. If the causes of faction are "sown in the nature of man" and the effects are seen in the "necessary and ordinary operations of the government," as Madison argued, an understanding of factional mobilization, as well as the associated organized competition for political influence, is essential for a coherent view of democratic government.

I WHO IS REPRESENTED?

1   Interest Groups That Speak for You and Me

When investigating which groups generate the most representation, the first question is, "Who is represented at all?" What
public groups generate organized advocates to speak on their behalf? Scholarship on interest group mobilization originally regarded this as a central question. The founding text of modern interest group research, David Truman's
The Governmental Process (1951), was concerned with whether social diversity
is reflected in organized representation. For a theory that takes groups as its
basic unit of analysis, it is quite important to identify the groups. Current research, however, has rarely revisited this question.

Interest-group researchers no longer use public groups as the starting
point for their studies. Instead, according to Allan Cigler (1991, 107), adjustments to the theories of collective action initiated by Mancur Olson dominate
interest-group-mobilization research: "By the late 1980s, a loosely integrated
body of 'incentive theory' literature had largely supplanted the pluralist model
as the subfield's main paradigm to explain group mobilization and development." Because Olson's *The Logic of Collective Action* (1965) gave scholars
less reason to expect public-group mobilization, the focus moved to the way
organizations mobilize members and away from which public constituencies generate representation. Meanwhile, however, scholars found that many
nonmembership groups represent public interests (Berry 1999). Investigating the dynamics of membership mobilization is not the same as studying

public-group representation. Scholars need to ask which public groups generate political spokespersons.

The Concept of Public Constituencies

The assumption that political leaders represent public constituencies is central to American governance. As Robert Salisbury (1992) explains, most political actors see themselves as representatives of societal segments and act in accordance with this social role:

> The most important concept in the American political system is constituency. It dominates the behavior of virtually every political actor and institution. Its corollary concept is representation . . . [In the American system,] political actors more or less consciously "look to" particular segments of the society as their primary reference points, as having by right first call over them, and see themselves as dependent on constituency approval, in this segmented sense rather than in the more general terms of "the people" or "the public interest," for their political survival. (149)

Legislators and political candidates make decisions by predicting how these public constituencies are likely to respond (Arnold 1992; Bishin 2009). Elizabeth Clemens (1997, 325) traces the development of this perspective on political leadership to the rise of advocacy groups: "In the place of a contest between 'the People' and 'the Interests,' American politics was rearranged as a contest of ever-multiplying 'partial interests' making demands on the state." Like elected officials, advocacy organizations claim to represent public constituencies. Because of the importance of this representative role, they are unlikely to arise and succeed independently of their claimed constituencies.

Political constituencies, in this book's analysis, are subpopulations of the public with a shared characteristic used by an organized leadership as the basis for representation. Constituencies vary along many dimensions, including whether their shared characteristic is an ethnic or religious tie, an occupation, a political viewpoint, or some other social quality. As examples, the NAACP claims to represent African Americans, and the Sierra Club claims to represent environmentalists. Instead of treating these types of constituencies as categorically distinct, both African Americans and environmentalists can be seen as examples of political factions; they serve as political constituencies for organized representatives.

Numerous interest organizations claim to represent social groups or public political perspectives. To capture the way these interest organizations relate to their constituencies, one can use an analogy to V. O. Key's famous tripartite division of the political party. Key (1964) sought to distinguish three of the following interrelated aspects of political parties: the party in the electorate, the party as organization, and the party in government. This theoretical frame still structures the study of political parties and the debate over their potential decline. It has the advantage of relating research on political parties to research agendas in the study of political institutions and mass behavior. It also clarifies the role of party organizations in relationship to other political actors. Interest groups can similarly be thought of as having three components, namely: (1) social, economic, or opinion groups with shared interests or concerns; (2) sectors of organizations that seek to represent those interests before government; and (3) factions within government that seek to advance the same agenda. This book focuses on the first two components, constituencies and the organizations that represent them.

The constituencies of concern here are subgroups within the American public. Scholars normally view "the public" as one unified entity or as disaggregated individuals with distinct interests and ideas. Similarly, the advocacy community is analyzed as individual organizations or one large community. The first step in this analysis is to move toward collective concepts by identifying public groups that correspond to sectors of organizations that claim to represent these groups, such as liberals, teachers, and Latinos. The second step is to redirect analysis to the group level, describing constituencies based on their aggregate characteristics and linking their group attributes to the success of the organizational sector that represents them. Some overlap occurs among these public groups and among these sectors of advocacy organizations. Nevertheless, the focus of this analysis is the potential for political mobilization associated with each group rather than the individuals belonging to multiple groups or the organizations representing multiple constituencies.

Identifying Organizations and Their Constituencies

The primary problem associated with assessing public group representation has been the lack of a population list of all potential political constituencies. This analysis circumvents the problem by looking first at the claims made by advocacy organizations for public representation. Without a complete population list of all potential political constituencies, one cannot analyze the factors that influence whether groups mobilize at all but can describe the breadth of representation.

The subpopulation of interest groups called "advocacy organizations" is the starting point. Many interest organizations act primarily as constituency representatives, behaving in a manner suggested by this function. Advocacy organizations are the subset of interest organizations that are intermediaries between public constituencies and government institutions. The constituencies may be social or occupational groups or groups with shared ideologies or issue perspectives. In their review of the division between research on interest representation in political science and sociology, Kenneth Andrews and Bob Edwards (2004) suggest the term "advocacy organizations" to include all organizations that "make public interest claims either promoting or resisting social change that, if implemented, would conflict with the social, cultural, political, or economic interests or values of other constituencies or groups" (481). This definition would include all of the organizations in this study's population.

Rather than assuming that mass membership mobilization is the process by which these constituencies become represented by interest organizations, this study outlines the distribution of organized representation among public constituencies and the structure of the organizations that seek to represent different groups. Because advocacy organizations seek to represent categories of people or public ideas, this study relies on claims of representation to link organizations with constituencies rather than membership affiliation.[1] Dara Strolovitch (2007) also locates public-group advocates by relying on their claims of representation, even though she argues that group leaders do not satisfactorily represent all of their claimed constituents.

This study compiles information about all organizations with a presence in Washington aspiring to represent a section of the public broader than their own institution and staff.[2] The names, reference-text descriptions, and websites of the organizations in the population indicate that they seek to represent American public constituencies in national politics.[3] This analysis combines the study of the organized representation of ethnic, religious, demographic, and occupational groups with the study of the organized representation of particular political perspectives (including both ideological and single-issue groups). The advocacy-organization population includes each of the organizations that Jeffrey Berry (1999) identifies as "citizen action groups," including those that others call "public interest groups" or "social movement organizations." This population is more expansive than the one used in the vast majority of interest-group analyses.[4] Of the major lobbyists identified in the most comprehensive recent study of lobbying (Baumgartner et al. 2009), the population here includes 56 percent of the participants, including those commonly classified as citizen groups, professional associations, issue coalitions, unions, and think tanks.

Not all interest organizations fall into this population of public advocates. Individual business policy offices, trade associations of companies, and governmental units are not included in this study. The population analyzed here thus excludes organizations of concern to other scholars, including most of those commonly considered "institutions." Salisbury (1984) argues that institutions are subject to different constraints in their mobilization and are unlikely to interact with policymakers as representatives of public constituencies. Even policy offices of nonprofit corporations like universities and hospitals operate like business policy offices; they primarily represent the interests of the institution, which has a nonpolitical primary orientation. As a result, this study does not use tax status to draw a line between for-profit and nonprofit organizations; many groups with the same tax status, such as a 501(c)3 designation, have very different purposes.[5] This study's population includes organizations that primarily represent public constituencies independent of the institution itself. Some organizations that Salisbury classifies as institutions, however, do claim to represent a particular social group or public issue perspective in national politics, especially church groups and ideological "think tanks," which are included in the analysis.[6] Using the same distinction, based on organizational purposes rather than tax status, Strolovitch (2007) also combines the study of membership groups with the study of some nonmembership advocacy organizations that Salisbury labels institutions.

In terms of the population of all interest organizations in Washington, the most important omissions from this analysis are individual business policy offices and business associations. Business policy offices and trade associations, according to David Hart (2004), mobilize and achieve influence through economic processes different from those used by organizations seeking to represent public groups or political perspectives. Hart recommends that scholars of business political activity use theories of the firm devised in economics, rather than theories created in interest-group studies.[7] Corporations are excluded from this analysis because their mobilization process is driven by different factors than those analyzed here, not because they lack influence.

Excluding businesses and their associations from the analysis means that this study cannot offer a complete picture of the interest-group universe.

Some scholars also separate professional associations and unions from advocacy organizations. Berry (1999), for example, analyzes "citizens' groups" independently of any group with an economic base for its political activities. The population of advocacy groups in this study is more expansive, including unions and professional associations because they seek to represent broad occupational categories rather than specific institutions.[8] For example, many professional associations, such as the AMA, claim to speak on behalf of physicians as a whole, rather than only those who join the group. Others, such as the National Medical Association (a group of African American doctors), represent ethnic and occupational subpopulations.

It is sometimes hard to draw the line between advocacy organizations and other interest groups, especially the line between occupational representatives and business associations. For example, the corn growers' association claims to represent all corn farmers, but the dry cleaners' association claims to be a business trade association, even though both represent primarily small business owners and gain disproportionate support from large members. There is some difference in their mobilization histories and public images, but it may not be of great importance. This study is generally inclusive in defining the borders of the advocacy community, even including representatives of entrepreneurs as a whole rather than industries.[9] Nevertheless, it excludes interest groups that are associations of businesses because they do not mobilize via constituencies of individual citizens and do not gain legitimacy as a representative of a public group. Whereas this distinction is less clear in marginal cases like that of corn growers and dry cleaners, it likely makes a difference in comparing associations of nurses and pharmaceutical companies or associations of professors and universities.

Methodologically, the lines drawn here raise two important considerations. First, the results of this study's findings cannot be generalized to all interest groups, only to those that claim to represent public groups or issue perspectives. Care must be taken in comparing this study's conclusions with those of research on all interest groups or on different subsets of the group universe. Second, the wide borders of the advocacy community defined here necessitate regular checks to ascertain whether subsets of the community have distinct characteristics that affect their mobilization or success. Notwithstanding these concerns, definitional decisions should be evaluated based on their usefulness rather than appeals to intrinsic meaning. Readers who prefer some other boundaries for defining the advocacy community are free to take note of divisions within the community as outlined here and to assume that organizations that are not included might operate differently. Alternate definitions or boundaries, however, would not invalidate any conclusions for the community of organizations studied here.

To attempt to locate the population of all advocacy organizations with a presence in Washington, this study uses data compilation with content analysis from reference sources and organizational websites. To identify organizations that seek to represent public constituencies with an office in Washington, I primarily used the directory of organizations in *Washington Representatives* but also checked for additional organizations in the *Encyclopedia of Associations, The Capital Source,* the *Government Affairs Yellow Book, National Trade and Professional Associations of the United States, Public Interest Profiles,* and the *Washington Information Directory.* With two research assistants, I content analyzed the reference-text descriptions and websites of all organizations in 2006 to confirm that they seek to represent public constituencies in national politics and to categorize them by the constituencies that they seek to represent.[10] These categorizations were consistent for more than 90 percent of the organizations. Many organizations were included in more than one category because they claimed multiple constituencies or were representing a subset of another organization's constituency. For example, an anesthesiologists' association was coded as representing that specific occupation as well as doctors (who were also represented by generalist associations). When available, this study compared the categorizations with those used by scholars of specific group sectors (Hertzke 1988; Hofrenning 1995; Berry 1999; Shaiko 1999; Hays 2001); the categorizations were consistent across studies for more than 90 percent of organizations.

The result of the analysis is the most comprehensive catalog available of the types of public constituencies represented by organized advocates in Washington. Previous studies of public representation (Strolovitch 2007; Bishin 2009) rely on lists of constituencies developed by scholars or political consultants. For example, Benjamin Bishin's study of group representation in Congress relies on a crude division of the American public into subconstituencies taken from the political consultant and pollster Stanley Greenberg (2004). With this approach, political elites' conceptions of their constituency may not match those of scholars. The organizations in this study, in contrast, define their constituencies through their written materials. Taking the representative claims of the organizations at face value enables a compendium of the groups in society with someone purportedly speaking on their behalf.

Many Public Groups Generate Organized Representation

The first important step in understanding organized constituency representation is to analyze its scope. This chapter summarizes the results of that analysis, but Table A.1 in the book's appendix provides the full list of represented social groups. The results show that at least 466 groups have generated an organization that claims to represent their interests in Washington. The nation's capital features representatives of forty-one ethnic groups, from Afghans to Taiwanese. The Formosan Association for Public Affairs, for instance, describes itself as a "Washington headquartered, non-profit organization that … [seeks] to advance the rights and interests of Taiwanese communities throughout the world," but is concerned primarily with American foreign policy toward Taiwan.[11]

Organizations are also associated with twenty-six religious groups, even including the Bahai and Seventh-Day Adventists. Groups like American Atheists represent the nonreligious; this organization is based in New Jersey but has a Washington presence and a PAC. The organization describes itself as the "premier organization laboring for the civil liberties of Atheists, and the total, absolute separation of government and religion."[12] In addition to organizations representing well-known ethnic and religious constituencies like African Americans and Jews, public advocates represent groups from across the identity spectrum.

Many economic public groups also generate representation. At least 256 occupations have generated representation, from compliance professionals to railroad engineers. An economy with a large number of occupations produces a diverse community of associations and advocates. Most occupational representatives speak for narrow occupations, but some diversity in scope and mission is present. The Association for Financial Professionals, for example, describes itself as "the global resource and advocate for the finance profession." Its public policy program, the website states, is "to ensure that the profession's point of view on critical finance issues is factored into public discussion."[13] The American Nephrology Nurses' Association, in contrast, represents only a subset of nurses but claims to "advance nephrology nursing practice and positively influence outcomes for individuals with kidney disease through advocacy, scholarship, and excellence."[14] Occupations of varying scope generate representations.

At least sixty-four intersectional groups are represented; these populations share multiple identities, such as ethnicity, religion, gender, or occupation.[15] Many of these constituencies are associated with a joint ethnic and occupational category, such as African American lawyers. Washington also features representatives of ethnicity–religion intersections, gender–occupation intersections, and religion–occupation intersections. Both Christian lawyers and blind veterans have their own representation. New public groups are created over time by the recognition of identity intersections; many of these social groups produce political representation.

In addition, seventy-nine social groups that do not fall into any of these categories have generated organized representation in Washington, including victims of diseases, enthusiasts of athletic activities, transportation users and owners, beneficiaries of specific government programs, consumers, and groups that share other demographic characteristics, such as gender, income, age, and location. Even graduate students and motorcyclists have their own leadership in Washington. Certainly many interest groups claim to speak for me; chances are, all citizens can find a few alleged constituencies that include them.

Divide the American public into dozens of social cleavages, and one will see organized groups on both sides of each divide, as well as some at the intersections of multiple divides. Even social groups that do not have clear opponents, such as hikers and dancers, are fair game for entrepreneurial activists seeking representative roles; both of these groups have Washington representatives. At first glance, few obvious social groups are missing from the list. In my undergraduate class on political parties and interest groups, I ask students to think of unrepresented groups; they rarely identify a group without an accompanying organization. Even some constituencies they identified that I initially thought did not have representation, such as parents who have their children taken away by child welfare agencies, Palestinian Americans, and fathers, have since begun to develop organized representation.

Many social groups have interest group representation, even if it is not necessarily extensive or effective. Bishin (2009, 20) argues that interest group studies miss the influence of unorganized constituencies. When scholars find that intense minorities, including small public groups, influence policymakers, however, they should not conclude that these groups are influential despite being unorganized. Most of the constituencies Bishin describes have generated some form of organized representation, even if most constituency members have never met and are not official organization members. Bishin reports that groups such as gays, religious Christians, African Americans, and Cubans all influence legislative behavior but concludes that this is evidence of the power of unorganized citizens. All of these groups, however, have organizations claiming to speak on their behalf. They cannot be categorized as unorganized.

Groups that share opinions rather than social allegiances are not omitted from the advocacy system. At least 146 different political issue perspectives have at least one organization that claims to speak on their behalf in national politics.[16] Table A.2 in the appendix lists all issue-perspective representatives encountered in this study. Washington features representatives of nine ideological perspectives, from economic conservatives to social liberals and libertarians. The traditional ideological categories of liberal and conservative are subdivided and augmented in the hands of the advocacy community.

At least fifty-six liberal issue perspectives also have some representation, from pesticide opponents to progressive taxation supporters.[17] Likewise, twenty-eight conservative issue perspectives are represented, from euthanasia opponents to supporters of right-to-work laws. Both broad multi-issue groups and narrow single-issue organizations represent each side of the ideological spectrum. Another twenty-five constituencies with issue perspectives that do not fall neatly on either side of the ideological divide also have representation, including supporters of wildlife management and opponents of child abuse. At least twenty-eight foreign-policy perspectives also have proponents in Washington. Supporters of international vaccine availability, for example, have their own lobby.

On some issues, Washington features multiple liberal and conservative sides. The Federation for American Immigration Reform, for example, describes itself as "a national, nonprofit, public-interest, membership organization" seeking to "improve border security, stop illegal immigration," and reduce legal immigration.[18] Such organizations as We Are America Alliance and the National Network for Immigrant and Refugee Rights, in contrast, support more open immigration policies. In other single-issue areas, however, a liberal perspective appears without an accompanying conservative single-issue perspective. Equine Advocates, for instance, describes itself as a "national non-profit equine protection organization" that advocates the abolition of horse slaughterhouses.[19]

Although substantially fewer sectors of issue representation develop than social group representation, it is difficult to think of a policy domain in which no organized representatives are active or to imagine a large public group associated with a single-issue perspective that is not represented. Even unrepresented single-issue constituencies identified by my undergraduate students, such as opponents of agricultural subsidies and proponents of college-loan forgiveness, typically have advocates working on behalf of somewhat broader agendas. The advocacy community represents not only the diversity of American society but also the diversity of its ideas about ideal policy and a substantial range of views about the relative importance of many public problems.

Americans should expect this proliferating representation to continue. Society includes a great diversity of public subsections that are potential constituencies for interest groups. Multiple mechanisms enable the number of public groups with political potential to diversify over time. First, existing public groups, such as those based on ethnic identity, often divide or proliferate along new dimensions. Second, existing groups may be amalgamated into new higher-level categories. Third, public groups are often formed via a mixture of incentives, based on both interest differentiation and changes in interpretations of self-identity; new groups can always emerge with new combinations of interests or ideas. The creation of new public groups is almost limitless, and the potential for politicization of some of these new groups is high. When new social groups or political perspectives emerge, they will not always be politically mobilized or represented. Nevertheless, many potential groups have developed representation in the past, and many more are likely to follow.

Many Nonmembership Organizations Represent Public Constituencies

Not all groups that claim to represent public constituencies actually involve citizens through membership and state or local chapters. A large and growing number of advocacy organizations make broad representative claims even with no discernable formal membership. Even though the collective action literature concentrates on explaining group membership, scholars regularly rediscover that it is not necessary for group creation or survival (Salisbury 1984; Walker 1991).

Indeed, membership is not a prerequisite for public constituency representation. It is not even the norm. A little more than half of advocacy organizations have no members at all.[20] The distribution of public members is decidedly uneven. The mean membership size is 186,000, but the standard deviation is more than 1.8 million. A few organizations, in other words, have most of the members; even among membership organizations, the median is well under 100,000. In addition, fewer than one-fifth of advocacy groups have any state or local chapters. Among those that do feature subnational organization, the majority sustains only minimal state-level affiliates. Membership and chapters are concentrated among professional associations, unions, and veterans groups, but some membership groups are found in almost every category.

For a sense of the variety, look at ethnic and religious representation. The Jewish sector of organizations includes twenty-five organizations, such as the American Jewish Committee; only thirteen have members, and six have chapters. Many offices for church denominations, such as the Washington office of the Presbyterian Church, claim large memberships. Most have a federal structure, but the membership is primarily church attendees rather than political advocates. The religious-right sector, with such organizations as the Christian Coalition of America, has four organizations with members and five without. The Catholic sector, with organizations such as the U.S. Conference of Catholic Bishops, has only six organizations with membership. Among ethnic sectors, the African American sector, including forty-two organizations such as the NAACP, has two-thirds membership organizations, including one-third with local chapters. The Hispanic sector, with thirty-five organizations, such as the National Council of La Raza, is the second largest ethnic sector in terms of organizations, but fewer than half feature any membership or chapters. Most of the other thirty-nine organizational sectors associated with an ethnic group are quite small, but most have at least one nonmembership organization.

Although the high number of advocacy organizations without members may indicate a lack of public mobilization, membership is not always an indicator of substantive participation. In some groups, membership is a formality used only to build direct mail fund-raising lists; in others, it conveys deep association with the group and constant interaction with other members. Many nonmembership organizations also have large followings. For example, some nonmembership organizations have thousands of pledged supporters on Facebook, thousands of followers on Twitter, and thousands of subscribers on e-mail lists. Many also regularly ask supporters to call members of Congress to convey their ideas. Having official membership, in other words, is often a decision based on self-identity or fund-raising considerations; it is neither necessary nor sufficient to promote public mobilization or allegiance.

The Largest Sectors of Advocacy Organizations Represent Diverse Interests

The broad categorization of organizations offers some important clues about the breadth of representation, but not all sectors of advocacy organizations are created equal. Descriptive data on sectors associated with different public constituencies can provide a sense of the distribution of organizations and their attributes across constituencies. This study reviews 211 sectors containing at least two organizations. Because these categories are not mutually exclusive, many organizations are included in several sectors. Some sectors, such as biological scientists, are subsets of other sectors, such as scientists. Table 1.1 reviews the largest sectors of advocacy organizations with information about the number of organizations in each sector, the number of in-house political staff at all organizations in the sector, the number of outside lobbyists the organizations have

TABLE 1.1. Largest advocacy organization sectors.

Constituency/sector	Groups	Political staff	Lobbyists	Members
Scientists/researchers	115	255	119	1,770,982
Environmentalists	87	292	48	9,782,026
Union members	86	306	108	36,599,015
Doctors	66	219	168	1,441,880
Sufferers of diseases	58	131	94	629,950
Government professionals	54	111	40	973,667
Health trade workers	54	145	90	2,030,903
Women	54	91	12	7,640,581
Biological scientists	49	77	61	663,743
Self-employed	49	162	108	1,708,978
Corporate professionals	49	102	34	733,000
Teachers	46	99	21	10,727,524
African Americans	42	79	14	5,722,018
Antipoverty/poor	42	94	26	326,991
General foreign policy	41	86	7	4,000
Foreign aid supporters	38	80	22	212,600
Lawyers	37	82	22	551,191
Veterans	37	104	26	5,487,854
Hispanics/Latinos	35	51	14	2,033,838
Liberals	35	125	11	373,300
Government employees	34	111	31	6,753,041
Consumers	31	88	68	6,075,050
Disabled/handicapped	31	79	21	1,516,000
Elderly/retired	30	104	24	37,196,654
Financial professionals	29	73	26	259,403
Conservatives	28	93	4	2,100,000
Child welfare supporters	25	44	13	787,000
Civil Rights Supporters	25	71	17	1,120,185
Engineers	25	58	8	2,886,248
General health care	25	60	27	8,000
Good government	25	53	10	630,000
Jews	25	71	8	732,000
Transportation trades	24	63	41	2,706,846
Building trades	23	60	16	2,725,189
Education expansion	23	49	15	408,700
Health coverage expansion	22	43	16	20,540
Farmers	21	85	24	6,305,586

NOTE: Table entries report the total number of organizations, political staff, lobbyists, and members associated with each constituency category.

hired from professional agencies, and the number of members they have mobilized.[21] This descriptive information provides a foundation for understanding the vast differences in representation afforded to different public groups.

Looking at the distribution of organized representation associated with each constituency makes it clear that the extent of representation varies considerably across public groups. Some sectors have many more organizations, in-house political representatives, lobbyists, and members. Among 211 sectors representing different constituencies, the average sector consists of approximately 13.7 organizations with only 35.5 total in-house political representatives and 12.5 external lobbyists. For all these indicators, the standard deviation is greater than the mean (16.8 for organizations, 48.6 for in-house political representatives, and 12.5 for hired lobbyists). In addition, the average sector has a little more than 2 million total members, but the standard deviation is more than 7 million. The distribution of each attribute across constituencies is highly uneven and skewed.

Which groups generate the most representation by organized advocates? Table 1.1 ranks the largest sectors of advocacy organizations by the number of organizations. A large number of organizations may sometimes represent diversity of viewpoints rather than effective representation, but sectors with more organizations are generally more prominent and involved in Washington. Chapter 2 introduces a new explanation for differences in the levels of mobilization associated with each public group. For now, it is enough to notice that the well-represented groups are difficult to place in any single category. Scholars will need more than general claims of categorical privilege or exclusion to account for the disparities in representation. In other words, political scientists cannot be satisfied with arguments that "disadvantaged" constituencies are less mobilized without more carefully defining what features of highly mobilized constituencies, which arise from many different types of interests, lead to their advantages.

The range illustrates the variation in levels of organized representation across groups. At least 115 organizations represent scientists, for example, but there are only a few organizations for most interests. The lobbying force of in-house representatives within these organizational sectors also ranges widely from 306 in-house political staff for one sector to one or two in many others. Public membership in the organizational sectors also varies. Some of the largest sectors in terms of number of organizations have a total membership of fewer than 10,000 people; others sectors have well over 10 million members.

Membership totals, therefore, do not seem to correspond with the number of organizations in a sector.

What Can Scholars Learn from Who Is Represented?

One cannot yet reach definitive conclusions about which types of groups are best represented from this list of highly represented sectors. Ad hoc theorizing is unlikely to be productive. For every reader seeing high levels of representation by scientists and health workers as surprising, for example, others see it as an obvious outgrowth of technological advancement. Citizens have a tendency to notice their own representatives or their opponents before digesting the full diversity of highly represented groups. Chapter 2 assesses several popular previous explanations for which groups are best represented. To begin, note the wide scope of organized representation, the large variation in levels of representation associated with each group, and the inability to place all of the well-represented public groups into any single category.

These descriptive results already point to some important conclusions. A large field of advocacy organizations has mobilized in Washington to represent the interests and ideas of a large and diverse set of social groups and political perspectives in national politics. Many public constituencies have generated organized representation in Washington, mobilizing in-house political representatives and external lobbyists to influence national politics. Many organizations and political staff represent single-issue perspectives, identity groups, and occupational groups. Some constituencies are much better represented than others, but the differences do not correspond to the ease of mobilizing members. Many organizations representing constituencies have members, and many sectors have some membership organizations, but large membership is not necessary or sufficient for producing a large sector of organized representatives.

One should be cautious, of course, in attributing biases to the interest-group system by examining only lists of organizations. First, as Lowery and Gray (2004) indicate, it is difficult to know what a system of unbiased representation would look like. Would it be unbiased, for example, to treat all groups equally or to differentiate by size or level of passion? Second, it is impossible to produce a list of every potential group that could mobilize to influence political outcomes. Nevertheless, by looking at the field of organizations representing public groups, one can identify the constituencies that have most successfully mobilized.

A Reassessment of Group Theory and
the Collective Action Problem

Most surprising from this initial analysis is the degree to which the current field of organizations was anticipated by Truman's (1951) accurate forecast. He argues that most Americans are members of many political constituencies and may devote their energies to one or more efforts to mobilize political interests and ideas. Truman identifies the following three categories of social disturbances that help to activate similarities among individuals and to distinguish their ideas and interests from other groups, providing the context for interest group organization: socioeconomic change, often driven by technological development (24); the behavior of allied groups and opponents (59); and changes in governmental institutions or policies (58).[22] In an interpretation of Truman's work offered by Salisbury (1992), the author has two major hypotheses. First, increasing social complexity produces more differentiated ideas and interests; this process increases the number of interest organizations making demands on government. Second, new organizations will regularly arise in a countermobilization against a current set of interests.[23]

As envisioned by Truman's (1951) "disturbance theory," Washington features many examples of groups that arose in response to socioeconomic change (including many new occupations and new categories of victims), in response to mobilization by others (such as opponents of tax cuts, anti-religious-right groups, and conservative women's groups), and in response to changes in government institutions (including beneficiaries of new government programs and proponents of new reforms). Given the large number of intersectional groups with organized representation in Washington, crosscutting individual identities may also promote diverse mobilization (as Truman suggested).

The increasing complexity of the economy and society seems to have led people with many different ideas and interests to mobilize in Washington. For example, the advocacy community contains representatives for occupations that did not exist a few decades ago as well as issue perspectives related to policy issues that are new to government. As Truman also suggested, many types of organizations seem to have arisen that seek to counter the influence of other groups. Some groups are organized around government programs, as he expected. Still others appear to have begun as social associations and gravitated toward the government.

In contrast, the scope of public representation in Washington is difficult to square with traditional models of collective action. In his classic work, Olson (1965) demonstrated that, given a set of rational expectations on the part of individuals, participation in interest organizations does not follow from agreement on public goods. If individuals follow their self-interest, they will not contribute to a mobilization whereby the cost of participation exceeds the personal share of the collective benefit expected from one additional participant. Given this cost–benefit calculation, he expects only very small groups to be able to motivate participation by appealing to collective goods. For all others, individual incentives will promote being a "free rider," relying on the work of others. Organizations of larger constituencies will need to provide "selective incentives," goods available only to members, to generate mobilization. Olson viewed his theory as a direct challenge to the group theory of politics advanced by Truman, even referencing it in the book's subtitle. As a matter of intellectual history, Olson's theory has superseded Truman's in importance. *The Logic of Collective Action* is cited more than twenty times as often in scholarly materials as is *The Governmental Process*.[24]

Truman ([1951] 1971) always maintained, however, that Olson's contribution was not useful for understanding much of interest group mobilization:

> Since many motivations in society . . . are not "rational" in the technical economic sense of self-interested, benefit-maximizing behavior, groups characterized by philanthropic, religious, or other technically nonrational or irrational motives may emerge and operate effectively on the political scene, without the need for coercion or special inducements. (xxix)

As Truman suggests, Olson's theory has not been supported empirically in interest-group studies. According to McFarland (1987), Olson did not successfully predict the emergence of new groups: "Not only did many lobbies exist that Olson implied should not exist, but clearly the number of such lobbying organizations had greatly increased, including lobbies for widely shared, diffuse interests" (140). Gray and Lowery also judge the theory inappropriate: "The Olson incentive theory . . . simply is not a useful guide to generating valid inferences about the societal-level properties of interest organization communities, largely because it ignores context, the environment in which interest organization takes place" (1996, 246). The environment consists of the groups in society that may mobilize to influence government: the original potential groups identified by Truman. The findings here confirm that small economically self-interested groups are represented in Washington, but so are many large social groups and many groups organized with the public interest in mind.

Because Olson's specific predictions primarily concerned individual-membership incentives, this analysis cannot assess the implied mechanisms directly. It is notable, however, that Olson's theoretical breakthrough does not seem to provide a useful set of hypotheses for understanding organized constituency representation in national politics. In terms of Olson's predictions about the likelihood of organized representation among constituencies, what he got right appears to have been predicted already by Truman. Olson predicted that some groups would find it easier to organize, but so did Truman. Olson predicted that many small economic groups would organize, as did Truman. Both Olson and Truman also predicted that not all potential groups would mobilize. The new predictions made possible by Olson's analysis do not comport with the empirical evidence. Many large public groups do organize political representation, overcoming any collective action problem. The groups that generate the most representation do not correspond to any single form of mobilization, such as one solely dependent on membership mobilization. Olson's claim that only small constituencies would be likely to organize absent selective benefits is not consistent with the evidence.[25] His suggestion that people need self-interested incentives to mobilize is similarly unable to account for many organized mobilizations of public constituencies.

The Differences in Levels of Group Representation Are Large and Unexplained

Given the current scope of organized constituency representation in Washington, it is disconcerting that so much scholarly energy has been expended to modify and extend collective action theory while little time or resources have been directed toward reformulating and advancing Truman's analysis. His core interests, the factors that influence the degree of organized representation among public groups and the factors that influence the success of representative organizations in influencing government, remain the key questions of interest group research (Baumgartner and Leech 1998). Rather than repeating claims that most groups cannot mobilize and extensively studying the dynamics of membership mobilization, scholars need to learn why some groups mobilize substantially more than others.

Based on the initial step of outlining the constituencies with some modicum of representation, the creation and survival of representative groups does

not appear to be the crucial step in what Schattschneider called the "mobilization of bias," the multistep process by which some interests gain more influence
than others through institutional development and government responsiveness. Instead, if organizational development is a major step in the mobilization
of bias, it is likely to be the degree of development that is important. Some
groups mobilize substantially more organizations, staff, and lobbyists to represent their concerns. The massive differences in the levels of organized representation associated with each public group remain largely unexplained.

2　One Person, One Lobbyist?

The Supreme Court famously ruled that the national system of legislative representation must reflect a principle of one person, one vote. No one has sought to impose a similar rule on public-interest representation. Instead, the national advocacy system responds to the behavior of each sector's constituency and the necessities of influencing government action. The results of this representative system are a reflection of relative constituency group mobilization.

How do characteristics of public groups promote the mobilization of advocacy organizations? Are larger groups able to generate more representation? If not, what other group differences explain the inequalities in the advocacy system? Why, for example, are gun-control opponents much better represented than gun-control supporters? Gun-control opponents, after all, are a smaller public group that is less affluent.[1] Why are lawyers better represented than engineers, even though both are small affluent groups?

Behavioral Pluralism, this chapter's new theory designed to answer these questions, contends that the process of organizational development is likely to be inseparable from the relative political capabilities of the constituencies that organizations represent. The characteristics of gun-control opponents in the mass public, for example, will likely influence the success of the NRA. The success of leaders depends on constituency support, which is likely to hinge on the civic and political capacity of the represented group. Groups consisting of individuals prepared and motivated to participate politically are likely to generate the most organized representation, no matter the shared social tie or political view motivating their action. Behavioral Pluralism draws on the insights of research on individual political participation and local civic engagement in analyzing the strengths and weaknesses of public constituencies for national political mobilization. To assess which types of social and political groups benefit most from the interest-group system, the analysis begins with the types of people most likely to participate in civic and political life.

Political factions differ in their degree of civic and political capacity, which can be thought of as a form of group-level social capital. Proactive central tendencies among group members enable constituencies to mobilize for political action through multiple mechanisms. First, more individuals within a constituency become leaders and organized supporters. Second, the group gains an image of high mobilization potential that group leaders and political elites heed. Third, networks of activists within a constituency are more likely to find one another and create dense attachments for mobilization and support. If gun-control opponents, for example, are highly socially active in their communities and motivated to participate in political activity, group leaders will be more likely to emerge, political elites will take the constituency seriously as a potential political force, and gun rights activists will find each other and join forces. These advantages are likely to matter not only for initial mobilization but also for building and maintaining more resourceful and prominent organizations over an extended period.

To test Behavioral Pluralism, this chapter compares the average characteristics of public members of each constituency with the degree of political representation of that constituency by an organized leadership in Washington. Most previous attempts to investigate whether some types of groups have advantages over others in the interest-group system have involved categorical counts of organizations with comparisons to the assumed size of their public populations of supporters.[2] Lowery and Gray (2004) contend that the methods used have been inadequate. Using these methods, scholars have pointed out that corporations and other institutions are overrepresented and all kinds of public groups are underrepresented (Salisbury 1984; Schlozman and Tierney 1986).

These previous analyses do not allow scholars to investigate the types of public groups best equipped to organize politically or the types of group attributes associated with high levels of organized representation. Most group theories of politics do not focus on business as one large group and society as another large group, but most of the tests of relative mobilization focus only on this distinction. Without reference to public constituencies, previous scholarship on interest mobilization has concentrated on the factors that allow organizations to assemble people and resources in order to survive (Olson 1965; Walker 1991; Baumgartner and Leech 1998). Nevertheless, the overall organizing process likely benefits some public groups more than others.

The Importance of Group-Level Political Participation

Many Americans view their participation in politics as part of a group's effort to influence policy outcomes. In Philip Converse's (1964) well-known study of public belief systems, more than 40 percent of the American public defined their political affiliation by associating the leaders they favor with a general effort to advance the interests of a social group. Even many people not on the official membership lists of national organizations see themselves as constituents of political causes or movements. Citizens may become single-issue voters or develop perceptions of political common fate with members of a social group without joining organizations. Yet some Americans also supplement their electoral participation with organizational involvement. Other than voting, affiliating with political organizations is the most common form of mass political participation (Verba, Schlozman, and Brady 1995). Whether consisting of official organizational affiliates or not, public groups sometimes act in unison to achieve collective goals and see themselves as doing just that.

Unfortunately, behavioral analysis traditionally avoids aggregating individual-level data into groups for fear of making an ecological fallacy by assuming that individual-level variable associations produce observed group-level associations. If Jews vote at high levels and have high organizational mobilization, it does not follow automatically that the individual Jews participating in elections also helped build advocacy organizations. In ignoring group-level associations, however, traditional behavioral analysis risks making an individualistic fallacy by assuming that observed individual-level associations are not affected by group context or relationships among individual actors within a group (Huckfeldt 2007). African American political participation, for example, may be explained by group-level attributes such as a history of successful social movements, relational attributes such as dense mobilization networks, or individual attributes such as socioeconomic status. Fortunately, the central tendencies within a group, such as group means or rates, influence all three types of causal mechanisms (Huckfeldt 2007). The aggregate density of factors relevant to political mobilization within a group is likely to affect group mobilization through many combinations of individual-level, group-level, and relational variables. Behavioral Pluralism relies on these mechanisms for predicting that the average characteristics of a public constituency will be related to its level of organized representation. The attributes of the average group member should matter not only for initial group mobilization but also for organizational maintenance and growth. Investigating public groups as collective entities avoids both ecological and individualistic fallacies by endorsing causal mechanisms operating at all levels of analysis.

The Type of Constituency May Not Matter for Mobilization Potential

This study's conceptualization of public groups as constituencies for political advocacy incorporates ideological or opinion-based groups, such as environmentalists, as well as social identity groups, such as African Americans. Constituencies organized around shared ideas may have a similar potential for political mobilization as those organized around shared identities. This notion is counter to the assumptions of most democratic theory and popular discourse. Because people acting in their own interests are commonly thought to be more normatively suspect than those acting on behalf of public-interested ideas, these two motivations are assumed to oppose each other and take different forms. For the purposes of organizational mobilization, however, there is no reason to assume that constituencies bound together by a shared perception of group interest will have a different capacity than those who share an ideology or a set of public policy views. Environmentalists, for example, will receive no automatic benefit for pursuing ideas in comparison to African Americans, who pursue their own interests. Instead, both groups will be dependent on their political capacity as constituencies for organized leaders. Some theorists, such as the late philosopher Richard Rorty, and some activists, including consumer advocate Ralph Nader, have long supposed that society could overcome interest-group politics by mobilizing around shared ideas that are in the collective interest (Rorty 1989). Yet if a group with shared ideas about the nature of the public interest, such as pro-life citizens, is just another public subpopulation with an organized leadership to speak on its behalf, these suppositions are naïve. Interest-group politics, despite its moniker, consists of both groups that share interests and those that share ideas.

More generally, scholars often make categorical distinctions between public constituencies that rest on unrealistic views of groups. Scholars divide public groups based on their presumed motivations and based on the way they define their membership, assuming that some group types will automatically mobilize whereas other groups will inherently face a more difficult road. Yet most public groups do not fit easily into common caricatures of the ideas or interests they share (Mansbridge 1992; Mathiowetz 2008). Most groups claim to have the interests of everyone in mind, but all political groups advance a particularistic view of society's goals and conflicts (Post and Rosenblum 2002). Although many differences in degree appear among the common categories of public constituencies, few genuine differences in kind make mobilization more automatic for any one category of groups. Whether public constituencies are identity groups, occupations, or opinion groups, they start as a subsection of the public with different political goals than others. Groups differ in ways that are pertinent to their potential for organized mobilization, but scholars are unlikely to find the most important differences by insisting on categorical distinctions premised on normative judgments.

The Behavioral Foundations of Interest Mobilization

Truman (1951) suggests that differences in the level of mobilization among groups are likely to be explained by their "strategic social position," that is, how others see them, and "internal characteristics," or the way they behave. Although vaguely outlined, Truman describes a large range of factors that may influence the relative mobilization of public groups. These factors include a constituency's resource levels, its degree of civic and political engagement, its degree of political participation, and its political views.

No scholarly literature compares constituency attributes across American public groups with information about the extent of their organized representation, but a large literature covers the kinds of individual attributes that are likely to promote individual political activity. Socioeconomic status, level of information and engagement, and attitudes toward government all affect political affiliation and behavior (Miller and Shanks 1996). Differences in engagement across individuals produce a community of political activists that is not representative of the American population (Verba, Schlozman, and Brady 1995). Similar attributes have also been used to predict substantial differences in democratic cultures between nations. Gabriel Almond and Sidney Verba

(1963) argue that the United States is a "participant civic culture" with high levels of political awareness, media usage, and civic engagement. These variables, they say, account for differences in modes and levels of participation between the United States and European nations.

Between the analysis of individual political behavior and the aggregation of public opinion to the national level lies the group level of analysis. In fact, group-level cooperation in service of competition with other groups may be the most common form of political engagement. Scholars can use findings from the literature on the way that individual attributes promote individual political involvement and local civic engagement to predict the way that similar group-level attributes promote the development and success of national advocacy-group sectors. As members of a public constituency develop the capacity and intention to become active in politics, the leadership of that faction should be more likely to expand its representative role and to gain advantages in political debate.

This constitutes the theory of Behavioral Pluralism. It is the result of an aggregation of previous individual-level research to the group level of analysis. The theory focuses not on the general population of activists but on a set of intermediary institutions (advocacy organizations) that claim to speak on behalf of public groups. It addresses the factions, rather than the individuals, that are advantaged. The theory is behavioral because it draws from the literature on individual political behavior in the mass public, rather than theories of organizational mobilization. It is a pluralist theory because it expects many different types of public interests to be associated with organized mobilization without a clear line separating the groups destined to be well represented from others. Regardless of the category of interests or ideas that a public group shares, it will need similar attributes to mobilize effectively.

In other words, there are substantial premobilization biases built into the interest group system based on the constituents that organizations attempt to represent. An organization seeking to represent high school dropouts would be at a significant disadvantage compared to one seeking to represent bankers. There would still be considerable contingencies associated with each mobilization, but a terribly managed bankers' organization might still outperform a brilliant attempt at organization by high school dropouts. Just as political scientists predict that electoral candidates with years of political experience will outperform an amateur, interest group research should acknowledge that political factions differ dramatically in their likelihood of success. As in the electoral context, strategic decisions, assistance from outsiders, and luck may help the occasional underdog overperform, but the broad predicted patterns will still be evident.

The important differences between groups will go beyond size and socio-economic status to incorporate civic engagement and political motivation. A constituency's level of attentiveness to political debate, the efficacy it perceives in political engagement, and its involvement in community organizations should all serve as indicators of its social and political capacity, along with its rate of traditional political participation. Group-level social and political capital will assist constituencies in generating leaders, building networks of interactive activists, and generating a reputation for political involvement, providing a focal point for mobilization opportunities. These mechanisms for increased political success should apply to both the initial mobilization of new organizations and the ongoing maintenance of existing organizational infra-structure. They will also likely influence the way that organized leaders are perceived by policymakers and other political elites, as leaders with stronger followings will be more credible.

Measuring Public Constituency Characteristics

To put Behavioral Pluralism to the test, this chapter considers the character-istics of 140 constituencies in the American public to see if attributes of the public groups are associated with their levels of organized representation. I identify the public constituency associated with each sector of organizations in the study's population using pooled public-opinion survey data from the General Social Survey (GSS) from 1972 to 2004. The cumulative GSS enables isolating a sufficient number of constituency members among the 45,803 total respondents to the survey. As a result, the study records the aggregate features of 140 of the constituencies associated with sectors of more than one organi-zation in Washington. It characterizes public groups like African Americans, environmentalists, and doctors that each have a sector of organized advocates claiming to speak on their behalf, relying on public opinion survey responses from members of each group. Based on the GSS race variable, for example, 5,660 African Americans were surveyed. The occupational code variable iso-lates 134 surveyed doctors. A question on national environmental policy iden-tifies 16,492 environmentalists. The appendix reviews all of the questions and answers used to identify public constituencies for each sector of groups. The study's population of public groups and their associated sectors includes four-teen ethnic groups, eight religious groups, forty-three occupational groups, eleven ideological groups, forty-eight groups of supporters for single-issue perspectives, and sixteen other social categories.

This approach differs from previous attempts to connect constituencies with organizations, which relied primarily on broad occupational categories. Kay Lehman Schlozman and John Tierney (1986), for example, compare the size of all professional workers with the share of the interest-group commu-nity that consists of professional associations; they compare the size of the nonmanagerial nonfarm working population with the share of the interest-group community that consists of unions. Instead, this analysis connects the specific occupational categories represented by each sector of professional as-sociations and unions with the population in each occupation. In their anal-ysis, Schlozman and Tierney associate only one type of interest group with each individual in the population; in contrast, this study often associates each survey respondent with multiple advocacy sectors. Some survey respondents are represented by ethnic, religious, ideological, single-issue, and occupa-tional sectors of advocacy organizations.

For each constituency, I record data on its demographic characteristics; its political opinions; its levels of political attentiveness, political efficacy, and civic engagement; as well as its rate of political participation. For example, I take the mean level of membership in civic organizations among all women, all African Americans, and all environmentalists in the survey. To alleviate prob-lems of incomparability across time, I record the attributes of constituencies by using the difference between the mean or proportion within a constituency and the mean or proportion among all respondents to the same set of surveys. For example, I compare the voting rate across constituencies like veterans and homeowners; because the questions I use to identify each constituency were asked in a different subset of years, however, I compare each constituency's voting rate to the overall voting rate in the surveys that asked each identifying question. I can then compare the voting rate of veterans and homeowners by asking how much higher or lower each constituency's voting rate is than the average. The appendix contains additional information about the coding and collection of all variables used to measure constituency attributes.

The basis of comparison between constituencies used here means that the study relies on the average characteristics of a group. Instead of counting the members of each group who watch the news, for example, this study looks at the average level of media attention within a group. This way of characterizing groups is consistent with the way constituencies often see themselves, the way they are seen by the organizations that represent them, and the way policymakers see the groups. Strolovitch (2007) finds that interest groups try to appeal to their typical member, ignoring issues or concerns of subgroups. The group leaders that she interviews report that policymakers also expect them to represent their average members rather than disadvantaged subgroups. Central tendencies within a group are also likely to affect group mobilization through individual-level, group-level, and relational causal pathways. Although many constituencies have some members who are affluent or politically engaged, the average member needs to possess these characteristics for the group to see itself, and be seen by others, as affluent or engaged.

Measuring the Extent of Organized Representation

To assess the representation of each constituency, I aggregate data for the sector of organizations that claims to represent each public group. For example, all organizations representing African Americans constitute a sector of organizations tied to African Americans as a group in the American public. I include organizations that claim to represent a subpopulation in each constituency's sector. Many organizations are therefore found in multiple sectors. An organization representing African American doctors, for example, is included in both the African American sector and the doctor sector. I record the number of organizations in each sector and the number of in-house political representatives in these organizations.[3] This reveals the number of leaders representing each group in the nation's capital. To assess the prominence of a constituency's representatives in the Washington political debate, I record the number of times that organizations speaking on their behalf were mentioned in the Washington print media from 1995 through 2004. I track mentions for any organization in each sector in *Roll Call, The Hill, National Journal, Congress Daily, The Hotline, Congressional Quarterly,* and *The Washington Post*.[4] These publications report on the important activities of the national political community and are among the first reads for policymakers.

To assess the involvement of a constituency's representatives in national policymaking, I use the number of times that organizations in each sector testified before Congress in committee hearings.[5] Appearances in hearings indicate that members of Congress are soliciting the views of a constituency's representatives. The collection of each of these indicators is explained in the appendix. Combined, the indicators provide a comprehensive and comparable aggregate-level assessment of the organized representation for each constituency (organizations and political staff), its prominence in Washington (mentions in Washington media reports), and its involvement in an important policymaking venue (testimony in congressional committees). In later chapters, I assess the determinants of media prominence and policymaking involvement for each organization, and I expand the analysis to other types of media and policy venues.

Descriptive Analysis

The units of analysis are the sectors of organizations associated with public constituencies. For each constituency attribute and each measure of the extent of its organized representation, I report the bivariate Pearson correlation coefficient along with an indicator of the results of a two-tailed significance test. The variations in political views, constituent resources, and engagement and participation levels that I analyze, however, are unlikely to be independent of one another. Sindey Verba, Kay Lehman Schlozman, and Henry Brady (1995) find that the main correlates of participation, resources, political engagement, and organizational mobilization, tend to follow from one another. Many of these group attributes are also not exogenous to the level of organized leadership that has arisen to promote a constituency's interest. Advocacy organizations attempt to promote political participation and public engagement. Even if these group attributes are associated with higher levels of organized representation, one cannot conclude that the attributes came prior to organizational mobilization.

The causal connections between constituency attributes and active organized representation are difficult to distinguish because the success of organized representatives may create feedback effects that change the character of their constituencies. Interest groups may stimulate passion among constituencies. Government action on behalf of a constituency may also activate group political motivation (Clemens 1997; Campbell 2003; Mettler 2005). Nevertheless, feedback effects whereby interest group sectors change the nature of their constituencies may be minimal. Most attributes associated with group-level social and political capital are stable traits that rarely change decidedly. Early interest group leaders were able to innovate in ways that mobilized previously apolitical constituencies, but the United States is now at an advanced stage of interest mobilization with less potential for innovation in mobilizing constituencies with low capacity (Clemens 1997).

Even if government action does stimulate mobilization, the mechanism is likely to include motivating constituencies rather than working through organizational leaders alone. Andrea Louise Campbell argues that feedback effects usually enable already-advantaged constituencies to consolidate their advantages through government policy. Policy feedback typically results in increasing returns for the groups that start out ahead (Campbell 2003, 136). In a comparison of retired people, veterans, and welfare clients, however, Campbell argues that the design of policies to help each constituency contributed to different effects, with welfare clients less mobilized because of means-tested benefits. Another possibility is that welfare beneficiaries might be inherently more difficult to mobilize than veterans or retired people.

No matter the strength of each direction of causality, the first step in generating an explanation of differences in organized representation is both important and achievable here: Analyze the associations between constituency characteristics and organized representation. Much of the theoretical interest for democratic theory and the empirical importance for policymaking derives from finding out which types of groups are best represented. In and of itself, this descriptive information helps demonstrate the biases in the system of organized representation. Without establishing baseline correlations between constituency characteristics and organized representation, one cannot assess claims about how and why some groups generate more representation than others. An account of which types of public groups are likely to be advantaged by organized representation is one important aspect of the "mobilization of bias" in American politics.[6]

This analysis makes it possible to assess which types of groups develop more extensive and active organized representation but not which groups influence or benefit from actual policy outcomes. It is likely that the groups represented in the advocacy system, in political debate, and in governing institutions have the capacity to influence government decisions and structure policy to benefit themselves. The system of representation through advocacy organizations is also worthy of scholarly interest, however, even if other factors explain policy influence. Being able to voice one's concerns in civil society, in the media, and in government institutions, in and of itself is a form of political power and an important goal of some movements and organizations.

It can be empowering to participants, raise new issues or concerns, or make people more satisfied with democratic institutions (Mansbridge 1992; James 2004). In addition to providing a type of descriptive representation, having interest groups speak on your behalf provides substantive representation analogous to symbolic policy votes in Congress. Advocacy group representation is thus important for political expression and democratic participation as well as for its potential to determine policy outcomes.

Constituency Characteristics and Group Representation

Although few prior studies have directly tackled the relationship between group attributes and organized representation, several prominent social theories do have alternative implications for this analysis. Collective action theory and spatial theories of politics, in particular, could lead analysts to consider constituency attributes other than those forwarded by Behavioral Pluralism.

Group Size

One basic demographic factor is of primary importance in several social theories: the size of a constituency in the American population. Democratic theory generally suggests that large groups should be represented more extensively than small groups (Dahl 1963). Although no one claims that a one-to-one relationship exists between group size and representation, principles of democracy imply an expectation that larger groups of citizens will have a louder voice in decision making. Olson (1965) famously suggests that the opposite will be more likely: Small groups will find it easier to organize for collective action because having fewer people makes it more likely that the benefit of any single person's contribution will outweigh the costs of his or her participation. Chapter 1 demonstrated that Olson was incorrect in assuming that large groups would not organize at all, but group size may still influence the level of representation afforded to public groups. Lowery and Gray (2004) also argue that smaller public groups are likely to be overrepresented in Washington. Studying subgroups within constituencies, however, Strolovitch (2007) finds that the size of a subgroup is not strongly associated with issue representation by organized advocates. Bishin (2009) finds that group size is rarely related to whether a legislator takes up a group's cause.

Is interest representation generally a function of a group's size in the American public? The results are not encouraging for demographic accounts of constituency mobilization. Table 2.1 reports bivariate correlations between constituency characteristics and organized representation. The size of a constituency does not appear to be a critical factor in determining representation; the percent of the American population that a constituency encompasses is not significantly correlated with any measure of its organized representation. The correlation is negative and insignificant for the number of organizations and in-house political staff that represent each group and positive but insignificant for their mentions in the Washington media and their committee testimony. In other words, measuring the size of 140 different political constituencies in the American public in aggregate survey data leads to no evidence that size matters for public group political advocacy. Larger constituencies do not systematically generate more extensive organized representation, but neither do smaller constituencies.

TABLE 2.1. Correlations between constituency characteristics and organized representation.

Constituency demographics	Number of organizations	Number of political staff	D.C. media prominence	Testimony in Congress
Constituency size ($n = 140$)	−.05	−.01	.13	.09
Extremity of opinion ($n = 140$)	.04	.04	.03	.01
Ideological cohesion ($n = 140$)	−.1	−.06	.05	−.02
Socioeconomic status ($n = 137$)	.28***	.22**	.04	.05
Media attentiveness ($n = 140$)	.19*	.21*	.13	.17*
Level of political efficacy ($n = 106$)	.3**	.28**	.19	.25**
Belief that government is responsive ($n = 127$)	.24**	.2*	.06	.05
Level of civic membership ($n = 132$)	.35***	.34***	.21*	.22**
Meeting/rally attendance ($n = 86$)	.27*	.24*	.2	.18
Voting turnout rate ($n = 140$)	.2*	.23**	.19*	.2*
Turnout * population size ($n = 140$)	.03	.08	.12	.13
Financial contribution rate ($n = 86$)	.27*	.23*	.15	.14

NOTE: Table entries are bivariate Pearson correlation coefficients. ***$p < .001$; **$p < .01$; *$p < .05$ (two-tailed)

Small constituencies such as doctors and scientists are well represented in Washington, as are such large constituencies as environmentalists and women. Being a large group does not guarantee a large representative sector; automobile drivers, for example, have produced only a small number of organizations despite their large size. The vast majority of constituencies are small, as are most organizational sectors in Washington. The results do not match the expectations of democratic theory or the predictions of collective action models. There may be offsetting benefits and costs associated with large group size, but most likely the theories underlying these predictions are incorrect. The number of members that organizations actually mobilize may be relevant to their prominence or involvement, but the size of their constituency or potential membership is not associated with the extent of mobilization.

Political Ideology

Other scholarship emphasizes the importance of political views in promoting success in the political system. Public-choice theories derived from Downs (1957) imply that the extremity of a group's political opinions will help determine its likely influence in the political system. Lowery and Gray (2004) similarly argue that groups "at the center of the distribution of opinions in society" will be overrepresented by interest groups. Scholars of particular interest group sectors (Staggenborg 1994; Strolovitch 2007) likewise argue that opinions viewed as radical are less likely to be represented by organized advocates. Popular commentators, however, often imply the opposite: The "special interests" are the "extremists" in American politics; they supposedly hold views outside the mainstream of opinion. Morris Fiorina (1999) also predicts that extreme groups will be better represented in Washington. He contends that extreme public voices have overtaken the political debate. Spatial models of party and interest-group systems (Axelrod and Bennett 1993) predict that the internal ideological cohesion of a group will also help determine its success, independent of average ideological orientation. Thinking in terms of electoral success, spatial theories generally emphasize moderate opinion and agreement on political issues. If politics is about competition in an ideological space, these same attributes may affect group mobilization in the advocacy system.

Yet these expectations do not match the results. Political views explain even less of the variation in the organized representation of public constituencies than group size. Extremity of opinions, measured by the total difference between a constituency's opinions and the opinions of the American public as a whole on four policy issue scales, is not significantly related to the extent of its organized representation. Comparing the average opinions of public groups with those of the public as a whole produces no evidence that groups with more extreme opinions, on average, have developed different levels of organized advocacy. The ideological cohesion within a constituency, measured as variance on a conservative–liberal ideological scale, is also unrelated to organized representation. The correlation coefficients are insignificant and negative for organizations, staff, and testimony and insignificant but positive for media mentions. Public groups that have a mixture of conservatives and liberals are not systematically advantaged or disadvantaged in comparison to ideologically consistent constituencies. The results do not provide much support for the applicability of spatial theories of politics to understanding organized representation. Popular complaints about the rise of the extremists over the moderates appear equally unhelpful. Constituencies with both moderate and extreme views are represented.

Neither models of collective action nor theories of spatial competition offer much explanatory power. Collective action theory unhelpfully offers one demographic variable as the likely explanation for differences in group mobilization, namely, group size. Spatial theories, designed to understand electoral mobilization but extended to the interest group domain by some scholars, identify factors associated with the political opinions of a group; these factors are not correlates of representation.

Socioeconomic Status

Behavioral Pluralism offers a different set of variables as likely predictors of organized representation. All of the characteristics likely to be associated with political participation may be connected to a single important individual characteristic: socioeconomic status. Verba, Schlozman, and Brady (1995) argue that socioeconomic factors account for much of the disproportionate involvement of some types of individuals over others in political activism. This basic demographic factor may account for differences in the political representation of public groups. Elitist theories about the role of class in democratic societies share this expectation with Behavioral Pluralism but generally suggest that class should be the only important factor in political mobilization (Mills 1956; Domhoff 1967). Based on these expectations, groups of high socioeconomic status should mobilize much more extensively, and the voices of their representatives should be incorporated into public debate and policymaking much more often.

How does this classic explanation for mobilization match reality? The mean socioeconomic status of a constituency is significantly correlated with the number of organizations and staff representing each public group. Public constituencies with higher socioeconomic status develop substantially more organized representation. Jews and lawyers, for example, are well represented by organized advocates; groups that are less affluent than the average, such as service workers and supporters of restrictive immigration policies, are not as well represented. Yet the organized representatives of affluent constituencies are not significantly more prominent in the Washington political media or more involved in committee hearings. Class differences do not appear to explain how often group representatives speak to policymakers and the media.

The results would be different if no professional associations or unions were established in Washington. Taking unions out of the population makes the advocacy system look more biased toward high socioeconomic status groups; taking professional associations out makes it seem less biased. Removing both groups leads to insignificant correlations with estimates in the same initial range. Professional associations and unions balance each other to some extent on this factor, with unions representing lower-status groups and professional associations representing higher-status groups. Of course, business policy offices are often seen as representatives of high-status populations; including this large interest group population in any assessment would lead to the conclusion that debate is tilted toward high-status groups.

Media Attentiveness

Behavioral Pluralism suggests that constituencies attentive to the workings of the political system and engaged in public life are likely to generate more extensive organized representation. John Zaller (1992) convincingly argues that individual political engagement follows largely from citizen attentiveness to current events in the news media. According to Zaller, individuals who regularly follow news are more informed about political issues and can identify differences among political leaders; they are more likely to form opinions on political issues and more likely to receive messages from political elites that motivate their actions. News media attentiveness also increases an individual's affiliation with political leaders who share her political predispositions. As Michael Delli Carpini and Scott Keeter (1997, 271) argue, groups that pay less attention to political debate are likely to be disadvantaged in mobilization: "Systematic differences in political knowledge have serious implications for the ability of some groups to perceive and act on their self-interest or their notion of the public interest." Similarly, scholars of "issue publics" (Krosnick 1990) contend that attentiveness is the key to understanding which sections of the public influence political debates. Particular public subpopulations pay close attention to each major policy area; these groups of attentive citizens are most likely to affect political decision making on each issue. Groups paying attention to public debate also understand policy issues as well as political disagreements and have information to use in mobilizing for political action.

The results confirm this expectation. A constituency's level of attention to current events through the news media is positively and significantly related to the number of organizations and in-house political staff that represent them. It is also positively related to the number of times that the constituency's representatives testify before Congress. Perhaps high levels of representation promote media attentiveness, but that would be contrary to research suggesting that attentiveness is a stable individual-level factor that promotes political involvement (Zaller 1992). The mean level of political understanding reported by constituency members, however, is not significantly related to any measure of their organized representation. A constituency's level of attention to news thus predicts greater levels of organized representation, but the relationship is not explained by greater perceived understanding. Instead, people attentive to current events also seem to be attentive to the need to mobilize politically.

Political Efficacy

Political involvement is typically stimulated not only by attentiveness but also by feelings of efficacy. Dahl (1963) contends that, to participate, citizens must believe that the government is likely to respond to their concerns. This belief stems from two sources: an individual's confidence that he or she has the capacity to effectively voice his or her concerns (internal efficacy) and an individual's assessment of the likelihood that government will respond to popularly expressed concerns (external efficacy). Scholars of individual political participation find that feelings of high internal and external political efficacy encourage political involvement (Rudolph, Gangl, and Stevens 2000). If political self-confidence and beliefs about political responsiveness differ across public constituencies, the variation should promote different levels of organized mobilization. If individuals become more involved when they have confidence that their messages will be heeded, groups of people with these beliefs will be more equipped to generate and sustain political support for their leaders.

Constituent views of their role in the political system are indeed associated with organized representation. A constituency's mean level of internal political efficacy is significantly related to the size of its sector of organizations and the size of its staff of political representatives.[7] It is also related to the number of times that its representatives testify in Congress and appear in the Washington media. Representatives of constituencies with higher-than-average political efficacy, such as public sector professionals and farmers, testify more often in Congress; representatives of constituencies with low levels of efficacy, such as college students and the nonreligious, testify less often. Many constituencies with average levels of efficacy have representatives who do not testify or speak to the Washington media very often. The most likely explanation is that feelings of political self-confidence, which are thought to be stable personal traits, help promote active constituencies that demand inclusion in the political system. Alternatively, public constituencies may accurately measure their effectiveness in politics; they may feel more efficacious if policymakers hear their concerns more often.

A constituency's level of efficacy is correlated with other significant variables, including socioeconomic status. Yet political efficacy appears to have an association with organized representation independent of socioeconomic factors. In a regression analysis reported in Table 2.2, the relationship between group efficacy and organizational testimony before Congress remains significant even after controlling for socioeconomic status and group size. Differences in efficacy are likely indicating some kind of underlying dimension of political preparedness levels across constituencies, over and above differences in social position. Efficacy acts as a kind of self-fulfilling prophecy, that is,

TABLE 2.2. Regressions predicting congressional testimony with constituency characteristics.

	Appearances in congressional hearings by organized leaders		
Constituency population size	.36	.8	.53
	(.31)	(.57)	(.54)
Mean socioeconomic status	.31	−16	−.33
	(1.24)	(1.1)	(.97)
Mean level of political efficacy	155.6*	—	—
	(65.2)		
Mean level of civic membership	—	90.7**	—
		(29.2)	
Voting rate	—	—	2.01*
			(.94)
Constant	80.6	56.2	72.6
R^2	.07	.09	.05
N	105	131	137

NOTE: Table entries are OLS regression coefficients with standard errors in parentheses. ***p .001; **p .01; *p .05 (two-tailed)

groups believing that they have the power to influence government act collectively to build organizational capacity.

The belief in government responsiveness among constituencies is also positively and significantly related to the number of organizations and staff that a constituency generates but is not significantly related to measures of the prominence or involvement of their leadership. Constituencies believing that government responds to ordinary citizens, such as scientists and civil rights supporters, generate more organized representatives; constituencies with a low level of belief in government responsiveness, such as supporters of animal rights and supporters of progressive taxation, generate less extensive representation. Yet the level of general confidence in government within a constituency is unrelated to its organized representation.

Civic Engagement

Success in group political mobilization is also connected to grassroots involvement. Public constituencies that become active in organizing their local communities should be expected to mobilize politically on a national scale. Scholars of civic engagement (Putnam 2000; Skocpol 2003) demonstrate that membership in civic organizations helps promote political involvement. When citizens join associations, they work together to solve problems and participate more extensively in civic life and democratic government. Theda Skocpol emphasizes that local civic groups provide training for participation in democratic institutions, especially when citizens participate in meetings. Oddly, both Putnam and Skocpol see national interest-group mobilization as a competitive rather than complementary style of mobilization, despite arguing that civic and political activities often go hand-in-hand. Even if groups are now more likely to organize national advocates than local meetings, however, the types of groups that organize locally are likely to be the same types that organize nationally.

Substantial evidence indicates that this emphasis on grassroots constituency activity is warranted. Civic engagement appears to be an important factor in constituency mobilization. The average number of nonpolitical civic organizations to which constituency members belong is consistently and significantly related to all measures of their national organized representation, prominence, and involvement. Local civic engagement is strongly associated with the number of organizations and staff representing a constituency as well as the prominence of its leaders in the political media and in Congress. Constituencies with higher levels of civic membership than the general population, such as law enforcement and teachers, have representatives who are much more prominent in Washington than constituencies with low civic participation, such as Asian Americans or supporters of criminal justice reform. In addition, civic involvement has an association with the prominence of a constituency's representatives independent of socioeconomic factors. In the second regression analysis reported in Table 2.2, the relationship between constituency civic involvement and leadership congressional testimony remains significant even after controlling for socioeconomic status and group size. According to this model, public groups whose typical members join one more civic organization have organized leaders who testify in Congress nearly ten additional times per year.

Despite any trade-off between local community organizing and national political mobilization, substantial national advocacy for public groups has not developed independently of local civic life. A constituency's rate of attending a local in-person meeting or rally for a cause is also significantly and positively related to the number of organizations and political staff that represent a constituency's interests in Washington. There may have been a shift toward Washington by all groups over the last few decades, but it seems to have empowered a set of public groups similar to those engaged locally.

Political Participation

From the perspective of Behavioral Pluralism, national organized representation should be dependent on the mass political participation of public constituencies. Voting is the most common type of political participation, and differences across groups in electoral turnout are often hypothesized to affect the relative influence of groups in the political system (Uhlaner, Cain, and Kiewiet 1989). For example, Campbell (2003, 14) calls seniors "the superparticipators of American democracy," finding that they are motivated, civically involved, and participate in all aspects of politics. Constituencies that participate in traditional electoral politics are likely to make themselves easy to mobilize by interest groups.

In fact, direct measures of political participation within a constituency are excellent predictors of the extent of a constituency's organized representation in Washington. The rate of voting turnout in a constituency is significantly related to the number of organizations and staff that represent a group and the number of times that their representatives are mentioned in the Washington media and testify before Congress. Constituencies with higher voting rates than the general population, such as nonprofit workers and economic conservatives, generate more extensive representation than constituencies with low voting rates, such as manufacturing workers and supporters of public housing expansion. Because advocacy organizations attempt to encourage voting among their constituents, one cannot necessarily conclude that the high voting rate preceded the development of organized representation. Nevertheless, voting is the most common type of political participation and may offer a signal of constituency importance, especially for elected officials. In the third regression equation reported in Table 2.2, a constituency's voting rate is a significant predictor of how often its leaders testify before Congress. According to the model, every percentage point increase in voting rate is associated with two additional hearing appearances.

The relationship between organized representation and voting rate, however, does not seem to be a product of a simple rational calculation by elected officials of the expected votes from a constituency gained by granting access to its leaders. The interaction between voting rate and constituency size, which is a measure of the expected number of votes from a constituency, is not significantly related to the number of organizations or staff that a constituency generates or its prominence in the Washington media or testimony before Congress. Elected officials are not simply counting potential votes. Instead, it appears that the process leading to electoral participation also leads to organizational mobilization.

Overrepresented constituencies in the national electorate are also overrepresented in the advocacy system. Because the relationship is not mediated by constituency size, overrepresentation by interest groups could be more significant. Doctors may vote at a substantially higher rate, but they still form a small proportion of any electorate. By mobilizing in the advocacy system, they achieve far more disproportionate representation. This critical distinction is likely to be at the core of most concerns about the advocacy system. Normative models of deliberation and democratic decision making often seek equal representation of citizens as well as equal representation of policy positions or stakeholders (Dahl 1963; James 2004). Nonetheless, these two positions are typically irreconcilable because different policy positions are associated with public groups of various sizes; all stakeholders are unlikely to be equal in size. The United States does not typically achieve either equality of citizens or equality of stakeholder groups. Electoral representation, however, tends to be closer to equal representation of citizens, whereas the advocacy system tends to be closer to equal representation of positions and stakeholders. Some groups are advantaged in both systems, but the advantage is moderated by group size in the electoral system. Doctors and lawyers participate more in both electoral and advocacy-group politics, but in the advocacy system they gain an advantage over groups of any size. In the electoral system, 100 percent voting participation by doctors and lawyers would still not lead to greater aggregate participation when compared to groups like African Americans or evangelicals. In both systems, groups having greater capacity are involved disproportionately. Because the advocacy system represents stakeholders independently of the size of their group, however, the lack of proportionality is far more dramatic in interest-group politics.

Other types of political participation are potentially important but do not generate the same broad-based results as the voting rate. A constituency's rate of contributing financially to a social or political cause is significantly and positively related to the number of organizations and political staff that represent its interests in Washington, but not to direct measures of the policymaking involvement of its leadership. On a similar note, the rate of contacting government officials within a constituency is related to their organized representation but not to the prominence or political involvement of their leaders.

Several robustness checks have confirmed the results presented here. Even though some constituencies were associated with small groups of survey respondents, the results are not affected by their inclusion. Correlation coefficients that include only cases where survey respondents numbered well above 100 generally matched those reported here. The scores for groups with more survey respondents also did not differ substantially from those with few respondents. The relative levels of social and political capacity used in this analysis also generally matched those found in subject-specific surveys, such as those targeted at African Americans or Jews. For groups that were identifiable on the National Election Studies survey, the relative characteristics of groups were also quite similar to those measured on the GSS.

Combining the Attributes

Many of the constituency characteristics analyzed here are highly correlated with one another. As a result of multicolinearity and the potential for reverse causality, it is difficult to build a definitive causal model of the attributes that lead to high levels of constituency representation. Attempts to assess the underlying dimensions of civic and political capacity associated with the measured attributes via scaling and dimensional analysis yielded distinct results under different specifications. Many of the attributes that help groups organize are related to one another, but none stands out as the crucial underlying factor driving the others. In a regression to predict committee testimony that includes all of the variables in Table 2.2, only civic membership remains statistically significant, although the size of its effect declines. Without observing changes in the attributes and organized activities of many groups over an extended period, scholars cannot be confident enough to move beyond descriptive associations.

Even a well-specified regression model incorporating multiple group attributes and interactions would not be equivalent to a causal model. Multiple causal paths allow group-level characteristics to affect organized representation. For example, high rates of political participation among environmentalists lead to organized advocacy for several reasons. First, as voters, individual environmentalists are more likely to participate in organizations. Second, leaders who seek to start environmental organizations view the constituency as a base that can be mobilized. Third, environmentalists who want to organize politically are likely to encounter others to join with them. All three of these processes depend on the average levels of capacity in each group and are likely to matter in organizational maintenance as well as initial mobilization.

Paired Comparisons

To see the way group-level relationships can help explain the differences in organized representation associated with different constituencies, returning to the examples introduced earlier may help. Figure 2.1 illustrates paired comparisons between constituencies on opposite sides of the gun control issue, with information about their standardized scores on the traits discussed in this chapter. The seven organizations that oppose gun control, such as the NRA, are more prominent in national politics than the six organizations that favor gun control, such as the Brady Campaign to Prevent Gun Violence. The public constituency that opposes gun control is smaller and less affluent than the constituency that favors gun control. The variables identified by Behavioral Pluralism offer some potential explanations for their differences in success in the advocacy system. Gun-control opponents are more attentive to the news media, more efficacious, and more civically involved than gun-control supporters. Gun-control supporters, in contrast, are below the national average on all three of these indicators. Opponents of gun control also participate more heavily in elections; their voting rate is 8 percent higher than that of gun-control supporters. The comparison also suggests that intensity of group preferences and the salience of their issue opinions are important variables in

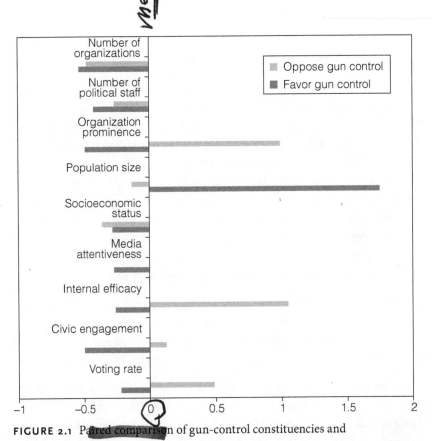

FIGURE 2.1 Paired comparison of gun-control constituencies and representative sectors.

NOTE: Each indicator is measured as the number of standard deviations above or below the mean group level. Organizations, staff, and prominence are characteristics of the organizational sector associated with each perspective. Other indicators are total and average characteristics of the public constituency.

understanding differential political mobilization; intensity may vary systematically with political engagement and civic participation.

Case studies of gun-control advocacy organizations and constituents find significant differences in the readiness of the two sides for political mobilization. In his book on gun-control politics, Robert Spitzer argues that the differential mobilization of the two groups is a classic case of the success of an energetic minority over a quiet majority:

The nature of interest-group politics is such that the energized and intense backers of the NRA have repeatedly proven the axioms that a highly motivated, intense minority operating effectively in the interest-group milieu will usually prevail in a political context over a larger, relatively apathetic majority. (2004, 141)

The NRA's success depends on its constituency, which Spitzer calls a "zealous, highly motivated, and readily mobilizable grassroots base" (107).

In her book exploring the lack of mobilization by gun-control supporters, Kristin Goss (2006) argues that constituency in favor of gun control does have intense beliefs despite its lack of organizing. According to Goss, missteps by organizational leaders and a lack of outside financial support hindered the development of a movement in favor of gun control. This study's results suggest that successful mass mobilization may be difficult when the base of supporters is inattentive and socially disengaged. The fate of the Million Mom March (MMM), a successful gun-control demonstration studied by Robert Spitzer (2004), illustrates the lack of sustained grassroots support:

> [MMM's] grassroots base was unable to sustain its momentum and mass involvement . . . The MMM's political and organizational arc again underscored limitations on the ability of gun control groups to establish and maintain the kind of political loyalty that has sustained the NRA for decades. (Spitzer 2004, 97)

Opponents of gun control are well known for their commitment to political advocacy. The NRA and its supporters are feared for their reported influence on members of Congress (Spitzer 2004), election outcomes (Wilson 2007) and even American culture (Melzer 2009). Harry Wilson (2007) reports that some voters have a stronger commitment to the NRA than they do to either political party; politicians perceive these voters and their organized leadership as potential kingmakers. Gun-control supporters lack this high level of political engagement; their reputation is one of a large but apathetic public group.

A second comparison between issue constituencies, this time on the issue of taxation, is portrayed in Figure 2.2. The six organizations in favor of progressive taxation are less prominent than the eleven organizations favoring tax cuts for everyone. Important organizations like Americans for Tax Reform favor lower taxes across the board, including cuts for the wealthiest citizens. These groups are tied to extensive local networks of antitax advocates and play major roles in Republican Party politics. Washington also features organizations that support higher taxes on the wealthy, such as Citizens for Tax Justice, but none of the groups in this sector are considered major players. The relative positions of these organizational sectors match the character of their two constituencies. The public constituency favoring broad tax cuts is

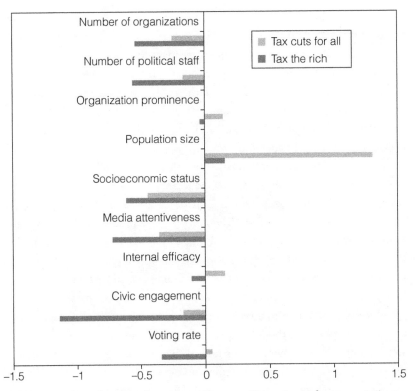

FIGURE 2.2 Paired comparison of taxation constituencies and representative sectors.

NOTE: Each indicator is measured as the number of standard deviations above or below the mean group level.

more involved in civic organizations, much more efficacious, and more likely to vote than the constituency that favors progressive taxation.

The comparison may help illuminate a puzzling trend in federal policy. Since 1978, federal policy has moved substantially in the direction of tax cuts for the wealthy. Many scholars see the move as a major factor in driving income inequality in the United States (Bartels 2008; McCarty, Poole, and Rosenthal 2008; Hacker and Pierson 2010). These scholars seek to explain the reason that policy moved in this direction even though the portions of the public favoring tax cuts and progressive taxation did not change substantially. Jacob Hacker and Paul Pierson argue that the relative influence of interest groups may offer an explanation. They find that antitax advocacy groups have grown in importance, noting "the emergence of a cadre of activists devoted to making tax cuts the durable, unquestioned foundation of Republican doc-trine" (247). Although these groups did not represent majority opinion, they convinced many candidates to take tax pledges and successfully threatened to intervene in primary elections to enforce their views. In their explanation, however, Hacker and Pierson focus on the relative balance of power between business and labor. A more parsimonious explanation might be that the anti-tax advocates faced no well-organized issue constituency advocating tax in-creases on the richest Americans.

The differential mobilization of the two sides has a long history. In a review of the tax revolt of the late 1970s that led to antitax initiatives like California's Proposition 13, David Sears and Jack Citrin (1982) argue that the public did not hold strident antitax views. The constituency in favor of large tax cuts, however, was more likely to vote and much more politically organized. They find a basic pattern of unbalanced mobilization (89–90). In a review of the property-tax revolt, Isaac William Martin (2008) concludes that, even though it originated in specific complaints about tax assessment, the antitax move-ment helped proponents of broad tax cuts gain a permanent advantage in state and national policy. Although many Americans favor progressive taxation, a similar single-issue movement for taxing the rich has yet to gain a foothold organizationally or within the Democratic Party. If the Occupy Wall Street movement that began in 2011 can sustain itself and coalesce around the goal of increased higher-income taxation, it may be the start of such a movement; yet that is made difficult by the likely character of its constituency.

Conservative positions win in both of these comparisons, but there are no consistent differences in levels of representation between sectors associated with liberal and conservative views. The differences are associated with the civic and political engagement of constituencies rather than general ideology. These comparisons also provide an alternative view of the reason that public opinion often fails to drive public policy. If policymakers respond to organized single-issue constituencies, the results might not match public opinion at large. If these single-issue constituencies gain prominence as a result of their political engagement, rather than the size of their public subpopulation of supporters, Americans should not expect the public opinion majority to rule the day.

These same differences in constituency engagement and participation also help to explain why some social groups are much better represented than oth-ers in national politics. Figure 2.3 illustrates a paired comparison between two religious constituencies. The organized representation of Jews is much more

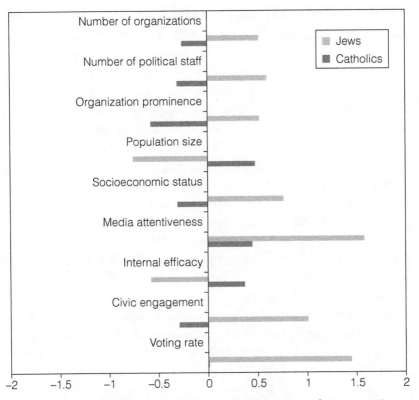

FIGURE 2.3 Paired comparison of religious constituencies and representative sectors.

NOTE: Each indicator is measured as the number of standard deviations above or below the mean group level.

extensive than the organized representation of Catholics, despite the much smaller size of Jews as a social group in the American public. The twenty-five Jewish organizations are substantially more prominent in national politics than are the Catholic organizations. Some potential explanations come to mind if one compares the characteristics of these two constituencies. In the American public, Jews have higher socioeconomic status and higher levels of media attentiveness and civic involvement than Catholics do. The voting rate among Jews is almost 17 percent higher than it is among Catholics. This higher rate reflects the importance that Jews attach to civic and political organizing and may explain their propensity to sustain advocacy groups.

Jewish political mobilization has been built on the broad pattern of successful Jewish social and economic advancement in the United States. American

Jews have had higher-than-average educational attainment, occupational status, and income than the rest of the population since at least the 1950s and have attained a disproportionate number of important positions (Burstein 2007). Paul Burstein (2007) offers several potential explanations: First, Jews accumulate more human capital, such as education. Second, Jews value mutual assistance. Third, Jews feel marginalized, stimulating creative endeavors. According to Burstein, combining these explanations points to the importance of group-level social capital, especially Jewish social networks and organizations.

This Jewish civic capacity also helps build political organizations. Stephen Schwartz (2006) describes successive waves of Jewish immigrants building a varied organizational infrastructure to protect rights, to advance ethnic interests, and eventually to support Israel. Mearsheimer and Walt (2007) argue that these organizations supported the interests of Israel above those of the United States, helping to redirect American foreign policy. Nevertheless, the key to the rise of these influential groups seems to have been the overwhelming activism and political orientation of American Jews. In his book criticizing Mearsheimer and Walt, Anti-Defamation League Director Abraham Foxman (2007) argues that Jewish leaders used the same methods of political organizing as have other successful advocacy groups like AARP and the NRA. He compares Jews to Cuban Americans, saying both motivated constituencies developed a shared interest in foreign policy.

Catholics have not had the same zeal for political organizing in the United States. Michael Sean Winters (2008) reports that Catholic citizens rely on bishops and Church institutions for political engagement, rather than organizing independently. Winters contends that Catholics became estranged from their leadership when such controversial issues as school desegregation and abortion came to the fore. As a result, Catholic organizations lost their constituency support and political leverage (144). According to Matthew Streb and Brian Frederick (2008), Catholic citizens do not rely primarily on their religious affiliation for guiding their political behavior. As a social group, Catholics are not as oriented toward collective political activity as are Jews. They do not provide an effective constituency for the public advocacy of their Church leaders.

There are similar potential explanations for differences in the mobilization patterns of occupational groups. Figure 2.4 depicts a paired comparison of lawyers and engineers. It demonstrates that, as one might expect, lawyers are more extensively represented in Washington than engineers. Their leadership is also more prominent in national politics. Both occupational constituencies

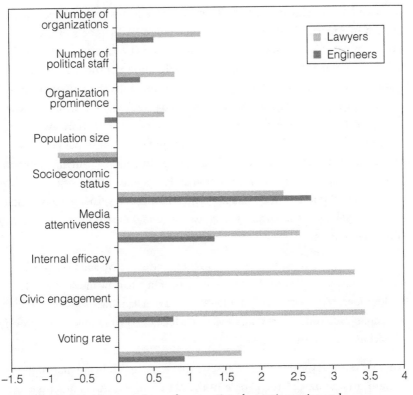

FIGURE 2.4 Paired comparison of occupational constituencies and representative sectors.

NOTE: Each indicator is measured as the number of standard deviations above or below the mean group level.

are small and affluent. Some clues to their differences as political constituencies appear in the results. Lawyers are more attentive to the news media, more civically involved, and more efficacious; moreover, they have a significantly higher rate of electoral turnout than engineers. Lawyers see an obvious and direct interest in government action. Their careers are tied to involvement in government institutions, and they may have been drawn to a life in the courts by an inherent interest in political issues. Engineers are affected by government policy, but they do not place the same emphasis on civic and political life; this difference is reflected in their group attributes and their relative lack of involvement in national political organizing.

These findings are consistent with qualitative analyses of the political activities of the two occupational groups. Mark Miller describes the prominent role that lawyers play in politics: "Lawyers are, and always have been, omnipresent in American political institutions" (1995, 1). Members of the profession dominate Congress, the administration, and the courts as well as political organizations for two reasons: First, people who enter the law already have a political orientation, and, second, legal training pulls them further toward political processes. As Stuart Scheingold (2004, 168) argues, the background and education of lawyers helps produce a political orientation. As a result of their political mobilization, lawyers have organized multiple policy areas around the concept of rights protected through litigation, ensuring their continued participation in policy formation and implementation.

Engineers' political activities are quite another story. In a personal interview, an engineering advocacy group executive told me that her constituency was difficult to mobilize:

> It is a patient process to even put together a letter . . . We still need to educate the membership. We are focused on putting out a narrow message in selected locations. [Engineers] are not interested in understanding the nuances of how Capitol Hill works. They want to see that a bill has been introduced and provide technical comments on it.

Another advocacy group leader representing engineers told me that engineers remain unorganized: "The people in the better position to contact [government officials] and have their voices heard are not as organized. They take up issues only on a local level." Overall, engineers have been much less politically important in the United States than in other nations; government officials rely on engineers less, and they are less likely to take up politics on their own (Tenner 2005). According to Ed Tenner, engineers have a public reputation as antisocial technicians and a self-image of narrowly focused specialists.

These paired comparisons are meant to illustrate the potential effects of constituency characteristics on organized representation; the differences between these groups are consistent with the descriptive associations. The results and their similarity to qualitative accounts offer substantially more support for a perspective that builds on theories of individual participation and local civic engagement than for traditional theoretical models focusing on the collective action problem or on spatial competition among ideological interests. Not all of the qualitative research on each group supports the broad patterns uncovered here. Case studies of particular political constituencies are more likely to focus on the strategies and tactics used by each organized leadership.

The broad associations, however, lend credence to the idea that some constituencies are more difficult to mobilize than others and less likely to generate a capable organized leadership. This does not mean that some constituencies succeed automatically and others are doomed to fail. Just as electoral politics features little-known candidates that defy the odds and some frontrunners that crash and burn, the advocacy community contains some sectors that are more or less successful than you would expect based on their constituency. Qualitative analysis of these cases, however, should not lose sight of the broad context that makes mobilization easier for some groups than others any more than analysis of individual campaigns should lose sight of underlying partisan trends and economic circumstances.

Assessing Behavioral Pluralism

Behavioral Pluralism identifies a specific set of constituency attributes that are associated with higher levels of organized representation. In contrast to rational choice theory, Behavioral Pluralism views attributes of groups as indicators of their propensity and capacity to engage politically rather than a set of given preferences and the costs associated with reaching them. It identifies stable attributes of groups that make them socially and politically distinct, not merely different in their current levels of resources or their contemporary agenda of political goals.

Public constituencies differ in ways that influence their success in political competition. Even though democratic theorists might expect more, the modern advocacy system is a product of decades of political mobilization by a multitude of constituencies. It reflects their relative success in organizing rather than any global effort to remedy inequalities or uniformly represent all public stakeholders. The relative mobilization of organized advocates is related to the underlying capacity of constituencies.

According to the results of this study, the strongest and most consistent factors associated with generating an extensive, prominent, and involved organized leadership are a constituency's political efficacy, its membership in local civic associations, and its voting rate. This corresponds to the traditional emphases of the scholarly literature on the political behavior of mass publics and of the literature on civic engagement in local communities.

Groups with higher socioeconomic status also produce more organizations and representatives to speak on their behalf; yet their leaders are not significantly more prominent in the Washington media or more involved in committee hearings. To paraphrase Schattschneider's (1960) famous statement, the heavenly chorus of organized representatives does sing "with an upper class accent," but it is not clear that members of Congress and reporters are more likely to listen to those with the loftiest intonation, at least when it comes to advocacy organizations. Schattschneider is concerned with the bias of the entire political system; his concerns cannot be fully addressed here. The "mobilization of bias" along class lines that occurs in the advocacy system, however, does not extend to organizational prominence or involvement.

Several other findings have broad implications for an understanding of democratic government. First, the size of a constituency does not appear to be a crucial factor in determining the extent of its organized representation, despite the important role of this variable in theories of collective action and in normative democratic theory. Because many small groups do not generate any organized representation, some minimum size may still be necessary for generating representation. Nevertheless, the striking lack of association between size and representation among the 140 groups analyzed here may be devastating for some normative theories of democratic competition based on rule-by-the-many rather than rule-by-the-few. Second, the extremity and cohesion of a group's opinions does not seem to have a direct relationship to the extent of their representation or their policymaking involvement. This suggests that spatial models of political mobilization based on the ideological spectrum may be incomplete. Popular caricatures of "special-interest" politics that pit the extremes against the center are also incorrect. Constituency political views offer poor predictors of the mobilization of advocacy groups. Third, even when constituency characteristics are related to whether a group generates organizations and political staff to represent its interests, the characteristics are not always related to the relative prominence or policymaking involvement of its representatives. One should not discount the important organizational factors that likely mediate the effects of constituency character on the involvement of organized representatives in national politics.

Are Organizations Representing Constituencies or Subgroups?

Even if a citizen is part of a constituency that is well represented, this does not automatically suggest that the citizen's personal concerns will be addressed or expressed by an organized leadership. Organizations are unlikely to represent the concerns of all constituents equally. Strolovitch (2007) convincingly argues that some subgroups within ethnic and economic constituencies with organized representation benefit more than others. Organizational leaders typically fail to represent the interests of disadvantaged subgroups within their constituency.

The assumptions behind this analysis, nevertheless, do differ from those of Strolovitch (2007) in some important respects. For each organization type, she assesses its attention to four types of issues: one concerning the group majority, one for an advantaged subgroup, one for a disadvantaged subgroup, and one for all citizens. For example, she assesses the importance of hate crime, affirmative action in government contracting, violence against women, and Social Security as issues for Asian American organizations. This study does not assess issue attention, but it does separate issue-based representation from identity-based representation. Some organizations and constituencies are specifically concerned with each of the four issues that she identifies as potential concerns for Asian Americans. Organizations designed around defense of entitlements, domestic violence, and government contractors would each be more concerned with one of these issues than any identity-based representative. Inequalities in representing ideas and social-group interests are both important to assess and may be driven by similar factors.

This chapter's results are potentially more devastating for the ideal of equal individual representation. Not only are some social groups much better represented than others, but also many of the well-represented individuals are likely to be connected to ideological or single-issue constituencies separately associated with high levels of representation. An elderly doctor in favor of abortion rights and Social Security protection, for example, is a member of many groups with high levels of representation. An unemployed teenage student in favor of guaranteed jobs and welfare rights is also a member of many constituencies, but each is associated with a low level of representation. Disadvantaged identities and viewpoints compound one another.

Helping to Answer Central Questions

By understanding which types of groups are advantaged in the "mobilization of bias" in America's political system, scholars can help move forward in the long-standing struggle to discover "who governs?" The advocacy system represents an important place for some groups to gain advantage over others. The system of organized representation of American public constituencies in national politics does not approach a "one person, one lobbyist" standard. As John Mark Hansen (1991, 230) concludes, interest groups are "both democratic and elitist" because they "represent popular demands," but they "represent only some demands, and by no means the most popular." Behavioral Pluralism has moved beyond this contention by identifying the attributes of the well-represented constituencies. The mobilization of bias in the advocacy system favors constituencies that are affluent, attentive to the media, politically efficacious, civically and politically engaged, and convinced of a responsive government. In contrast to judgments by some commentators, the process of organizing political representation does not necessarily favor the large or small, the extreme or moderate, the cohesive or conflicting.

The relative prominence of some groups in politics is not necessarily evidence of a conspiracy on the part of the advantaged group. Jews and lawyers, for example, may just be more politically engaged than other social groups. Supporters of progressive taxation, on the other hand, may not have much capacity to mobilize around this single-issue perspective. Just as everything must go right for a challenger candidate running against an incumbent in a good economy, leaders of progressive taxation organizations need more luck to be heard.

If the views of some groups are better represented in the policy debate and in important policymaking venues, citizens are justifiably concerned that some interests may be advantaged over others in the political system. When aggregated to the group level, many of the individual attributes that produce an unrepresentative group of American political activists also produce an unrepresentative population of organized political representatives in national policymaking. The political science debate over the relationship between inequality in political influence and inequality in economic outcomes (Bartels 2008; Hacker and Pierson 2010) should take note of the advocacy system. Both in particular issue areas, like taxation, and in competition between social groups, the differential representation of some constituencies over others may be part of the explanation for why the American political system produces unequal economic outcomes.

The civic and political attributes of public constituencies should be considered important features of any social group that seeks to have its views included in public decision making or any group of supporters for either side of a policy debate. Basic differences in the capacity of public groups to participate in political life promote the interests and ideas of some groups more than others in the advocacy system. Where groups stand in national political institutions depends on the way they score on traditional indicators of political engagement compared to other groups, rather than categorical distinctions that separate the winners from the losers. Just as some groups benefit more from electoral politics than others, even though there are many enfranchised groups, some groups also gain more from the interest group system despite its inclusion of advocates for many different perspectives. The advantages are traceable, in large part, to the civic and political capacity of the constituencies that organized advocates represent.

3 The Skew and Diversity of Organized Advocacy

Not all advocacy organizations with the same constituency are created equal. The NRA, for example, has a large Washington operation and millions of members; they are mentioned in the Washington news media more than 300 times per year. Gun Owners of America (GOA), in contrast, has five in-house political representatives and is mentioned in the Washington news media fewer than fifteen times per year. These groups tend to take the same positions on policy issues and claim to speak on behalf of the same supporters; yet one has more resources, is substantially more active in the national policy debate, and is called on far more often to speak on behalf of gun owners in opposition to gun control.

Chapter 2 analyzed the sectors of organizations speaking on behalf of each constituency, such as the opponents of gun control. Nevertheless, broad and stable working coalitions of organizations that correspond to each constituency are rare (Hojnacki 1997). Advocacy groups act primarily as individual organizations making decisions based on their own considerations. The NRA and GOA may be working on the same side, for example, but they are also somewhat independent actors who are sometimes in competition with each other. Most organizations representing similar constituencies, such as the environmental sector or the women's sector, line up with each other even less predictably and obviously. In the crowded Washington advocacy community, it is difficult to be familiar with all of one's potential allies and opponents, and it is often unclear against whom one is competing for resources and attention.

In an important sense, each organization is competing with all of the others. Attention from policymakers and reporters is limited, and not all organizations make the cut for regular inclusion in policy debates.

This chapter outlines the distribution of resources across the advocacy community, reports information about the community's activities, and puts forward some measures to assess the success of each organization in Washington. One can learn a great deal about the advocacy community from the way important attributes are distributed across organizations. The picture that emerges is one of uneven distributions as well as wide and skewed variation in success. This variation presents a puzzle that Part II of the book seeks to explain.

Investigating the distribution of organizational resources, the variation in activity profiles, and the differences in prominence and involvement across the advocacy community is an important component of assessing claims about the structure of interest group politics in the United States. Traditional pluralist models of governance assume that many different types of stakeholders generate resources for political advocacy, participate in political debate, and gain a voice in public political discussion and national policymaking. Traditional elitist models of governance assume that a small group of major players dominates the political arena by amassing resources and gaining disproportionate access to media and policymaking institutions.

These frameworks, however, are not mutually exclusive. A small subset of advocacy-organization leaders may amass disproportionate resources and gain preeminence, and yet this subset may seek to represent many different types of public constituencies. In this case, organized advocacy in Washington would be both skewed in its resource and activity distributions and diverse in the content of its advocacy. If some organizations are much more successful than others, this does not necessarily imply that the successful groups share the same views or represent the same type of interests. One might see diversity in type, even given a low rate of overall success. Prominent and successful groups may include representatives of ethnic, religious, occupational, ideological, and single-issue advocacy groups; yet, in each sector, only a few groups may be conspicuous for their high levels of resource mobilization and involvement.

The Washington advocacy community, in other words, may be analogous to a zoo. Zoos need several examples of each species or family but do not seek to represent each type of animal in proportion to its natural occurrence. Visitors take the animals on display as representative of the broader community. They hear a cacophony of animal noises and rarely fear missing the sounds of the kingdom. Some animals gain disproportionate attention, space, and care in the zoo. A single elephant or lion may drown out many other creatures. The zoo accommodates visitors who want to see variety but selects a few animals to place on prominent display. An ardent egalitarian may fear that the mice and crickets fail to generate equal attention with the elephants and the lions, but most visitors are astonished by the assortment on display. Likewise, policymakers may hear from an assorted set of voices even as organizations achieve vastly different levels of success. The content of advocacy may be diverse even while the relative prominence of organizations varies dramatically, with a few groups from each sector standing out in the crowd.

Organizational Resources and Activities

For a sense of the character of each organization, this study uses information about organizational resources, that is, the size of an organization's political staff and external lobbying force, its ties to PACs and local chapters, its membership size, the breadth of its issue agenda, and its age. The data collection includes most of these data for all 1,621 organizations in the population.[1] To explore the Washington activities of the advocacy community, this chapter uses data on organizational participation in public political events in the nation's capital from 1995 through 2004. To assess the public mobilization strategies of organizations, it analyzes data gathered from a content analysis of organizational websites in 2005.[2]

This type of data compilation, like all research methodologies, has strengths and weaknesses. The primary strengths are the breadth of coverage and the use of measures based on observed structure and behavior. The primary weakness compared to survey-based research is the reliance on information that is publicly available. Nevertheless, the data compilation offers the first comprehensive view of the complete advocacy community; it reports information on all organizations in the population rather than only a limited sample of survey respondents. The review is also the first attempt to look at distributions of resources and activities across that entire community.

To see the way resources are distributed across different types of organizations, this chapter reports the proportion of resources and political activities accounted for by several broad and mutually exclusive categories of organizations. The advocacy community is partitioned into the following three broad sections: occupational groups, identity group representatives, and issue advocates. Each of these categories is then divided based on the type of constituency organizations claim to represent. Using the content analysis of websites and reference-text descriptions, organizations fall into categories based on the specific type of social group or political perspective they claim to represent.[3] Occupational groups are divided between professional associations and unions. Identity-group representatives are placed into smaller categories: ethnic groups, religious groups, gender groups, other social groups, and intersectional groups representing people with multiple shared identities (such as an occupation and ethnicity). Issue advocates are partitioned based on whether they represent a liberal or conservative ideological view; a single-issue perspective of a liberal, conservative, or nonideological variety; or a foreign-policy, environmental, or consumer perspective. The categorizations are consistent with those used by other scholars (Hertzke 1988; Hofrenning 1995; Berry 1999; Shaiko 1999; Hays 2001) for most organizations. Later chapters analyze whether these categorical distinctions best predict organizational behavior or whether other organizational attributes are more important. This chapter seeks to describe the lay of the land in the advocacy community.

The Skewed Distribution of Organizational Resources

The results reveal that most resources are distributed unevenly across the advocacy community. Political staff size is a useful starting point. The average advocacy organization has 2.5 political representatives on its Washington staff, but the standard deviation is 3.2. The middle 50 percent of organizations have between one and three in-house political representatives. Groups like AARP and the AFL-CIO (American Federation of Labor and Congress of Industrial Organizations) have large staffs of dozens of political advocates to speak for their constituencies, but these large groups are a small minority of the advocacy community. Most groups, including the Citizens Committee for the Right to Keep and Bear Arms and the American Alliance for Health, Physical Education, Recreation and Dance, have only one or two political staff members.

The distribution of external lobbyists hired by advocacy organizations from professional lobbying firms is also skewed. The average number of hired lobbyists is less than one per organization, but the standard deviation of hired lobbyists is 2.5. The bottom 75 percent of organizations hired either one external lobbyist or none at all. Most advocacy organizations, including groups like the International Reading Association and American Friends of the Czech Republic, do not hire lobbyists to advance their agendas. Others, such as the American College of Gastroenterology, hire dozens of lobbyists. Whether measured in terms of staff or lobbyists, some organizations have a substantially larger force of boots on the ground than others.

Other important organizational attributes are also unevenly distributed. The average advocacy group is a little more than four decades old, but the median organization is only thirty-one years old. Several older groups raise the average above the median. The middle 50 percent of organizations range from nineteen to fifty-eight years old, but the standard deviation of organizational age is thirty-two years. Most organizations are young. A few, like the American Automobile Association or the International Brotherhood of Teamsters, have been active for more than a century.

The size of organizational issue agendas matches a similar distribution. The average organization has a small issue agenda that includes approximately two major issue areas. The standard deviation of issue areas per organization is greater than four, signaling that some groups cover the issue spectrum broadly while most focus narrowly. A few generalist organizations, like the ABA and the National Taxpayers Union, take positions in more than a dozen issue areas.

Other attributes are quite scarce in the advocacy community. Fewer than one-fifth of advocacy groups have state or local chapters. Although Chapter 2 demonstrated that local civic involvement is related to national organized advocacy among public groups, most of the advocacy organizations themselves are unlikely to be tied directly to local mobilization. This result is consistent with Skocpol's (2003) concern that national advocacy groups are no longer tied to local organizations, even though the population here claims to represent public groups.

In addition, a little more than one in ten Washington advocacy organizations have an affiliated PAC to fund campaign contributions. Most of these PACs make quite limited contributions. PACs associated with advocacy groups donate substantially less than PACs associated with members of Congress or corporations. Unions were the only sector of advocacy groups making significant use of PACs in the last five election cycles.[4] Only a small minority of advocacy groups have an affiliated PAC; those that do mostly donate inconsequential amounts. If organizations have to pay-to-play in Washington, only a small proportion of the advocacy community is prepared.

Which types of advocates have the largest share of resources? If boots on the ground in the national capital are indicative of the representative capacity of each type of group, the distribution of organizations and resources among these types of organizations is likely to have an impact on whose voice is heard in Washington. The results reveal that occupational groups, identity groups, and issue advocates all constitute large shares of the organizational population. Table 3.1 reports the distribution of organizations and resources in the advocacy community. Professional associations account for 33 percent of advocacy organizations in Washington, and unions account for 5 percent. Representatives of identity groups account for 24 percent of all advocacy organizations, with the largest total shares constituting ethnic-group representatives, intersectional groups, and other social group representatives (such as veterans' associations). Representatives of issue perspectives, rather than social groups or occupations, account for 38 percent of advocacy organizations. Among issue advocates, liberal single-issue groups comprise the largest proportion of the total. This total does not include representatives of consumer concerns and environmentalists, some of which are commonly viewed as liberal single-issue groups. Conservative single-issue groups account for substantially fewer advocacy organizations.

TABLE 3.1. Distribution of advocacy organizations and resources by constituency type.

	Organizations	Political staff	Lobbyists	Members
Issue groups				
Conservative ideological	1.5%	2%	0.2%	1%
Liberal ideological	2.1%	3.2%	0.5%	0.4%
Conservative single-issue	4.2%	3.9%	5.1%	3.2%
Liberal single-issue	17.2%	17.5%	16.3%	4.6%
Environmental	4.1%	5.4%	2%	2.6%
Consumer	1.3%	1.4%	3.8%	2%
Foreign policy	2.2%	2.7%	1.2%	0.6%
Other Issue	5.5%	4.1%	5.8%	0.7%
Vocation				
Union	4.8%	7%	6.6%	11.9%
Professional	33%	34.1%	43.4%	23%
Identity groups				
Ethnic	6.1%	3.4%	3.5%	1.6%
Religious	3.7%	3.8%	1.6%	6.4%
Gender	1.7%	1.1%	0.4%	0.6%
Intersectional	4%	2.3%	1.4%	10.2%
Other social group	8.6%	8.1%	8.1%	31.1%

NOTE: Table entries report the percentage of total advocacy organizations, staff, lobbyists, and members accounted for by each category of organizations.

Liberal single-issue and ideological groups outnumber conservative groups by more than three to one. This distribution confirms Berry's (1999) finding that liberal-issue organizations vastly outnumber conservative groups but clarifies that liberals possess a substantially greater share of single-issue advocacy organizations rather than a greater share of generalist ideological groups. One should not jump to the conclusion that liberal interests dominate Washington, however. The organizations in this population do not include individual business policy offices or trade associations, which are often spokespeople for conservative issue positions. In addition, the cacophony of liberal advocates for different perspectives in Washington is often seen as a disadvantage for reaching consensus around policy proposals (Hacker and Pierson 2006). Nonetheless, Berry argues that the large array of liberal spokespeople helps these groups shape the Washington agenda. Whether or not it is an advantage, the large number of liberal single-issue organizations is an underappreciated basic fact about the advocacy community that contributes to its collective behavior and image.

Chapter 2 demonstrated that ideological differences among public groups do not contribute to the relative mobilization of different constituencies; a general mobilization advantage does not seem to be held by liberal public groups. Other potential factors may explain why liberal single-issue organizations are more common. First, many of these liberal single-issue organizations search diligently for a slice of the federal budget; sectors of organizations are associated with a variety of federal programs. The conservative opposition to these sectors consists primarily of generalist antispending or antitax groups rather than small sectors opposing spending on each type of program. Second, the Democratic Party has been known as a coalition of many minorities since Franklin D. Roosevelt's New Deal. The Republican Party also has divisions, but they are largely based on the relative emphasis of social and economic ideological concerns.

If more organizations are not always indicative of more representation, one needs to look at the resources mobilized to represent each type of constituency. One important resource is the scale of an organization's internal staff of political representatives. The proportion of all in-house political representatives associated with each category, however, is roughly proportional to its share of advocacy organizations. Identity organizations have 19 percent of the total political staff for all advocacy groups in Washington, occupational groups account for 41 percent, and representatives of issue perspectives have 40 percent of all staff. Some differences occur across categories, however. Liberal and conservative ideological organizations have a larger share of political staff than their share of organizations. In addition, unions account for more staff, but ethnic groups have a smaller share of staff than their share of organizations. Intersectional groups, many of which claim to represent ethnic groups in particular occupations, also represent only a small share of all in-house staff. With that said, most categories receive similar shares of organizations and political representatives.

The distribution of hired lobbyists across organizational categories, in contrast, is not proportional to the distribution of organizations. Many categories have a much smaller share of lobbyists than organizations. Ideological groups, for example, have less than 1 percent of lobbyists, and environmental groups have only 2 percent. All identity representatives combined have only 15 percent. The categories that account for disproportionately large shares of external lobbyists include consumer groups, unions, and professional associations. Professional associations disproportionately use lobbyists rather than internal staff. On the other hand, ideological groups rely more on staff than lobbyists. Unions have more personnel of both kinds working on their behalf.

The distribution of members across organizational categories is equally disproportionate. As Truman (1951) and Olson (1965) predicted, unions have an easier time generating members than other groups, accounting for 12 percent of all members. Identity groups, however, generate most advocacy-organization membership (50 percent). Religious groups, for instance, generate a greater share of members than their share of the organizational population. Groups organized around issue perspectives generate little of the total membership (15 percent). An ideological disparity also prevails. Liberal ideological and issue groups generate fewer members per organization than conservative ideological and issue groups. This provides some support for Berry's (1999) contention that conservative organizations rely more on membership mobilization than do liberal organizations. Overall, the findings reveal that organizations and staff are distributed similarly across advocacy categories, whereas lobbyists and members are more common in particular categories. The disproportionate use of lobbyists by professional associations and the disproportionate membership size of unions and identity organizations are likely to be stable and significant distinctions in Washington representation.

Public Events and Mobilization

Advocacy organizations use their resources to educate policymakers and the public about their policy positions and to attempt to persuade others to support their views. Advocacy organizations often interact in public events such as panel discussions and conferences. These events can stimulate media coverage and the attention of government officials. Regular participation serves as an indicator of general visibility in the Washington advocacy community. How active are most advocacy organizations in these events? Here too, the variation is wide and skewed. It can be measured by the number of mentions of each organization in daily Washington event calendars.[5] The average advocacy organization participated in approximately four public political events per year, but the standard deviation of event calendar mentions was more than 15. The bottom half of organizations participated in fewer than one event annually. These event calendars include both large and small events, but they are seen daily by thousands of participants in Washington policymaking. The advocacy community's presentation of itself in Washington makes it appear skewed toward issue advocates of a particular kind. Representatives of issue perspectives accounted for a disproportionate share of appearances at Washington events (53.3 percent). Organizations specializing in foreign policy were especially prominent and account for approximately 13 percent of all appearances. Just as a tiny minority of organizations account for most of advocacy group resources, a small subset of the advocacy community participates most in public events. The population of organizations participating in public events, however, is less representative of the wider advocacy community.

Washington event participation provides only one indicator of policy-relevant advocacy group activity, but the distribution reveals that a small number of organizations, especially single-issue groups and think tanks, are much more active than others. For example, a 2010 panel on the American response to flooding in Pakistan drew officials from the Brookings Institution and the New America Foundation along with government officials.[6] Another 2010 panel discussion on endangered species included representatives from Competitive Enterprise Institute and the Heritage Foundation.[7] In that same year, a "Dialogue on Iran" featured staff from the Center for American Progress, the American Action Forum, and the Foundation for the Defense of the Democracies.[8] These events are typically held at think tanks or the Capitol and allow policymakers to speak with advocates.

Policymakers are not the only intended audience of advocacy organizations. Some groups seek to mobilize and involve public supporters of their positions. Nevertheless, mobilization activities are again concentrated among a small minority of groups. Organizations vary dramatically in how much they attempt to mobilize public constituencies for direct participation. The results from my content analysis reveal that the average organization makes 2.3 requests for public or member political action on its website. The standard deviation of these action requests across all groups is 4.5, meaning some groups make many more requests of their supporters. More than half of advocacy organizations request no political action from their online supporters. The most popular type of request focused on calling a member of Congress; 24 percent of advocacy organizations make at least one request of this kind. Almost one in three advocacy organizations mentions pending legislation on its website. CQ-Roll Call sells an online product to help advocacy groups enable calls to members of Congress on their sites. The organization has enrolled dozens of advocacy groups and integrated all of their calls for action into a central portal. In 2010, advocacy groups sent alerts through the site regarding gays in the military, food safety legislation, and immigration policy. Congress remains the focus of advocacy group online mobilization. A little more than 1 percent of advocacy groups mention pending administrative actions on their sites and even fewer mention court cases. To the extent that they mobilize constituents at all, most advocacy organizations ask supporters to call Congress.

Requests to attend local meetings or participate in protests are much less common. Only 5.1 percent of advocacy organizations mention an in-person meeting on their websites. Advocates are not promoting the archetypal social-movement activity, public protests. Only 0.1 percent of advocacy organizations are promoting a protest. Public mobilization is part of the advocacy community's tactical repertoire but not its primary style of activism. The use of these tactics across organizational categories is roughly consistent. In all categories, some organizations make a small number of requests of their constituents, primarily focusing on action in Congress. Social-movement-style activities seem secondary to other forms of traditional interest group advocacy.

Measuring Success

If the Washington advocacy community features wide variation in the resources, structures, and activities of its organizations, great variation in the success of these organizations should also be expected. Nevertheless, scholars have thus far been unable to measure adequately which advocacy organizations are most successful in Washington. In their research review, Andrews and Edwards (2004) call for more research on the most obvious indicator of success, namely, organizational influence on policy outcomes. Unfortunately,

that research is easier said than done. Political influence is notoriously difficult to measure (Polsby 1963), and interest-group research has been hindered
by this difficulty (Baumgartner and Leech 1998). Attempts to investigate influence have mostly been limited to analyses of specific policy areas (Heinz et al.
1993; Fernandez and Gould 1994), specific sectors of organizations (Skrentny
2002; Berry 1999), or specific tactics of influence. Research on the influence
of PAC and lobbying activity has demonstrated mixed results, but political
scientists have accumulated little evidence that these tactics approach the
scale of influence that popular commentators assume they do (Baumgartner
and Leech 1998). Instead, PAC contributions increase the amount of time that
already-allied legislators spend on issues of concern to resourceful interest
groups (Hall and Wayman 1990), and lobbying may provide a staffing subsidy
for allied legislators (Hall and Deardorff 2006).

In a recent comprehensive investigation, Frank R. Baumgartner, Jeffrey M.
Berry, Marie Hojnacki, David C. Kimball, and Beth L. Leech (2009) look for
evidence of interest-group influence on policy change. These scholars review
policy issues on which there is active lobbying. They discover that many issues
have interest-group lobbying on both sides, sometimes tied to specific legislation and at other times tied to more general policy goals. They conclude that
opponents of policy change have tremendous advantages when compared to
proponents because of built-in biases toward the status quo. These scholars
also conclude that moneyed interests do not always prevail over other groups
because groups with fewer monetary resources have some other tools and allies at their disposal. Although the researchers find little evidence of successful
attempts by interest groups to change public policy, they conclude that interest-
group influence may be baked in to the status quo; current policy, in this view,
is already a consequence of the success of the most influential interest groups
in previous battles. As Christine Mahoney (2008) points out, however, evaluating lobbying success is not the same as proving influence. Comparing winning
and losing sides in interest group battles cannot help discern whether factors
related to interest groups had much to do with policy outcomes.

Case studies of the policy process in specific areas provide evidence that
advocacy organizations often play a central role in defining options and influencing decisions. Shep Melnick (1994), for example, argues that organizations
representing the handicapped, welfare recipients, and antihunger activists
were instrumental in the development and enforcement of public policy. John
Skrentny (2002) profiles the success of representatives of ethnic groups and

women in achieving fundamental policy change. Long-term analysis of policy-debate progression also highlights the importance of advocacy groups. Frank Baumgartner and Bryan Jones (1993), for instance, provide evidence that organized scientists, antitobacco and safety advocates, as well as environmentalists all had major effects on policy development. Elizabeth Clemens (1997) finds that organizations representing farmers, women, and laborers all had a significant impact on progressive-era reform. Berry (1999) reviews the more recent activities of "citizen groups," primarily liberal single-issue advocates, over several years and concludes that they often direct the agenda in Congress.

In their meta-analysis of research on the influence of political organizations in sociology and political science, Paul Burstein and April Linton (2002) find that interest groups are often found to have a substantial impact on policy outcomes, especially when they represent widely held public perspectives. According to their evidence, issue-directed advocacy has substantial effects on policy outcomes in most studies of influence, whereas electoral activity and resource mobilization have significant effects less often. Burstein and Linton also claim that political parties and interest organizations have a similar level of impact on policy outcomes.

Studies of public-policy conflicts also find interest group influence. In most areas of policy subjected to close analysis, the influence of interest organizations has been visible and widespread (Wilson 1995; Baumgartner and Leech 1998). Nevertheless, some analysts claim that the unorganized public interest sometimes triumphs over the organized interests of those with a direct stake in the action (Birnbaum and Murray 1987). Even in these cases, however, the policy outcome does not remain immune from organized representatives. Analyzing the quintessential instances of the supposed failure of interest organizations, including the Tax Reform Act of 1986, Patashnik (2003) finds that public-interest policies are commonly altered after their passage to fit the interests of organized constituencies. Overall, the case-study research suggests that interest groups, including advocacy organizations, are often influential throughout the policy process. They help set the government agenda, propose policy options, assess alternatives, and direct policy implementation.

Few studies, however, generalize across a large range of cases and contexts. Baumgartner and Leech (1998) contend that the small scale of most interest-group research has been a major limiting factor in the accumulation of knowledge and in the ability of scholars to create and test theories of group influence. Wider survey-based studies have offered a poor indication of influence whereas studies of policy influence have been too narrowly focused. Recent studies (Holyoke 2003; Heaney 2004) use interviews with participants in a particular issue domain to assess behavior; their evidence relies on self-reports of success. Most knowledge of organizational success is therefore based on two problematic sources: asking organizations themselves about the way they succeed or relying on post hoc explanations of the determinants of particular policy enactments. Scholars have extensive information about how organizations mobilize in Washington but limited information about the way they succeed once they arrive in the nation's capital. As a result, scholars have difficulty comparing across types of organizations or testing theories of how organizations gain advantage in political debate and policymaking.

Yet there are important intermediary steps in the process of organizing political interests to influence policy outcomes. Many advocacy organizations survive, but few become prominent players in political debate and regularly involved actors in national policymaking. To advance the state of the field, scholars can use indicators of these intermediary steps. The prominence of organizations in political debates in the news media and the involvement of organizations in policymaking venues can be thought of as measures of success. Prominence and involvement each come after mobilization but prior to influence. They are precursors to policy influence that are more likely to produce influence than a mere presence in Washington. Policy influence is a concept that must be assessed on a case-by-case basis; scholars must assess which policies are considered and analyze the determinants of every policy outcome. In contrast, prominence and involvement are generalized concepts; scholars can productively assess the overall level of prominence and involvement for each organization.

Neither prominence nor involvement is the same as the notion of access, which typically points to the opportunity to obtain a meeting with a policymaker, but each concept implies that a group has developed a similar capability.[9] Rather than conceptualize the intermediary step between mobilization and influence as reaching a set bar of access, assessing prominence and involvement has the advantage of differentiating the various levels of success associated with a multitude of organizations. Two organizations may each be able to obtain a meeting with an administrator or member of Congress, for example, but those meetings are unlikely to be equally important if one organization is much more prominent and more regularly involved.

Measuring organizational prominence and policymaking involvement across a broad range of organizations does not require making slippery judgments about the relative effect of interest-group actions and the many other factors that determine policy outcomes. Prominence and involvement can be seen as necessary but insufficient conditions for major policy influence. If organizations are regularly included in media reports and invited to participate in policymaking venues, they have achieved much more than survival but have not necessarily influenced particular policy outcomes. If an organization generates attention from policymakers and reporters, that organization has become a prominent player in national policy discussion. Organizations that achieve this status should be seen as successful; from a position outside the government, they have become active participants in public debate and policymaking institutions. They have the access, experience, and capacity to influence government decisions.

To measure organizational prominence, this analysis uses data on the number of times that each group was mentioned in major news reports. I count the number of references to each organization in Washington print media and in national and local television news broadcasts from 1995 to 2004. Television news broadcasts are the primary political information source for the public, while Washington print publications are the main source of information for political elites and government insiders; this study thus uses one measure of group prominence in media directed at political elites and one measure of their prominence in media directed at the public. Chapter 2 used the measure of Washington print prominence. The new measure of television news prominence derives from transcripts of all network and cable news broadcasts as well as summaries of local news broadcasts in major markets. To see if the changing media landscape alters the relative prominence of organizations, I also use an indicator of each organization's prominence in new media. I count the number of links provided by other Web publishers to each organization's site on the World Wide Web. The Web is the primary vehicle for new media outlets, including online magazines, blogs (Web journals), and individual websites. Search engines use the number of links to a website as a measure of prominence online.[10] In Chapter 5, I use these same measures to predict which organizations are most prominent in each type of media and compare my explanation to that offered by scholarship on media and journalism.

To analyze organizational involvement in national policymaking, I use indicators of involvement in the following four different venues: committee hearings in Congress, announcements by the president, administrative agency rulemaking, and federal court proceedings. In analyses of particular issue domains, measures of organizational participation in these venues are common (Salisbury 1984; Laumann and Knoke 1987; Berry 1999; Hays 2001; Holyoke 2003). Yet no one has collected general measures of involvement level in policymaking venues across many different types of advocacy organizations.[11] As used in Chapter 2, I measure the number of times that each organization testified in congressional committee hearings from 1995 to 2004. To assess involvement in presidential policymaking, I search for organizational names in the *Papers of the Presidents* over the same period. This database includes the writings, press releases, executive orders, proclamations, and other materials issued by the White House under two presidents: Bill Clinton and George W. Bush. Furthermore, it includes transcripts of radio addresses, presidential speeches, and news conferences. The database is used by scholars of the presidency to assess each president's attention to various issues and his participation in policymaking. To assess organizational involvement in the bureaucracy, I search for organizational names in the final rules and administrative decisions issued by more than 100 executive branch decision-making bodies. Advocacy organizations commonly appear in these rules and decisions if they are participants in an administrative dispute or if administrators are responding to their written comments submitted in a public review of proposed rule changes or public-comment period. To assess organizational involvement in the third branch of government, I search for organizational names in federal court proceedings, including case law and legal documents from the Supreme Court, all federal district courts, and courts of appeal, as well as several specialty federal courts. Advocacy organizations commonly appear in these decisions and documents if they are participants in litigation or submitted amicus curiae ("friend of the court") briefs to federal courts.[12] In Chapter 6, I predict which organizations are most involved in policymaking using these same measures; I compare my general explanation of organizational success to venue-specific theories of how organizations become involved in policymaking.

The measures I use include broad information about policymaking involvement across all branches of government. They do not offer direct evidence of influence on any specific policy enactment, but they do offer an underlying indicator of the capacity for influence. One advocacy-group leader stated that his organization views congressional testimony as an indicator that someone is listening to their views: "Testifying gives a platform, allows the press and public to hear, and helps membership. You can shape debate and they hear your arguments." The same groups that appear regularly in the public record are also active in direct talks with policymakers. One former Hill staffer, who is now an official at a prominent advocacy organization, explained the reason that testimony is a good indicator of involvement:

> I would say [that testimony] is a measure of involvement. It is objective criteria . . . It is a way of validating, even your opposition. It is not [directly influential], but two of the things that cause you to be invited to testify [also] cause influence: The committee staff have respect for [the organization]. That helps your case; you have credibility. [Second,] they are aware of your work. If your name does not come to mind for a hearing, it is not likely to come to mind when they are considering legislation.

Similarly, an advocacy-organization representative regularly participating in rulemaking told me that the list of organizations that are referenced in an agency's final rules represents the major actors: "The key stakeholders weigh in, and there is certainly no surprise about that. [The agency] knows who the stakeholders are." Undoubtedly, not every influential exchange between policymakers and advocacy organizations appears in the public record. Nonetheless, advocacy groups not involved in these policymaking venues, such as those that never testify or never have their comments referenced in final agency rules, are unlikely to influence government action. When policymakers officially and repeatedly solicit the views of some advocates and ignore others, they signal which interests they seek to appease and which organized leaders they believe represent those interests.

This perspective contrasts with the long-held suspicion among scholars that many influential moments in policymaking occur behind closed doors. This may be true of influence by corporations or administration officials. Nevertheless, advocacy organizations generally conduct their affairs in public and seek to generate publicity (Berry 1999). Each organization attempts to influence policymaking before and after public airings of their views, but there appear to be few phantom advocacy groups who appear only in private. In five personal interviews that I conducted in Washington in June 2006 with congressional committee staffers, no one could name a single advocacy organization that regularly worked with them but did not appear commonly in testimony before their committee. Based on their judgments, the most prominent and involved advocacy organizations in testimony were also the most involved in policymaking behind the scenes. Similarly, in interviews with administrative-agency officials and advocacy-group leaders, each individual

identified the same central actors in their fields who appear as regular participants in rulemaking. Studying which advocacy groups are most involved in
four venues is a window into which advocates can generally speak on behalf
of the public to policymakers. The testimony or mentions themselves may not
lead to policy change, but the regular heeding of some advocates over others is
likely to affect policy outcomes eventually.

The Skewed Distributions of Prominence and Involvement

All measures of organizational prominence and involvement indicate that
most organizations are not very prominent or involved; the distributions are
uneven and skewed, with some organizations acting as much more important
players in public debate and policymaking. In terms of media prominence,
this is true of both media directed at elites and the public as well as all forms
of media. The average organization is mentioned in the Washington print media on eighty-five occasions over a decade, but the standard deviation of print
media mentions is 284. The middle 50 percent of organizations in this distribution are mentioned between three and fifty-four times, but a few organizations are mentioned much more often. The range was large: 150 organizations
are never mentioned, but one organization (the AFL-CIO) is mentioned more
than 5,000 times. As a result, policymakers are more likely to read quotes
from some advocates than from others. For example, *Roll Call* quotes AFL-
CIO officials responding to the 2010 midterm election, arguing in support of
immigration reform, opposing tax cuts, challenging President Obama's position on trade, and supporting "card check" legislation to ease unionization.[13]
The newspaper rarely quotes the many other groups that have positions on
some of these issues.

The viewing public also sees a limited community of advocates regularly
speaking on political issues. Television news mentions are even more skewed
than Washington print media mentions. The mean number of mentions in the
television news media per organization was 463, but the standard deviation
was 2,404. The middle 50 percent of organizations were mentioned between 2
and 136 times, with a median of 21. The range was again quite broad: several
organizations were mentioned more than 20,000 times on the television news
over a decade, but 291 advocacy organizations were never mentioned at all.
As a result, Americans come to hear repeatedly the views of the same orga-

nizations. In the month of November 2010 alone, the LexisNexis broadcast-transcript database recorded ninety news reports including the NAACP. The organization's views were displayed on CNN, MSNBC, Fox News, National Public Radio, and dozens of local television programs.

Prominence in online media is somewhat less skewed than television news but still far from even across organizations. Based on data from 2005, the average organization has 615 links from other online publishers to its website, but the standard deviation is 1,347. Links are highly concentrated. The middle 50 percent of organizations have between 46 and 577 links pointing to their site. The most prominent online organization, the American Civil Liberties Union (ACLU), has 15,700 links to its website. Many bloggers, local advocates, universities, online newspapers, students, librarians, churches, governments, and wikis all link to the ACLU. Most organizations have a few links pointing to their sites; only forty-six organizations have none at all.

The measures of direct involvement in the policymaking process also have extremely skewed distributions. For testimony, the mean among all advocacy organizations is 4.6 appearances during the decade with a standard deviation is 13.1. The median organization testifies only once, and 747 advocacy organizations do not testify at all for ten years.

Five organizations testify at least 100 times, including the Heritage Foundation, AARP, and the Center for Strategic and International Studies. For example, representatives from the American Enterprise Institute, the National Wildlife Federation, Environmental Defense, and the Union of Concerned Scientists all spoke alongside government officials and corporations at a 2009 hearing on national energy policy. Participation by each of these organizations is common, whereas other groups rarely testify.

Mentions in the *Papers of the President* are also skewed. The attention of the president appears to be quite a scarce resource; 1,331 organizations are not mentioned in presidential papers over ten years, including both the Bush and the Clinton years. The average number of mentions is only one, but the standard deviation is 4.5. Nevertheless, organizations like the ABA and AARP are mentioned at least sixty times in presidential papers. President Clinton spoke to AARP and mentioned them in remarks to senior centers, university gatherings, and radio programs; President Bush thanked AARP as he signed the 2003 Medicare Prescription Drug Bill, mentioned them during visits to hospitals, and responded to their views in radio addresses. This level of presidential attention is quite rare.

Within the executive branch, most organizations had less difficulty being noticed by administrative agencies. The distribution of involvement, however, remains skewed. A total of 780 organizations are not mentioned in the final rules and decisions of administrative agencies and departments over this ten-year period. The mean number of mentions is forty-one, but the median is only one mention; 75 percent of the organizations have fewer than eight mentions. Nevertheless, seven organizations are mentioned more than 2,000 times, including multiple veterans' organizations, unions, and professional associations. For example, the concerns from lawyers at the ABA were mentioned in the proceedings of the Securities and Exchange Commission, the IRS, the Federal Trade Commission, the Federal Deposit Insurance Corporation, the Federal Communications Commission, and the Federal Reserve. Most advocacy groups do not gain this broad attention from government agencies.

As for the federal courts, the average organization is similarly uninvolved, while a small group of organizations dominates the distribution of involvement. For federal court documents, the mean number of mentions is thirty-two, but the median is only one; a total of 790 advocacy organizations are never mentioned in any court documents. As in administrative agency mentions, 75 percent of the organizations have fewer than eight mentions in court documents. Yet ten organizations are mentioned more than 1,000 times over the decade, including environmental groups, unions, and professional associations. Dozens of lawsuits and amicus briefs from the Sierra Club, for example, are referenced throughout the federal court system. Many advocacy groups, in contrast, are never to be found in the courts.

The Implications of Organizational Inequality

Some organizations are clearly taking the lion's share of attention from policymakers and the media. Washington features a diverse advocacy community full of organizations that make claims to public representation and aspire to be involved in public debate and the policymaking process. Nevertheless, these organizations are certainly not created equal. They have different basic attributes, resource levels, and constituency connections. The prominence of these advocacy organizations ranges from peripheral players almost never called by reporters to household names appearing in the news media on a daily basis. Their levels of involvement also range from almost never appearing in the governing process to being called regularly to participate in all branches of government. These vast inequalities are important indications that only a minority of advocacy organizations is successful.

Returning to the zoo analogy can help clarify. The Washington advocacy community is analogous to a zoo in several respects. A zoo reflects the diversity of the animal kingdom but does not put animals on display in proportion to their occurrence in the wild. Similarly, the advocacy community includes representatives of many types of constituencies, but not all organizational sectors are equally present. Within this community, some organizations from each sector are regularly featured. Like the giant pandas of the Washington zoo, a few very successful organizations rise to great prominence and stimulate interest. New exhibits come and go, but these veterans remain. Each section of the zoo gets its share of exhibit space and visitors, but only a few examples of each animal are widely noticed. Likewise, the distributions of resources, prominence, and involvement are highly skewed, but the most resourceful subset of organizations is quite diverse in the content of its advocacy, representing constituencies of many types.

The results also have an important implication for research design: Some previous studies of interest groups may have offered a limited view of interest-group strategy and behavior. Survey-based research relies on self-reports from a cross section of the community; this cross section is likely to provide knowledge about the activities of the average organization but may not offer a complete picture of the advocacy community. Surveys, after all, generally have low response rates. The two famous interest-group surveys by Walker (1991) have response rates of 55 percent and 65 percent. Strolovitch (2007) reports a 40 percent response rate for her study of advocacy groups. Scott Furlong and Cornelius Kerwin (2005) report response rates of 15 percent and 25 percent for their two surveys of interest organization participation in rulemaking. By relying on public evidence of organizational characteristics and behavior, I am able to collect information on organizational prominence and involvement for nearly 100 percent of advocacy organizations as well as complete data about the vast majority of the organizations in this study's population (85 percent). It is unlikely that the response bias in organizational research is random; busier organizations and those having risk-averse staff may be less likely to return printed surveys.

In a community of organizations with such concentrated resources and involvement, analyzing organizational behavior based on the central tendency of the population is unlikely to offer a reasonable view. If 5 percent of organizations account for half of all participation, for example, researchers must cover that 5 percent to understand the dynamics of the advocacy groups that are involved in policymaking; sadly, one may not learn much from the opinions or behavior of most advocacy groups. Any distribution of survey responses, such as the distribution of self-reported success, is also unlikely to match the extreme skew of the genuine distribution of organizational prominence and involvement. If a scholar predicts whether groups rate themselves as highly successful or not very successful on a survey, that surveyor is unlikely to be assessing the true magnitude of differences across organizations. By several measures, after all, some advocacy groups are more than one hundred times as successful as others.

The consistently skewed distributions imply that some major players achieve vastly disproportionate success. Although many organizations claim the same constituencies and policy positions, a few organizations rise above all the others to speak regularly on behalf of those constituencies and positions. Another pertinent analogy might be the box-office success of feature films. Only a few movies are hits at the theaters, with most gaining little following. Nonetheless, theater multiplexes provide considerable choice, appealing to moviegoers who want comedies, dramas, and action films. The Washington advocacy community likewise features a limited subset of disproportionate participants, but they do not fall into any single category.

Finding out why distributions are so uneven and skewed requires an investigation of how and why some advocacy organizations become the most prominent and the most involved by such large margins. To augment my theory of Behavioral Pluralism, a theory of the success of individual advocacy organizations in political institutions and public debate is needed. The next chapter outlines that theory, and the following two chapters test it. The challenge for this theory is not only to account for which organizations succeed but also to explain the puzzling concentration of prominence and involvement among a small subset of advocacy organizations that do not represent any single type of constituency. From the distributional information, one already knows that the advocacy community is wide in scope but that organizations have narrow opportunities for success.

11 WHOSE VOICE IS HEARD?

4 Institutionalized Pluralism

Among the advocacy organizations in Washington, whose voice is heard? Organizations generate unequal attention from political elites and are unequally equipped to participate in policymaking. Relatively few of the more than 1,600 advocacy organizations in Washington become prominent players in national politics. Although most groups struggle to be heard, some advocacy organizations are able to ascend to preeminent positions in the nation's system of governance and assumed roles in the society and polity.

The success of these few organizations does not mean that everyone in the political process agrees with their goals or sees them as allies. In fact, some of the best evidence for their assumed social roles arises from the bizarre rituals of elected officials kowtowing to their presumed political opponents and from the reaction when they try to avoid it. When George W. Bush came into office, for example, he decided not to speak at the NAACP annual convention. Many elites saw this as an affront to African Americans as a public group; Bush eventually relented and spoke to the organization. During the 2008 election, John McCain spoke before the group's convention, despite facing the first African American major party nominee and having little chance of winning many African American votes, especially those of the political activists present at the convention. The NAACP has reached such a status as the representative of African Americans that missing their event is taken as tantamount to offending a large public group. How did the NAACP achieve such a status?

Scholars must take this problem seriously to understand the way that advocacy organizations succeed. The key lies in thinking more like sociologists, but political scientists typically think like economists. For this problem, they might consider the incentives of the NAACP and the politicians and then evaluate their potential exchanges, rather than considering status and social norms. This chapter seeks to remedy this theoretical imbalance in interest-group research by focusing on the sociology of organizations. It will cast familiar dynamics in somewhat unfamiliar theoretical terms. Economic theorists in political science have often been given leeway to pursue such re-evaluations; most famously, Mayhew (1974) reformulated theories of Congress by assuming that members of Congress were single-minded seekers of reelection, and Downs (1957) asked scholars to think of election outcomes as sales contests between candidates competing on one ideological dimension. The payoff for these kinds of theoretical advances does not appear until one sees the full implications of the theory for guiding observations. This study does not presume to replicate these remarkable contributions but similarly deviates into basic theory to understand how organizations become institutionalized into accepted social roles.

My theory, labeled Institutionalized Pluralism, suggests that institutionalization is the crucial dynamic explaining advocacy-group success. Because public representation and policy deliberation constitute the two accepted democratic values that supposedly animate the interactions of policymakers, media elites, and organization leaders, advocacy groups succeed if they become recognized as constituency representatives and informed policy-position proponents. Rather than actively evaluate organizational pretentions, however, political elites take for granted that organizations can serve these purposes to the extent that their attributes make them seem like stable embodiments of their presumed roles. The NAACP, for example, is taken for granted as a representative of African Americans and an informed advocate for their positions in policy debates. AARP serves an analogous role, representing retired people and defending the major government entitlements that serve them. In both cases, they have achieved their status as a result of their scale and longevity as well as their formal ties to public supporters and policy issue positions. These structural features institutionalize a few organizations as assumed representatives of public constituencies and informed position advocates in policy debates.

Institutionalized Pluralism explains why some advocacy organizations succeed while others fail. It does not pretend to explain the historical process of every organization's development, only to predict which organizations will succeed today. This chapter seeks to identify the factors that lead some organizational voices to be heard over others. In Chapters 5 and 6, I compare the expectations of Institutionalized Pluralism with those of other theories. If it succeeds, Institutionalized Pluralism can help interest-group scholarship address questions of wide concern to social science. Knowledge of the causes of generalized advocacy organization success should be useful to scholarship on specific social groups or on policymaking within specific issue domains or institutions.

The Obvious Players

The first lesson of understanding advocacy organization success is that everyone seems to find the list of participants in any given area rather obvious. Reporters, congressional staff, administrative-agency officials, and advocacy-organization leaders commonly assert that the actively involved community in their area is readily apparent. In interviews, this set of organizations was referred to as "the usual suspects," "the primary stakeholders," "the short list," "the universe of groups," and "the obvious players." One advocacy-organization leader combined these concepts into an explanation for his invitation to participate in a hearing:

> There was a slot we filled . . . we are very visible, in a prominent position . . . on the usual suspects list and a natural choice [based on] our established reputation.

A sense prevails among participants that everyone agrees on the list of the most important actors. Nevertheless, it is one problem to list who is at the table and quite another to understand why they were included and how they became the obvious participants.

It is not intuitively clear why any nongovernmental organizations should be involved in policymaking. These unelected organizations have generally not been appointed by elected officials to perform any tasks. They lack clear sources of direct power in government or universal legitimacy with the American public. These organizations claim to represent the public interest or the interests of public groups; yet, it is not a trivial problem to understand why advocacy organizations gain this status without any legal justification or electoral process.

In institutional theories of organizations developed in sociology, scholars have long studied the problem of how organizations legitimize their activities and become stable embodiments of a social purpose. Philip Selznick (1957, 17) defines institutionalization as the "[infusion] with value beyond the technical requirements of the task at hand." Expanding this concept, John Meyer and Brian Rowan (1977, 143–144) argue that particular organizational forms and behaviors become the taken-for-granted means to achieve social goals.

That organizational roles become "taken for granted" moves beyond traditional notions of legitimacy. It emphasizes that neither those involved in an organization nor outsiders have to accept consciously the normative premises that underlie organizational behavior. Whether or not individuals have strongly held beliefs about the goals of an organization or about its effectiveness, they often behave as if they acknowledge some collective agreement on its function. Institutions are built on highly symbolic "standardized interaction sequences" in which relationships among actors are defined by their social roles (Lawrence and Suddaby 2006, 216). Not everyone has to believe that the NAACP accurately represents African American views, but everyone acts as if everybody takes it as a given that representation is the organization's role. McCain speaking at their convention is one of many standardized interaction sequences, a symbolic act built on the organization's role in representation.

Individuals come to take the role and status of an organization for granted by relying on shortcuts in individual cognition. In the case of advocacy organizations, group leaders, reporters, and policymakers all make assumptions about the roles served by each organization. Individuals learn routines that standardize their assumptions, including their views of legitimate organizational purposes (Friedland and Alford 1991, 251). Using schematic views about organizational roles, individuals accept implicit assumptions about an organization's role that they never fully justify to themselves (DiMaggio 1997, 270–271).

Actors use cognitive shortcuts that answer internal quandaries with appeals to basic assumptions and norms. For example, policymakers and reporters sometimes invite the NAACP to speak on behalf of African Americans because they implicitly grant the NAACP their representative status without thinking through the assumptions. Alternatively, they may question whether the NAACP is the proper choice but rely on the need for someone to speak on behalf of African Americans and the assumption that everyone else has accepted this organization's representative role. As one congressional-committee staffer matter-of-factly described his decision to invite a similar advocacy group to testify, "They represent a constituency, and they bring knowledge and perspective."

These largely automatic processes, however, do occasionally surface to become a part of conversation; the language used by advocacy organizations sometimes mirrors that used in sociological analysis. For example, one official mentioned that his involvement in administrative rulemaking was the product of collective assumptions: "I think it was taken for granted that we would participate. We were one of the organizations working on the program, and we had an interest in [continuing to be involved]." When asked if their participation was a conscious step to achieve a goal, the official said they had only a general interest in continuing their involvement: "You want to get on the record. Often times there is a sense that you're bearing witness . . . you know you are not going to carry the day . . . you just want to be part of it." Strolovitch (2007, 104) quotes a Latino organization representative saying that the organization gets involved in issues "just for symbolic purposes, because . . . it's important to lay a marker and say this is where we stand even though we may lose." These attitudes are conscious reflections of the process of role acceptance.

Adapting generic institutional theories of organizations to the unique institutional environment that political advocates face requires acknowledging the particular symbolic logic that structures behavior in American democracy. As Roger Friedland and Robert Alford (1991, 248–249) contend, that logic is "participation and the extension of popular control over human activity." The logic provides a "set of material practices and symbolic constructions . . . available to organizations and individuals to elaborate." In representative democracies, the most legitimated goal of political actors is the representation of public interests and ideas. As Dahl (1961) argues, competition and compromise among political elites are justified by their presumed role in representation:

> because a democratic creed is widely subscribed to throughout the political stratum . . . overt relationships of influence between leaders and subleaders will often be clothed in the rituals and ceremonies of "democratic" control, according to which the leaders are only the spokesmen or agents of the subleaders, who are "representatives" of a broader constituency. (102)

For government officials, the process of legitimizing governing activities through elections and policymaking institutions is typically direct and unproblematic: They are elected or appointed. In contrast, advocacy organizations must become recognized constituency representatives and position advocates in policy debates without an obvious path.

Advocacy organizations are able to fill these legitimized roles because the policymaking process is justified by the presumption that the process receives public input and considers alternative views. This presumption is widespread and customary across national institutions. As Hertzke (1988) argues, "[The] consensus-seeking Congressional process aims to accommodate simultaneously many conflicting interests and values." A "White House veteran" interviewed by Bradley Patterson (2000) stated that the same is true of the White House:

> The Public Liaison Office, the Public Affairs Office: they have people in there who are assigned to very small constituencies . . . as soon as you assign someone to constituency X, constituency Y begins to demand White House time. What Presidents have done, over the decades, is to incur an expectation for attention on the part of all kinds of people in the American public. (175)

This need to hear from representatives of different interests and perspectives extends to some degree to the administrative state (Kerwin 2003) and to the courts (Kagan 2001). American political institutions do not always incorporate the many perspectives that they hear, but participants feel obliged at least to go through the motions of listening to and claiming to be responsive to a wide array of interests and ideas.

Because policymakers cannot hear from everyone, policy deliberation among large populations requires group-based representation, with some people speaking on behalf of large categories of others. All attempts to incorporate public perspectives will thus advance some leaders as spokespeople. Policymakers seek to hear from representatives for constituencies, but they rely on the signals they receive from organized leaders about which constituencies care about which policies. Members of Congress assume that relevant constituency leaders come from the organized advocates that approach them (Miller 2007).

As a result, advocacy organizations seek to develop an identity as a representative of a social group or an advocate of an issue perspective in national politics. Michael Heaney (2004) discovers that most organizations attempt to shape their identities as constituency representatives and position advocates; they adjust their behavior to instill that identity among policymakers. Hansen (1991) also argues that interest groups gain attention and respect by representing constituencies.[1] Kristina Miller (2007) finds that policymakers do not form lists of all constituents that may care about an issue and seek to hear from all of them; instead, they rely on organized advocates to present themselves as constituency spokespeople. How can the notoriously despised "special interests" gain this status? As Clemens (1997) notes, complaints about interest groups have a long history but have not undermined the assumptions that lead to group legitimacy:

If the normative attack on interest group politics persists, even to the present, this form of political organization has become thoroughly taken for granted in other respects. Political analysts routinely begin by identifying the "interests" of contenders; public programs are implemented with formal provisions for participation by all stakeholders. (324)

The roles that advocacy organizations fill are taken as a given part of democratic governance.

Advocacy organizations make their way onto the internal lists of obvious participants in the heads of policymakers by playing these social roles. Government officials may never be consciously convinced that advocacy organizations should substitute for public stakeholders or widely held policy positions, but they behave as if they take it for granted because public representation and policy deliberation are the animating principles supposedly behind their work. As a result of the recognized social roles associated with these principles, advocacy organizations are engaged in two interrelated forms of institutionalization: They are attempting to become the taken-for-granted representatives of a public constituency and the taken-for-granted informed position advocates in policy debates.

These roles are available because they are tied to central assumptions about democratic practices. Americans ask their leaders to incorporate competing policy perspectives and to hear from everyone concerned with each issue. In practice, these values are vague idealizations that may not be achieved by involving advocacy groups in governance. Normative expectations nonetheless provide an opportunity for organizations to perform these legitimized roles.

The availability of these roles means that organizations that make claims to represent constituencies and take formal positions in policy debates can gain the attention of political elites, but it does not mean that all organizations that make these claims are seen as legitimate. To understand which organizations achieve this status, institutional theories of organization suggest that one look at the structural attributes of organizations and how well they match the institutional logic governing behavior in their environment. This view is consistent with prior evidence that the basic characteristics of interest organizations, such as their links to members and supporters, often determine the way that outsiders see them (Anderson and Loomis 1998). Advocacy organizations become taken-for-granted representatives and policy advocates by aligning their structure with the democratic purposes of policy deliberation and constituency representation. If organizations are in Washington for an extended period and have a large political infrastructure, they come to be seen as permanent instantiations of their claimed roles. If they have formal ties to public supporters, they gain credibility as representatives. If they are known for informed advocacy of policy positions, they gain credibility for their role in deliberation.

Many of these organizational characteristics are the outcomes of the constituency mobilization process analyzed in previous chapters. As Behavioral Pluralism argued, particular constituencies are more likely to mobilize extensive organized representation to speak on their behalf. Organizations rely on these constituencies for ongoing maintenance and development, in addition to initial mobilization. In contrast to economic accounts of organization that focus on resource preservation, however, sociological accounts emphasize that institutionalized organizations must build and sustain myths regarding their social roles and infuse their claimed purposes into their daily routines (Lawrence and Suddaby 2006). Maintaining institutions can take considerable work, well beyond fundraising for survival. Engaged constituents help their leadership maintain organizations as well as the myths that uphold their representative role.

Contingency in Organizational History

Moving from engaged constituencies to particular successful organizations, however, involves some contingencies. McGee Young (2010) finds that it is difficult to predict which organizations will succeed within a constituency sector when groups are in their early stages. The first organization founded does not always gain preeminence; if not, it is often replaced by an organization that compensates for youth with increased membership or issue position leadership. Clemens (1997) argues that interest groups can sometimes challenge "logics of appropriateness" and undermine institutional configurations. They can pursue and legitimize new strategies by combining scripts in use by other constituencies with standard operating procedures associated with their own constituencies. Clemens shows that organized labor, agriculture organizations, and women's groups all repurposed innovations that were already legitimized by business lobbies to create public advocacy sectors.

There are many possible historical paths associated with these groups, though tracing sequences does not necessarily indicate causal path dependence. Many paths may be consistent with the same end result. The United States now has a more mature institutional environment than when many innovative interest groups were founded. Today's interest groups are conscious of the many different organizational histories that came before them and can learn the most acceptable means for interest advocacy. As Clemens (1997, 58) argues, "Shared or taken-for-granted strategies or scripts facilitate cooperation and exchange; shared strategies even channel or focus conflict. Thus, the greater the diffusion of an alternative model, the greater its capacity for coordinating action and the costlier its abandonment." By 1925, according to Clemens, "The components of modern interest group politics were in place" (314).

We are unlikely to see a new wave of organization development that is not built on previous efforts. Even recent innovative mobilizations have eventually emulated traditional forms of advocacy. The Tea Party movement, for example, not only was reliant on long-running conservative advocacy groups but also built new interest groups with organizational structures copied from existing groups. Likewise, the Internet-based organization MoveOn.org followed traditional tactics to intervene in elections and partnered with existing liberal organizations.

Several features of the contemporary advocacy community were probably inevitable. With large populations of interests and organizations and limited attention from political elites, the skewed results found in Chapter 3 may not be dependent on historical accident. The diversity we see within the community of the most involved actors is also likely to come about in any system built on norms of democratic representation and deliberation.

A Circumscribed Theory

I label my theory "Institutionalized Pluralism" to indicate that it is an attempt to synthesize traditional group theories of politics (Truman 1951) with institutional theories of organizations to help understand the representation of public constituencies by advocacy organizations. The theory is "pluralist" because it relies on the role of democratic norms suggesting inclusion of many different public groups and views in political decision making. The theory incorporates "institutionalization" because it borrows from sociological accounts of the way organizations reach a taken-for-granted role in public life. The theory does not seek to adjudicate long-standing debates over the sources of political power or the degree of inequality in influence over policy outcomes. It can serve as a guide for understanding a large and important subset of the interest group universe, but it does not aspire to explain the workings of the political system as a whole. Kernell (1997), in contrast, uses the same moniker of "Institutionalized Pluralism" to suggest a bygone era in which presidents used existing party coalitions to advance their legislative agendas prior to the rise of the "going public" strategy. This study does not seek to challenge that set of findings or the research agenda that it spawned. Nevertheless, "Institutionalized Pluralism" is alive and well in the interest group system: Organized leaderships commonly represent public factions in American governance.

The Role of Organizational Attributes

Institutionalized Pluralism focuses on the way that some organizations become institutionalized as public constituency representatives and informed position advocates in policy debates. This dual institutionalization process is predicted to lead to the success of particular advocacy organizations. It also explains the dominance of public political debate and the policymaking process by a small number of institutionalized actors. Chapter 3 argued that advocacy group success could be measured by looking at the prominence of different organizations in news-media reports and their involvement in policymaking venues. It demonstrated that three different indicators of media prominence and four different indicators of policymaking involvement are distributed very unevenly across the advocacy community. This chapter now seeks to move from the theory of how advocacy organizations succeed to empirical expectations about the factors that influence organizational prominence and involvement, producing these skewed distributions. Later, Chapter 5 tests these predictions as applied to organizational prominence in the media, comparing them to traditional theories of reporting; Chapter 6 applies the predictions to policymaking venues, comparing the predictions of Institutionalized Pluralism to those offered by scholarship on venue selection and interest-group strategy.

Which characteristics of advocacy organizations will lead to institutionalization into constituency representatives and policy position advocates? To determine whether an organizational attribute is likely to influence institutionalization, I ask two key questions. First, does the attribute help to align the organization's structure with its presumed role in policy deliberation or constituency representation? Second, does the attribute encourage outsiders to view the organization as a stable embodiment of its purposes? Table 4.1 reviews the expected effects of different attributes on each institutionalization process. It indicates that some attributes will promote both types of institu-

TABLE 4.1. Organizational attributes associated with institutionalization into two roles.

Organizational attribute (variable)	Associated with: Institutionalization as representatives of public political constituencies	Associated with: Institutionalization as position advocates in policy debates
Longevity (organizational age)	Yes	Yes
Scale (political staff size)	Yes	Yes
Ties to constituency (membership size)	Yes	No
Local organization (chapters)	Yes	No
Nonprofessional interests (not professional association)	Yes	No
Agenda scope (size of issue agenda)	No	Yes
Research expertise (think tank identification)	No	Yes
External lobbying force (number of lobbyists hired)	No	No
Campaign contributions (affiliated PAC)	No	No
Ideological orientation (conservative or liberal)	No	No

tionalization, whereas others will help with only one process. Yet some attributes often thought to influence advocacy group success will not help with either process. Policymakers do not typically think about these attributes as legitimizing or delegitimizing, but the attributes cause political elites to assume that an organization is a legitimate player of their proscribed roles.

Organizational Age

Two crucial attributes of advocacy organizations should help contribute to both institutionalization processes, namely, an organization's longevity and the scale of its national political operations. As previous research suggests (Smith 1984; Schlozman and Tierney 1986), organizations with a long tenure in Washington become better known as policymaking participants and develop the capacity to act as informed participants in policy debates and mobilize their constituencies effectively. As institutional theory suggests, longevity also indicates that insiders and outsiders perceive the organization as a stable actor with a coherent purpose. The age of an organization is commonly used as a proxy for institutionalization because extended survival proves that an organization has adapted to the requirements of operating in its sector. For advocacy organizations, longevity signals a history of presence in policy debates and support from some constituency. In a personal interview, one advocacy group official stated that age is a signal of capacity in multiple venues: "Older groups have maturity in policymaking. They understand the role of regulatory agencies and Congress." Another advocacy-group leader lamented that his organization was too young to be taken seriously: "You became institutionalized at some age. We have transitioned from the founders, but we are still young. We are not to the same level [as other groups]." Longevity in Washington, then, is a signal that an organization should be taken seriously.

Organizational Scale

The other major indicator of an organization's stable presence and purpose is the scale of its national political operations. Previous research (Schlozman and Tierney 1986; Walker 1991) suggests that a large political staff in Washington enables organizations to establish a reputation with many policymakers and to become visible to stakeholders. A large staff size also increases the number of distinct tactics that organizations can use and increases their coalition partnerships (Mahoney 2008). Institutional theories further suggest that organizations of greater scale have mobilized more people to support the organization's operations and purposes; this can inspire outsiders to take their function and their behavior for granted. A large political staff indicates that an organization seeks to professionally participate in policy debates and to represent its constituency regularly and actively. An advocacy-group leader mentioned that building a large staff also allows the organization to expand the breadth of its role: "Our staff increase coincided with an expanded issue agenda . . . we added more experts, new issues, and expanded capacities." A congressional-committee staffer also mentioned that organizations of greater scale are relied on more often: "I would like to believe that size is not determinative . . . but we do turn to the huge organizations more often . . . we do want depth of experience." A large scale provides capacity and is taken as evidence of importance.

Ties to Membership

In addition to incorporating these hypotheses of previous interest group research, Institutionalized Pluralism suggests additional unique predictions. First, institutionalization as a representative of a political stakeholder will be advanced if organizations have formal connections to a public constituency. If an organization nurtures a large individual membership, it will be assumed to be acting in a representative role. As an advocacy-group official stated, organizations with members are seen as leaders of constituencies: "[Government officials] get associations to be the voice of constituents. Views [coming from] the grassroots are less discounted." Another group leader said that older membership groups are treated as especially credible spokespersons: "We have more credibility the longer we are around . . . [and] we get some more credibility from our members."

If organizations are tied to an active membership through federated local or state chapters, they are also likely to be seen as maintaining in-person ties with their public supporters. Organizations with local chapters and members engage in more outside lobbying and public mobilization (Mahoney 2008). Recent critics of the decline in civic engagement, however, have implied that mass organizations no longer wield the power they once did. Skocpol (2003), for example, bemoans the decline of locally organized mass-membership groups and the shift in emphasis to Washington. Institutionalized Pluralism, however, suggests that local organization and national representation do not conflict. Individual membership will help an organization to be recognized as a representative of a public concern. Local chapters will help indicate that an organization is linked to its constituency via a multilevel structure of representation.

Professional Interests

Although individual membership is a visible signal of constituency support, some types of membership organizations are more likely to be seen as spokespeople for private interests without active political support. If advocacy organizations must be seen as representatives of public constituencies, organizations that arise to promote professional development should face a disadvantage in being seen as representatives of their supporters' political ideas. Olson (1965) argues that the ease with which small economic groups organize represents a distinct advantage over other social interests, but this mobilization around narrow goals lacking political content is unlikely to produce an organized leadership seen as representing a political constituency. Most professional associations began with broad social advocacy but now focus on internal maintenance and operations rather than public political goals (Brint and Levy 1999). As a result, professional associations have become less identified as public advocates and more associated with occupational advancement. Reporters and policymakers will discount professional associations when comparing them to other groups.

The Breadth of the Agenda

Institutionalized Pluralism suggests that a different set of factors may help organizations become institutionalized as informed position advocates in policy debates. First, the scope of an organization's political agenda helps establish it as a presence in multiple areas of political discussion. Organizations that produce a large agenda of public policy goals are likely to see themselves as participants in more debates; policymakers will also remember them more often as they consider various policy issues. Previous research contrasts with this emphasis. William Browne (1990), for example, argues that interest organizations adapt to potential competition by finding a policy "niche," a smaller issue agenda with a smaller constituency. Institutionalized Pluralism suggests that niche-seeking organizations will incur a clear cost; that is, organizations will be obvious participants in fewer policy debates. Speaking in a personal interview, an advocacy-group leader said that a large issue agenda conveys a sense of broad expertise: "We are identified with a range of issues. We produce public data . . . We have scientific, economic, and legal experts." Articulating multiple policy views increases the likelihood that an organization will be seen as a credible spokesperson for positions relevant to current debates.

Think Tank Reputation

The second factor that should influence organizations' institutionalization as participants in policy debates is formalized expertise on policy issues from a particular political perspective. In previous research, Andrew Rich (2004) argues that "think tanks," providers of expert policy information from a political perspective, have become central actors in national politics. Almost all advocacy organizations, however, claim to produce expert information (Schlozman and Tierney 1986). These groups gain access from policymakers to the extent that they provide policy information and political expertise for a side in a policy debate (Hall and Deardorff 2006). Institutionalized Pluralism suggests that organizations that can establish an image of fulfilling the formal role of expert policy proponents will gain advantage. Although some academics suggest that think tanks are attempting to depoliticize themselves, policymakers and reporters know them as informed advocates of particular perspectives. No one doubts that the Cato Institute, the Heritage Foundation, or Resources for the Future represents partial views of policy. Because they enter a political debate in which organizations need to be identified with one side and easily placed into categories, this combination of expertise with position taking is their strength, not their weakness. Policymakers will call on groups more often if they see them as experts at representing an issue perspective.

External Lobbyists

Institutionalized Pluralism also distinguishes itself from other theories by identifying factors that should not produce prominence or policymaking involvement. First, previous research suggests, but does not conclusively demonstrate, that mobilizing resources to hire lobbyists will increase the success of an interest organization (Heinz et al. 1993; Wright 1996). Building from a simple resource-mobilization model, this hypothesis seems straightforward. Nevertheless, hiring external lobbyists does not help an organization become a stable leadership for a public constituency or assist it in establishing itself as an informed position advocate in policy debates. An organization with outsiders working on its behalf, rather than internal staff, is unlikely to be seen as the site of public representation or the site of expertise for policy deliberation. It may even suggest that an organization is attempting to compensate for its lack of internal leadership by looking outside organizational boundaries. As an advocacy-group leader stated, "Internal staff have knowledge and drive. We have rarely had cases where [external] lobbyists were valuable." Another group official agreed: "[People] are skeptical if they think they are talking to a lobbyist that is self-serving. Staffers have something to say that they believe." External lobbyists are thus not interchangeable with internal political staff.

Political Action Committees

Previous research has also suggested, but not demonstrated, that PAC contributions are a route to political involvement and influence (Smith 1995; Mahoney 2008). Establishing a PAC, however, does not help an organization become a recognized advocate for a constituency or a policy position. It may even convey the message that an advocacy organization plans to gain influence by providing financial contributions rather than by representing public interests and participating in policy discussion. Because Institutionalized Pluralism suggests an inconsequential role for PACs and lobbyists, one can distinguish it from a simple resource-mobilization perspective. If policymakers are merely accumulating campaign contributions, all signals of financial support should suffice to improve a group's standing. If they are instead seeking public-constituency representatives and expert policy debate participants, policymakers should not respond to all expenditures of resources.

Prominence in Particular Media Outlets

The same factors that lead organizations to become institutionalized spokes-people for public factions and participants in policy debates should also make them attractive sources for political reporters. When these factors are used to predict the prominence of advocacy organizations in the news media, they should not need to be substantially adapted to account for the causes of prominence in particular mediums. Some previous scholarship treats media usage as an interest group strategy that organizations are able to choose (Mahoney 2008). Institutionalized Pluralism, in contrast, suggests that organizations that have the capacity to act as spokespeople, through extensive staff and membership, longevity, and broad issue expertise, will have their voices amplified by the media. Both Washington reporting aimed at elites and national news broadcasts focused on the public present political stories as conflicts among groups with different interests and perspectives. Reporters for both audiences must rely on entrenched spokespeople for these perspectives. Advocacy organizations that are prominent insiders are thus also likely to succeed in gaining mass media attention.

Ideological Bias

This reliance on institutionalized actors has important implications for theories of political debate in the news media. If reporters are reliant on the advocacy community's structure, rather than their own decisions about framing political competition in their news stories, advocacy-group involvement will not reflect the internal biases of the news media. Reporters will not be more likely to call liberal or conservative organizations for comment, even if they agree with the views of some organizations more than others. Instead, reporters will be more likely to call institutionalized organizations across the ideological spectrum.

Differences in Web Prominence

Nevertheless, the basic theory of Institutionalized Pluralism must accept nuances if it is to make predictions for prominence in all types of media. In addition to talking to reporters, most advocacy organizations have now attempted to take advantage of the new media to reach potential supporters. The characteristics that promote success in the offline world, including internal resources, expertise, and constituency support, should also be relevant to gaining attention online. Web publishers will not be immune to relying on recognized spokespeople for political perspectives. Nevertheless, a few political factions have highly concentrated support from Web publishers. Most Web publishers are members of technological occupations and have an inherent interest in supporting the free flow of information on the Web. In particular, Paulina Borsook (2000) contends that the creators of Internet technology tend to be libertarian in ideology and particularly concerned with civil liberties and the free use of technology. Web publishers may be more likely to advance advocacy groups associated with these interests.

Chapter 5 assesses these expectations using data on the prominence of advocacy organizations in print, television, and online media. It compares the explanations for prominence offered by Institutionalized Pluralism to traditional explanations of media source use offered by scholars of news media. The goal is to apply the theory to an important set of outcomes that shape public debate on political issues. The analysis will also demonstrate that the theory offers insights unavailable if scholars use a media-centric explanation of the news media's actions.

Involvement in Particular Policymaking Venues

Policymaking does not always take place in view of reporters. If Institutionalized Pluralism aspires to be a theory of advocacy organization success, it must also explain the direct involvement of organizations in the policymaking process. This chapter has offered several organizational attributes that should promote high levels of involvement. How do these expectations apply to particular policymaking venues? The American political system, after all, is notoriously fragmented. Each policymaking venue offers different rules and different decision makers. What factors influence an organization's level of participation in each venue?

Interest-group research has traditionally viewed these questions as part of the discussion of organizational strategy. This strategy research has produced alternative expectations about the way that advocacy organizations become involved in policymaking, which are reviewed in Chapter 6. In contrast, Institutionalized Pluralism suggests that advocacy organizations are playing out generally accepted social roles in government, not succeeding in one place by making successful calculations about receptive venues. After organizations have defined their constituency and their goal to influence national policy, the proscribed routes of participation limit remaining strategic action. A group's basic structure and external image will provide a certain capacity to be involved in policymaking across the board.

Differences across Policy Venues

Yet, Institutionalized Pluralism must be refined to make it useful for understanding policymaking in every branch of government. Advocacy organizations are in the midst of a generalized process of institutionalization as well as specific attempts to become participants in each venue. Even if the requirements for participation in each venue leave little room for strategic decisions by organizational leaders, this does not imply that the exact same distribution of actors will be active in all venues. Instead, differential participation across venues will be a product of the barriers to entry in each arena and policymaker control over the scope of participation. Policymakers, if they have a choice, seek to hear from multiple taken-for-granted spokespeople for public stakeholders.

Previous research indicates that congressional committees and the president play an active role in empowering certain organizations to participate in their venues (Shaiko 1998). Administrative agencies, in contrast, are required to publicly announce their rulemaking procedures and proposals as well as to be somewhat responsive to the official comments they receive (Kerwin 2003). Courts hear only cases brought to them by litigants and primarily reference briefs that are submitted by interested parties (Kagan 2001). Although each set of policymakers will seek recognized voices of stakeholders and recognized advocates of policy positions, each of those political leaders has a different level of control over advocacy organization involvement. Congressional committees make collective decisions to solicit information from the sides of political debates and the representatives of public stakeholders they seek to appease (Wright 1996). Presidents are interested in responding to the broad national constituencies they seek to represent (Patterson 2000). Administrative agencies and courts, which have less control, primarily enable involvement by those having the capacity to participate. In a personal interview, an administrative-agency official agreed that their population of advocacy-group participants was likely to be less representative of the constituencies of interest than the population in Congress:

> We are careful to respond to everyone [who submits comments]. If they file a comment, it is addressed . . . [Congress] gets to invite a broad cross-section. They get to pick anyone for group A and anyone for group B. We do not.

Agencies and courts also have greater barriers to successful entry as a relevant expert. One former Office of Management and Budget official, now an advocacy-group leader, compared the barriers to participation in Congress and the administration:

> Most lawyers in Washington work the Hill . . . The price to [the administrative] game is a pretty high price . . . It's detailed work . . . Congressional staff [will often listen because they] are overwhelmed . . . You go talk to [an agency,] there's someone who worked on that rule for eleven years . . . there's very high barriers to entry in this game.

Robert Kagan (2001) argues that the barriers of administrative procedures correspond with the high complexity of participation in the courts. Advocacy-group involvement in the judiciary, he reports, is often tied to previous administrative policymaking. Advocacy-group involvement in congressional and presidential policymaking is thus likely to be more representative of a cross section of the advocacy community than involvement in administrative agencies and courts.

Institutionalized Pluralism, therefore, makes two unique predictions about differences in the processes that lead to policymaking involvement across venues. One prediction leads to similarity in the actors involved in each venue, but the other leads to some dissimilarity. The two predictions are not mutually exclusive or contradictory, however. They suggest that the organizational attributes that lead to institutionalization will be the same across all venues but that the types of organizations responsible for the bulk of involvement across venues will be distinct. Institutionalized organizations will be most prominent in all venues, but only Congress and the president will have the ability to create a representative cast of participants in their venues. Congress and the president possess more power to shape participation in their venues, and they will use it to select institutionalized organizations from many different categories of constituencies, whereas agencies and courts will merely respond to whichever categories of institutionalized organizations submit comments and cases in their venues.

How to Evaluate Institutionalized Pluralism
Chapter 6 assesses the expectations of Institutionalized Pluralism using data on organizational involvement in all four policymaking venues. It evaluates whether the same factors are operative in promoting some organizations to

high levels of involvement in each venue and whether the distribution of the types of involved actors varies across venues. Chapter 6 compares the explanations offered by Institutionalized Pluralism with different explanations that focus primarily on venue selection or resources.

Institutionalized Pluralism predicts which organizations will be most successful, given their current characteristics, rather than explaining the historical process behind organizational development. It is possible that the success of each organization is contingent on many steps and decisions made earlier in its evolution. Alternatively, the eventual success of an organization might be held within narrow bounds based on its constituency, image, and competition. How much organizational history matters is an open question. In all likelihood, success generally breeds more success, and organizations that become prominent and involved may build on their strengths. Institutionalized Pluralism, however, is not intended as a theory that specifies a first-mover advantage in organizational development. There may be many cases where an initial leader lost ground and was never institutionalized as a constituency's representative (Young 2010). The theory is meant to explain why certain groups are much more successful than others but not to adjudicate whether their success is contingent on particular historical circumstances.

The theory also does not rely on or challenge the well-known idea that the policymaking system has a status quo bias (Baumgartner et al. 2009). Constituencies who seek to change public policy are prominently represented alongside constituencies that seek little change. Despite their representation, the proponents of change will still face an inherent disadvantage because of the multiple veto points in the policy process. Institutionalized Pluralism identifies the process by which advocacy organizations come to be relied on by policymakers, but this is largely independent of the underlying ability to shift policy from the status quo position.

AARP as an Institution

Institutionalized Pluralism can also be helpful in understanding particular cases, such as AARP. The view of this organization changes when one sees it as a representative institution. AARP is an undeniably important and successful advocacy organization in American politics. It places among the most successful 5 percent of advocacy organizations on every indicator of resources, activity, prominence, and involvement considered here. It is also recognized as a major actor by nearly all observers of Washington politics and regularly brought into policy discussions concerning elderly Americans, especially any debate involving the two largest entitlement programs, namely, Medicare and Social Security. How has it achieved this role?

In the traditional view, AARP is successful because it is an organization that happens to possess a great many resources. Because it offers an array of consumer discounts, it has a large dues-paying membership. It generates income from selling or sponsoring mutual funds, advertising, credit cards, pharmaceuticals, and annuities as well as health, home, life, and auto insurance. As a result, it has a great deal of resources to spend on a byproduct: political advocacy. Journalists and policymakers are drawn to what it can offer because of these resources. In this view, if AARP chose to represent young people with their resources, rather than retired people, they would be just as prominent.

Institutionalized Pluralism, in contrast, would see AARP as the institutionalized representative of older Americans. It is successful because it is considered the main organization representing the views of retired people. Policymakers, reporters, and other interest groups take for granted that AARP can substitute for older Americans. When the elderly are a constituency of interest, people consult AARP. It has reached this status because it possesses attributes consistent with its representative role, including a large staff and membership as well as longevity; it developed its reputation and has maintained it. Its ostentatious downtown Washington headquarters, its unrivaled membership, and its huge operation encourage everyone to see it as a permanent institution. Even if reporters or policymakers dislike the leadership of AARP or question whether its views are consistent with those of older Americans, they still behave as if they take its representative status for granted. It is one of the usual suspects, and all of the other participants in policymaking believe it will continue to serve that role.

Nevertheless, AARP was created with some commercial interests in mind and generated resources for use in politics via its commercial success. Ethel Percy Andrus and Leonard Davis founded AARP in 1958. Andrus had founded the National Retired Teachers Association eleven years earlier, and Davis was an insurance agent selling group health insurance who wanted to expand his mail-order business (Morris 1996). AARP has since become an amalgam of advocacy organization and commercial enterprise; it even agreed to several payments of back taxes and postal-service fees for improperly using its nonprofit status to sell to its members (Morris 1996). In one sense, therefore, AARP embodies Olson's byproduct theory of collective action: Its commercial success enables its political activity.

This commercial success is only part of the story, however. Andrus appears to have been driven by a political agenda from the beginning. Commercially providing health insurance to the low-income elderly seemed an implausible business in the time before Medicare. In the 1970s, AARP does appear to have been partially controlled by its insurance partner, Colonial Penn. After a *60 Minutes* television exposé in 1977, however, AARP experienced a tumultuous separation with the company (Morris 1996). It now sponsors an alternative policy and competes with its original partner. Since the separation, AARP has become much more prominent. As seniors benefited from government policy and became a more active constituency, AARP membership expanded dramatically (Campbell 2003). It has generated more than 40 million members and emerged as one of the most credited and feared political organizations. It wields an extensive lobbying staff, sponsors voter-mobilization programs, and produces an annual book of policy proposals for members of Congress. AARP is not afraid of direct policy advocacy; it is credited with helping George W. Bush pass prescription drug coverage and for intervening on behalf of Barack Obama's health care reform law. It is also known for its ability to block changes to entitlement programs, such as Bush's proposed reforms of Social Security. It brings a powerful representative message to its political work: "One out of every two people over age 50 is an AARP member," its lobbying director says regularly.[2]

Other organizations actively challenge AARP for its role as the representative of older Americans. The limited success of its competitors, however, makes the institutionalized role of AARP more apparent. The National Council on Aging predates AARP but is academic in orientation. The National Council of Senior Citizens is an AFL-CIO offshoot that represents unionized seniors. The National Committee to Preserve Social Security and Medicare is involved in lobbying and election campaigns but is seen as a Democratic Party coordinating mechanism. The three conservative challengers are the Seniors Coalition, USA Next (formerly known as the United Seniors Association), and 60 Plus; the same direct-mail magnate founded all three. The conservative groups have been active in criticizing AARP but have had trouble generating a large membership, starting their lobbying operations, and gaining a hearing on Capitol Hill (Van Atta 1998). A retirement report reviewing all of the organizations told retirees that AARP was the most important organization and that the others were appropriate only for those who want to take a more liberal or conservative stance on current legislation.[3]

The conservative groups have made the most frequent efforts to dislodge AARP from its role as the representative of older Americans. They sent direct mail to seniors attacking AARP for its support of several Democratic policy proposals. The groups' spokespeople appear regularly on Fox News Channel with the same message. The organizations claim to have a membership but report no money received from membership dues and a large budget from the pharmaceutical industry.[4] AARP refers to them as front groups for business. As of 2010, USA Next seems to have disbanded, and the Seniors Coalition has only a minimal presence online and almost no reports in the news media. The 60 Plus Association is still active but acts more like an occasional vehicle for directing donor money rather than a consistent lobbying force. It spent $5 million in independent expenditures for the 2010 elections opposing the Obama healthcare plan; it had not been very active in campaigning in previous years. In 2002, the association similarly reported a spike in lobbying expenses to $11 million but has reported only thousands of dollars in lobbying expenses since that time.[5]

In short, the conservative groups claiming to represent seniors are not institutions. They are sites for occasional resource mobilization. They can generate sporadic media attention when their issues top the agenda and when they provide an issue perspective different from AARP. Nevertheless, they lack the structural features that make AARP a representative institution: a large and stable internal staff, long-running research expertise, and a large credible membership. When they are given a voice in Congress or in media coverage, it usually takes the form of a notice that not all groups share the views of AARP. The competitors are merely treated as marginal participants in policymaking; they are included only when AARP is already regarded as a major player. AARP is still universally known as "the premier lobbyist for elderly causes" and the "eight-hundred pound gorilla" (Morris 1996, xxi).

The history of AARP's interaction with policymakers also supports the view that the organization has become institutionalized in its representative role. In 1995, Senator Alan Simpson sought to discredit AARP with a series of congressional hearings, but his efforts only reified its role in the policy process by convincing everyone that the organization could not be disregarded (Morris 1996, 5). Policymakers will often admit that they rely on AARP because of its assumed role in representation or because they believe everyone else takes that role for granted. In a personal interview, a congressional-committee staffer stated "AARP is the largest advocacy group for the elderly. Their views are always considered . . . They are available [to speak at hearings], they speak well . . . [and they] lend credibility . . . we need someone representing seniors." As *The Economist* magazine reports, politicians depend on AARP:

> If pensions are the third rail of American politics, the AARP generates much of the lethal current . . . Although the AARP does not give a dime . . . its imprint is on dozens of laws affecting entitlement programs. AARP's strength lies in its 35 million members—far more than any other politically active group. The old vote in higher numbers that the young do, and the AARP is better at rounding them up than anybody else.[6]

Even when politicians doubt the practical power of AARP, however, they still view its participation as sending important signals. Then-Congressman Rahm Emanuel told the *New York Times* that he did not receive calls from constituents animated by AARP's positions, but that its voter mobilization threat was only one source of its influence: "The threat of AARP has always been on two fronts: their ability to mobilize members at a local level, and their Good Housekeeping Seal."[7]

The notion that AARP must be consulted is most evident when recognized by opponents. In the 2005 debate over Social Security reform, Senator Charles Grassley told *The Washington Post*: "It will be very difficult to do anything without AARP's support. And it would be a heck of a lot easier if they came along." When faced with likely opposition, reform proponent John McCain still said, "I want to say to our friends in the AARP—and they are my friends—come to the table with us." Having quoted these officials, the *Washington Post* compared AARP to its competitors: "USA Next's claimed membership of 1.5 million is tiny compared with AARP's. AARP dwarfs every other group that represents older people."[8] Whether successful policies actually require AARP support, the common belief that they are the major player to appease on any issue concerning America's oldest citizens is sufficient to make them a constant participant in policymaking.

It remains unclear how contingent the success of AARP is on its own history or external factors like the introduction of government programs to help the elderly. The advent of Social Security and Medicare mobilized the elderly as a political constituency in the mass public and had some role in supporting organizational development (Campbell 2003). My two theories provide no reason to challenge these previous findings. Behavioral Pluralism suggests that, given that older Americans were a motivated and socially engaged constituency, they would likely develop substantial organized representation to speak on their behalf. Institutionalized Pluralism additionally suggests that representing the elderly and defending government entitlements for them both constitute legitimized political roles that would have provided an opening for an organization to fill, whether or not it was AARP. Together, the theories suggest that the particular historical contingencies of AARP development are less important to contemporary political outcomes than the relative capacity of the elderly compared to other groups and the importance of the structural features of organizations like AARP in determining their success.

The Use of the Theory of Institutionalized Pluralism

Institutionalized Pluralism offers expectations about advocacy-group involvement in every branch of government and all types of news media. The theory incorporates some information about each target institution and medium, but it relies primarily on an explanation of the way that organizational characteristics lead to a taken-for-granted status as a public representative and as a position holder in policy debates. In addition to providing a new view of specific organizations like AARP, the theory advances a new and testable baseline causal model of the way that advocacy organizations become successful in Washington. The theoretical predictions are tested in the following two chapters, one focused on prominence in the news media and the other on involvement in policymaking venues.

The theory is meant to be useful not only for its testable empirical implications but also for its new perspective on the roles played by advocacy organizations. The theory offers an explanation for the reason why any nongovernmental organizations are brought into democratic decision making. By incorporating ideas from cognitive psychology and sociological institutionalism, it explains why official actors take the role of organized advocates for granted in the American political system.

As a stand-alone theory, Institutionalized Pluralism offers several potential insights. First, it provides a reason to expect the broad and skewed variations in prominence and involvement across the advocacy community found in Chapter 3. Second, for studies of media reports and policymaking venues, it directs attention to the way that advocacy organizations reach their exalted positions of obvious players, rather than assuming that policymakers or reporters drive the process. Third, the theory elevates advocacy organizations to the status of political institutions in their own right. It connects Americans' normative views of the roles that should be played by actors in civil society with the assumptions that contemporary actors use in their relations with advocacy organizations. These organizations are imbued with Americans' collective expectations of the role that civil society should play in government.

Whereas the theory of Behavioral Pluralism is meant to explain why some groups generate more representation than others, Institutionalized Pluralism is meant to describe how and why some organizations play an active role in American governance. Together, the theories refocus attention on the intermediary role of advocacy organizations as incarnations of the political organizing of public factions and as established institutional actors in national politics. The types of organizations that can play proscribed democratic roles are likely to be developed by the types of groups in society that begin with social capital and political motivation. Each theory suggests that the intermediary roles played by advocacy organizations have their basis in Americans' collective expectations for a vibrant civil society built on the civic engagement of its citizenry. Attention to the empirical processes by which particular public groups use their social capital to engage politically should lead people to question whether group political engagement leads to egalitarian democratic competition. Attention to the processes by which particular advocacy organizations become institutionalized actors, in contrast, should lead Americans to reconsider their expectations for a robust system of democratic debate and decision making. Americans' expectations create the political functions of group representation and policy deliberation that civil society actors serve.

Institutionalized Pluralism may therefore offer insights for normative discussions of the civil society's role in democratic deliberation and governance. Americans expect a democratic system to bring different views into the political discussion and to hear from all stakeholders. These expectations may entrench some actors as permanent spokespeople for the public and stimulate the development of new institutions of American governance not called for by the Constitution. As this book assesses the empirical hypotheses associated with Institutionalized Pluralism in Chapters 5 and 6, it seeks not only to challenge our current theories of how advocacy organizations interact with reporters and policymakers but also to illustrate the trade-offs inherent in Americans' expectations for democracy and the civil society that they have empowered to achieve them.

5   The Supply Side of Media Bias

One of the primary goals of political organizations is generating media attention for their activities and then speaking through the media to gain public and elite support for their positions. The media, in turn, are dependent on advocacy organizations for informed comment on policy issues and often look to organizational leaders as spokespeople for important political perspectives. Advocacy organizations and the media rely on one another to set the political agenda and engage in debate over major public issues. This codependence has engendered criticism from all sides of the political spectrum; we all seem to believe that our perspective is underrepresented because the media turn too often to our opponents. Critics also bemoan the "he said, she said" structure of news coverage, which often lacks close examination of either side's claims.

Advocacy organizations are major actors in the contemporary highly mediated public deliberation over policy issues. Rather than interview random members of the public, reporters rely on spokespeople for perspectives. Berry (1999) finds that advocacy organizations are the dominant actors in political debate in the news media, outpacing the prominence of corporations and trade associations. He reports, for example, that public advocates account for more than half of group interviews on television news. In a finding that hits close to home for political scientists, he also reveals that advocacy-group research is featured more often than any academic scholarship. Advocacy-group prominence in the news media is likely to have important implications for the way that political issues are framed and whose concerns are recognized as important and valid by the public and by policymakers (Corrigan 2000; Callaghan and Schnell 2001). Given this influential position in the media debate, just who are these talking heads and quoted experts?

Media scholars attempt to provide an empirical basis for concerns over the role of media in politics by analyzing the constraints that the media face and the process by which they select topics and present the multiple sides of political disagreements. They argue that reporters face constraints that promote reliance on interested advocates; that is why these experts are chosen. As a result of research on the media, scholars have learned a great deal about why journalists search for subjective voices on political issues and the way they go about describing political debates. In other words, scholars know much about the demand side of expert sourcing, that is, why reporters demand spokespeople.

This scholarship, however, underestimates the importance of the supply side. The character of the organizations that mobilize to enter the political debate should affect the structure of media political discourse. This chapter takes the supply side seriously by examining the population of advocacy organizations that seek to affect political discussions in the media. It asks whose voice is heard within this population and why some groups succeed where others fail. Prior attempts to answer these questions have been framed as a discussion of ideological bias; scholars have asked whether the media amplify some voices at the expense of others. Rather than acting as independent arbiters of political stakeholders' claims, however, Institutionalized Pluralism suggests that media rely on the organizations that have most effectively mobilized to participate in national politics.

The theory predicts that organizations that have become institutionalized as representatives of public constituencies and position advocates in policy debates will be most prominent in all types of media. An organization's scale, longevity, and ties to public membership and breadth of expertise will determine its level of prominence, producing a small subset of organizations that are much more prominent than most. As a result, the theory predicts that ideological bias will not be a relevant predictor of prominence. These predictions are tested in this chapter. Though Chapter 5 acknowledged that the most prominent actors online would differ slightly from those in the traditional media, in that organizations representing technologists and libertarians would be advantaged, the theory largely expects similarity across mediums. The products that one sees in newspaper reports, television-news broadcasts, and online commentaries will all generally reflect the structure of the interest-group environment. This does not imply, however, that the media debate is fair and balanced. Rather, as Behavioral Pluralism has shown in Part I of the book, some political perspectives are more frequently heard in the media because they are better represented by organized advocates.

The View from Media Studies

Media scholars have generally assumed that the use of interest group sources is dependent on the constraints of news coverage and journalistic judgments about news values. Gaye Tuchman (1978), for example, contends that journalists are subject to professional norms that encourage regular patterns of source usage. Herbert Gans (1979) demonstrates that journalists share elite values that promote the use of government-related sources. David Weaver and Cleveland Willhoit (1991) further suggest that characteristics of journalists are the chief factor encouraging the use of experts in reporting. Stephen Hess (1989) argues that political reporters, in particular, face important pressures that promote reliance on elites. Dorris Graber (2002) contends that the need to generate audiences under structural and economic constraints governs the relationship of journalists to political elites. Robert Sahr (1993), in contrast, contends that journalists often make independent decisions in selecting their sources based on source credibility and public opinion. Whatever the reasons for their choices, journalists are the crucial agents in theories of news media and politics.

Most studies of expert sourcing in political reporting emphasize government sources, but a few studies focus on media coverage of advocacy organizations. Some research investigates whether organizations arising in social movements are mentioned in the news media and whether their portrayal is positive or negative (Terkildsen and Schnell 1997; Smith et al. 2001). Studies of other interest-group involvement in media debates have concentrated on case studies of particular policy areas. Relying on the Clinton health care reform debate, Matthew Corrigan (2000) reveals that interest groups sometimes have great success in generating media attention. Karen Callaghan and Frauke Schnell (2001) analyze debates over the Brady Bill and the assault-weapons ban and spotlight how journalists borrow some frames from advocacy groups but also invent their own story lines emphasizing different arguments than those used by advocates. Based on a study of abortion coverage in print media, Nayda Terkildsen, Frauke Schnell, and Cristina Ling (1998) conclude that the media and advocacy groups jointly structure the messages in policy debates. Competition among groups in the media affects the kind of information available to the public about abortion. They argue that journalistic norms rather than actual interest-group strength account for differences in success among groups.

In the major aggregate study of interest-group participation in media political debates, Lucig Danielian and Benjamin Page (1994) study the sources used on television-news programs in eighty policy issue debates. They find that interest organizations are common sources, particularly businesses, trade associations, and "citizen action groups." Labor organizations and ethnic minority groups are cited in some cases, but agricultural interests, professional organizations, and religious groups are rarely mentioned. These scholars conclude that businesses are overrepresented but do not compare the sources mentioned with the population of organized advocates available for comment. Berry (1999), in contrast, compares the population of organizations with the interest groups that are quoted and finds that advocacy groups are more likely to be quoted than business representatives. Scholars have thus shown that advocacy groups can be influential in media discourse on policy issues but not why some groups succeed in spreading their message where others fail.

In public debate about media reliance on political spokespeople, a consistent focus remains on bias. Bernard Goldberg (2003), for example, claims that the mainstream media engage in consistent liberal bias. In his best-selling account, he presents examples of alleged bias from his years in the news business. In a best-selling rejoinder, Eric Alterman (2004) disputes Goldberg's findings and general claims of media bias; he quarrels that the media have become biased toward conservatives from a fear of appearing too liberal. Both sides of the public debate insinuate that news outlets call the shots, either by advancing their own positions or in response to public claims of bias. Each side uses examples of the media's reliance on advocacy groups to present particular sides of political debates.

Some scholarship also contends that media bias should be expected. David Baron (2006), for example, predicts media bias based on a formal model of journalists and competitive news organizations. Nevertheless, the evidence is mixed. In a meta-analysis of many studies of media bias in elections, Dave D'Alessio and Mike Allen (2000) find no ideological bias in print publications; they find a small, but inconsistent, bias for television news. One account of media bias has generated attention by claiming to produce a comparable measure of bias across media outlets and members of Congress: Tim Groseclose and Jeffrey Milyo (2004) construct a measure of media bias based on mentions of liberal and conservative think tanks. They find that most outlets have a slight liberal bias, when compared to the average member of Congress. A few media outlets, such as the *Washington Times* and Fox News, score conservatively. They do not claim to identify the reason that certain organizations are included in media debates, only to produce a comparable descriptive measure of bias. As a result, they do not account for differences in resources and attributes across organizations. Based on the limitations of their data analysis software, they also choose to limit the population of organizations in their study to fifty for some analyses. The organizations included are those thought to be influential and to possess a clear ideological perspective. In another analysis that received less attention, Rich (2004) analyzes many of the same organizations as Groseclose and Milyo, including Washington think tanks. He finds contrary results; according to Rich, organizational attributes rather than ideological tendencies explain most of the relative prominence of think tanks in media coverage. Without analyzing the characteristics and prominence of a large sample of advocacy groups, scholars cannot conclude that liberal or conservative organizations encounter more difficulty making their way into news reports.

An Organizational Explanation

Institutionalized Pluralism offers a supply-side explanation for patterns of media-source usage. As the current literature suggests, reporters are reliant on established leaders and organized political interests for comments on public policy and political conflicts. This does not reflect independent ideological judgments about whom to call for comment, however. Journalists rely on the population of constituency representatives in Washington, reflecting the more numerous and better-equipped organizations representing particular perspectives. The characteristics of each group determine its prominence relative to other groups.

The constraints and norms of journalism do affect two crucial aspects of reporting on political issues. First, reporters face economic, political, and structural constraints that promote the use of sources viewed as "experts" in political stories (Graber 2002). Second, journalists commonly observe norms of balance that encourage them to search for sources that speak from different political perspectives and on behalf of different groups (Gans 1979).

Missing from this discussion, however, is an acknowledgment that the political landscape offers differential ease of access to spokespeople based on the degree of each political interests' organized mobilization. The structural constraints of the media promote reliance on representatives of the recognized sides of public issues and political conflicts. Advocacy organizations fill the space of spokespeople for these political ideas and interests. As one group official stated in a personal interview, reporters see her organization as an easily accessed spokesperson: "We have a reputation as a media source. [Journalists] understand why we speak and where we see problems." As this book has argued, the population of available spokespersons is driven by the relative capacity of different political constituencies. The success or failure of each organization in becoming a recognized spokesperson, in turn, is driven by whether its structural attributes match its proscribed roles of public representation and policy advocacy.

Journalists' choices about which political elites to reference in their stories, in other words, are not typically independent judgments of the merits of their political beliefs. The media tend to exercise at least moderate due diligence in presenting the sides of political conflict, but they rely on the types of policy experts and spokespeople easily available and notable to them. Based on this perspective, neither liberal nor conservative organizations should suffer any inherent disadvantage in gaining media attention.

Institutionalized Pluralism's organizational explanation of media reliance on advocacy groups also involves a reevaluation of the effects of major changes in the structure of the media. Scholars of new media often contend that the rise of Internet publishing heralds a new era of political debate in which old assumptions about the role of the political establishment do not hold. Anderson (2002), for example, argues that the Internet will successfully empower new voices in issue advocacy. Davis (1999), in contrast, contends that the Internet will enable organizations that already have political advantage to extend their control over the political process. Institutionalized Pluralism suggests that both claims are unfounded; organizations that had an advantage in the offline world will have the same advantage in online media. Yet the theory acknowledged an important nuance: Differences in the types of organizations that succeed online are likely to be tied to the specific interests of Web publishers rather than to any general change in the characteristics of prominent groups.

A supply-side explanation for the prominence of advocacy organizations in the media takes into account the factors that influence the success of advocacy organizations and the constraints of the media. Testing the theoretical predictions across three types of media allows one to evaluate which factors are universally important for advocacy organizations and which are important only for gaining attention in a specific medium.

Distributions of Media Prominence

The descriptive patterns for media usage of advocacy-group sources are instructive. As a reminder, this book uses three indicators of media prominence: mentions in the Washington print media that are directed at policymakers, mentions on the television news (which is directed at the public), and links from Web publishers to an organization's website. Table 5.1 compares these distributions based on the organizational categorizations used in Chapter 3, with fifteen specific categories that correspond to the types of constituencies that organizations claim to represent. The table indicates that each type of media features some important differences in organizational prominence, but the diversity of coverage generally matches the diversity of advocacy groups. The distribution of elite and mass media mentions and Web links across

TABLE 5.1. Distributions of media prominence by constituency type.

		Organizations	D.C. print mentions	TV news mentions	Web links
Issue groups	Conservative ideological	1.5%	3.9%	1.5%	2.2%
	Liberal ideological	2.1%	4.4%	2%	2.7%
	Conservative single issue	4.2%	4.7%	2%	2.2%
	Liberal single issue	17.2%	15.8%	14.3%	18.5%
	Environmental	4.1%	6%	4.9%	5.7%
	Consumer	1.3%	1.7%	3.8%	0.8%
	Foreign policy	2.2%	4%	1.8%	3.5%
	Other issue	5.5%	3.2%	1.7%	3.9%
Vocation	Union	4.8%	9.5%	6.9%	2.7%
	Professional	33%	23.1%	22.8%	38.6%
Identity Groups	Ethnic	6.1%	3.8%	5.1%	2%
	Religious	3.7%	4.4%	12.4%	4.5%
	Gender	1.7%	2.3%	1.8%	1.6%
	Intersectional	4%	1.7%	0.6%	1.2%
	Other social group	8.6%	11.5%	18.5%	9.9%

NOTE: Table entries report the percentage of total advocacy organizations, Washington print media mentions, television news mentions, and web links accounted for by each category of organizations.

different types of organizations largely reflects the distribution of organized representation in Washington.

In the Washington media directed at policymakers, mentions of advocacy organizations are closely reflective of the organizational population. Organizations representing identity groups receive 24 percent of mentions, equal to their share of organizations. Religious representatives, such as the Christian Coalition, receive a little more than their organizational share, and ethnic representatives, such as the NAACP, receive less. Occupational groups are referenced in Washington media reports in approximately 33 percent of Washington media mentions, but unions receive more mentions per organization than professional associations. Professional groups, such as the AMA, receive more than twice the total share of unions, but they are more than six times more numerous. During the 2009 health care debate, *The Hill* newspaper quoted an NAACP official calling for the inclusion of the public option for insurance coverage; they also repeatedly referenced the AMA's support and opposition to different versions of the bill.[1]

Reporting aimed at political elites more regularly references organized representatives of issue perspectives. These groups receive 44 percent of Washington media mentions, more than their share for organizations. Liberal and conservative ideological organizations each account for more mentions than organizations. Liberal-issue organizations like NARAL Pro-Choice America (formerly the National Abortion Rights Action League) far outpace conservative-issue organizations like the Right to Work Coalition. For example, *The Hill* referenced NARAL's opposition to abortion-restriction language included in the 2009 health care bill passed by the House.[2] In total, liberal-ideological and single-issue organizations account for 20.2 percent of total mentions (or 27.9 percent, including environmental and consumer interests in the liberal category).

At first glance, this evidence appears to confirm the long-held conservative suspicions of media liberalism. The difference in Washington media mentions, however, mirrors the clear difference in the organizational population. Liberal-issue organizations are simply more numerous in Washington. A recent story in *The Hill* about a Supreme Court case involving animal protection, for example, quoted only animal-rights groups like the Humane Society of the United States.[3] There was no obvious conservative interest group to quote in opposition to regulation designed to prevent animal cruelty. Overall, the distribution of Washington media mentions is quite similar to the distribution of organizations.

Television news media mentions follow a similar pattern, with a few striking differences. Television reporters rely more often than Washington print reporters on representatives of identity groups, which account for 38.4 percent of all mass-media mentions. The likely explanation is that reporters for public audiences emphasize the effects of policy on social groups. For example, a CBS News report on the original GI Bill and its recent extensions referenced veterans' groups like the American Legion.[4] Occupational interests are again heavily represented in mass media debate, but not quite in proportion to their organizational population; they account for 30 percent of television-news mentions, with professional associations responsible for most of the total.

Television reporters rely less often on representatives of issue perspectives than Washington print reporters; issue-based organizations account for only 32 percent of mass-media mentions. Conservative ideological and issue organizations account for only 3.5 percent of all television-news mentions. Liberal-ideological organizations receive only slightly more mentions than conservative-ideological organizations; yet, together, television reporters rely on liberal-ideological and single-issue advocacy organizations more than four times as often as conservative organizations. Including environmental and consumer interests in the total, liberal groups account for one-fourth of all mentions. Television journalists rely more on consumer organizations like Consumers Union to comment on everything from drug safety to the digital-television transition to food prices. Television reporters appear to take the consumer organizations seriously as representatives of their own consumers' concerns, namely, those of the viewers. Overall, identity groups and consumer groups receive more mass-media mentions per organization, and occupational groups receive fewer mentions per organization.

Minimal differences also appear in the prominence of types of advocacy organizations on the World Wide Web. In comparison to traditional media, occupational organizations gain share, and identity groups lose share. The distribution of links to organizational websites is close to the distribution of organizations in Washington, except that identity groups account for only 19 percent of all links; ethnic and religious organizations are particularly less prominent online. Occupational organizations account for 41 percent of links to organizational websites, with professional groups leading the way. Members of professional associations apparently use the Web to publicize their organizations in a way that the traditional media do not allow. Groups like the American Nurses Association, for example, have links originating from all over the Web, from personal websites to university field descriptions and government guides to nursing.

Organizations representing issue perspectives account for almost 40 percent of all links to advocacy-organization websites. Liberal single-issue organizations and environmental groups account for more links online than conservative single-issue groups or either sector of ideological groups; this mirrors the organizational population. Liberal groups account for a total of 21 percent of links (or nearly 28 percent, including environmental and consumer interests). Because liberal single-issue organizations outnumber conservative issue organizations by more than three-to-one, however, this result is not surprising or necessarily indicative of the bias of Web publishers.

One can use a Herfindhal index to measure the concentration of media mentions across types of organizations. In this index, 0 indicates low levels of concentration, and 1 indicates high levels of concentration in only a few sectors of advocates. Based on this measure, all types of media tend to amplify a similar diversity of organizational spokespeople. Using a fifteen-category index, the advocacy-organization distribution has a score of .16. Washington media mentions and television-news mentions are slightly less concentrated in these categories, with Herfindhal scores of .12 and .14, respectively. The distribution of Web links across these categories has a score of .2. Web links are therefore more concentrated in a few sectors of advocacy groups. Nevertheless, the distribution of media prominence across categories is not extremely concentrated in any medium.

The similarity of the distributions of media prominence and organizations across categories is remarkable given the highly skewed distribution of media mentions across organizations. Chapter 3 demonstrated that a small number of organizations account for most media mentions in every medium. Combined with these results, it appears that Washington features a few prominent organizations in each category. The diversity of organized mobilization is reflected in media debates but dominated by a few organizations representing each type of interest. Again, the advocacy community resembles a zoo with a few prominent animals of each type. It does not quite match the equality in the biblical description of Noah's ark, with two animals from every species, but the advocacy community represented in media reports is quite diverse. Nevertheless, just as most of the animals get left off Noah's boat even as two of their breed make it to safety, most advocacy organizations are rarely included in media debates, even though the overall distribution reflects the organizational population.

Not surprisingly, organizations prominent in one medium are likely to be prominent in others as well. The correlation between Washington print-media prominence and television-news prominence is nearly .6, suggesting that organizations have a similar level of prominence in the mass and elite media. Only a few advocacy organizations appear to be prominent Washington insiders without generating mass exposure. The number of links that the organizations generate on the World Wide Web is also highly correlated with both indicators of their prominence in the traditional media but Web links are more highly correlated with Washington media prominence ($r = .51$) than with mass media prominence ($r = .34$). This initial evidence suggests that the Web may empower Washington insiders rather than organizations prominent in the mass public, to the limited extent that they constitute different populations. Across all of these mediums, prominence is likely to mushroom once organizations gain status as media spokespeople. Because the media rely on organizations that they have called previously, there is likely to be a lock-in effect whereby organizations are placed in media Rolodexes and remain as the dominant spokespeople. In other words, one should not expect the skewed but diverse distributions of media prominence to change anytime soon.

Predicting Media Prominence

With a multivariate framework, one can better understand the causes of organizational standing in the media and identify differences in the factors that lead to prominence in the Washington media, in the television news media, and on the World Wide Web. Table 5.2 includes the complete results of negative binomial count models to predict organizational prominence in these three types of media.[5] In the first two cross-sectional models reported, I predict the total number of media mentions of each organization in the population from 1995 through 2004.[6] In the third model, I predict the number of links to each organization's website as of 2005. All of the models include the size of the political staff and membership, the age of the organization and the breadth of its agenda, as well as dichotomous indicators of whether each organization has federated chapters and whether it is identified as a think tank. The models also include a seven-category organizational type variable where

TABLE 5.2. Predicting the prominence of advocacy organizations in three types of media.

	D.C. print mentions	TV news mentions	Web links
Political staff size	.21***	.18***	.13***
	(.02)	(.02)	(.02)
Age of organization	.01***	.01***	.01***
	(.002)	(.002)	(.001)
Breadth of issue agenda	.02*	.05**	−0
	(.01)	(.02)	(.01)
Number of external lobbyists hired	−.015	.03	.01
	(.014)	(.02)	(.02)
Organization has associated PAC	−.33*	−.31	−.21
	(.13)	(.19)	(.13)
Size of membership (log)	.07**	.07*	.09***
	(.02)	(.03)	(.02)
Organization has state or local chapters	.23	.73***	.07
	(.12)	(.17)	(.11)
Organization is identified as a think tank	1.4***	1.2**	1.1***
	(.3)	(.5)	(.3)
Organizational type — Professional association	−.64**	−1.2***	−.31*
	(.14)	(.2)	(.14)
Union	−.3	−.87**	−1.6***
	(.22)	(.31)	(.2)
Identity group representative	−.07	−.04	−.27*
	(.13)	(.18)	(.13)
Liberal perspective	.3*	−.04	.06
	(.14)	(.19)	(.14)
Conservative perspective	.48*	−.06	.34
	(.19)	(.26)	(.19)
Environmental perspective	−.21	−.38	−.35
	(.19)	(.27)	(.19)
Consumer perspective	.24	2.2***	−.07
	(.32)	(.4)	(.31)
Organization has (civil) libertarian perspective	—	—	1.3**
			(.44)
Organization represents technologists	—	—	.97**
			(.37)
constant	2.8	4.3	5.4
Log likelihood ratio index	.051	.033	.021
Maximum likelihood R^2	.397	.314	.262
N	1373	1373	1271

NOTE: Table entries are negative binomial regression coefficients, with standard errors in parentheses. The excluded type is organizations representing nonideological issue perspectives. *$p < .05$ **$p < .01$ ***$p < .001$ (two-tailed) the excluded category happens to be organizations representing nonideological issue perspectives. This type variable differentiates between whether the organization represents a liberal, conservative, or nonideological perspective.[7]

As expected, the results indicate that the structural characteristics of advocacy organizations are significantly associated with their prominence in the news media and account for most of the explained variance in each model. Organizations of different types occasionally have different levels of prominence in each medium, but neither conservative nor liberal views have an advantage that is independent of their organizational characteristics.

For Washington media mentions, the size of an organization's internal staff of political representatives is significantly associated with prominence. Each additional staff member increases the expected number of mentions by 23 percent. Organizational age also has a statistically significant relationship to Washington media prominence. Each decade of experience in Washington increases the expected number of mentions by 10 percent. The breadth of an organization's issue agenda is also a significant factor, as is think-tank identification. According to the model, think tanks generate more than four times as many mentions as other advocacy groups. As also predicted, public membership has a significant effect; the log of membership size is significantly related to organizational prominence, although having state and local chapters is not significant. Using the log of membership generates a substantially better fit. Including a direct measure of the number of members in each organization makes the membership variable insignificant but makes the variable for state and local chapters statistically significant. Theoretically, this pattern of results indicates that organizations do not gain as much for additional members once they reach a large membership size. Unexpectedly, having an associated PAC significantly reduces prominence in Washington print-media reports. Hiring lobbyists has no discernable effect.

Controlling for these factors, some types of organizations are mentioned more than others in the Washington media. Professional associations are significantly less prominent than organizations representing nonideological issue perspectives. According to the model, they are expected to generate a little more than half of the mentions. Liberal organizations are slightly more prominent than nonideological groups, as are conservative organizations. Nonetheless, there is no statistically significant difference between conservative and liberal group prominence.

The model for prominence in the television-news media reveals similar results. Political staff size is significantly associated with prominence, as are the organizational age and breadth of issue agenda. For both print and television reporters, it appears to be useful to have established broad advocates rather than narrowly focused groups on their speed dials. According to the model, each additional political staff member increases the expected number of mentions in television-news broadcasts by 20 percent, and each additional issue on an organization's agenda is expected to increase prominence by 5 percent. Organizations with state or local chapters are also significantly more prominent in the mass media than those with only a Washington office; having chapters is expected to more than double television news mentions. Local television reporters likely rely on organizational spokespeople who are more accessible at the local level. Membership size also has an independent significant and positive effect. The membership effects are generally small; yet, because some organizations in the population have recruited millions of members and most large membership organizations also have chapters, the aggregate predicted effect can be quite large. Issue expertise is also valued. Think tanks are significantly more prominent in mass media than other advocacy groups; being identified as a think tank more than triples the predicted number of media mentions. As expected, hiring external lobbyists and establishing a PAC are not associated with mass-media prominence.

In addition to these effects of organizational attributes, some types of organizations have different levels of mass-media prominence. Occupational representatives, for example, suffer a significant disadvantage in gaining exposure in the mass media, including professional associations and unions. According to the model, being a professional association rather than a non-ideological issue organization generates only 30 percent as many mentions; being a union generates a little more than 40 percent as many. Despite the high aggregate level of occupational representation in the mass media, each occupational organization is disadvantaged in media prominence. Their high level of prominence in the aggregate is simply a product of the large number of organizations representing occupational groups. In contrast, organizations representing consumer concerns are significantly more prominent in the mass media than are other issue advocates. Consumer organizations are approximately nine times more prominent; television reporters rely on them to deliver information to their own consumers. As hypothesized, representing liberal or conservative ideological or issue positions has no significant effect on organizational prominence.

Together, these two models of media prominence indicate that many of the same factors generate prominence in media directed at policymaking elites and at mass television audiences. Washington print reporters rely more often than television reporters on organizations that focus on ideological issue perspectives, whether those groups are liberal or conservative. Yet there is no support available for liberal media bias in these results. Liberal advocacy organizations are referenced in the mass and elite media more often because of their numerical advantage in the population, not because reporters provide advantages to liberal organizations.

The model of World Wide Web prominence provides evidence that the process generating new media attention is similar to the process generating traditional media attention, with the exception of the specific interests advantaged in the online world. Larger organizations are significantly more prominent online. Every additional political staff member is expected to increase the number of links from other Web publishers to an organization's website by 14 percent. Unlike the popular caricature, these data do not support the claim that the Internet is heralding an era of successful new organizational upstarts. Older organizations are more prominent online, just as they are in the offline world. Scholars may focus on well-known Web upstarts such as MoveOn.org, but they are likely outliers. Organizations identified as think tanks are also significantly more prominent online, generating approximately three times as many links. Organizations with a larger public membership do benefit from their mass mobilization in becoming more prominent online, but locally organized groups with chapters do not gain an advantage in Web prominence. Organizations with a wider issue agenda are not advantaged online, even though they are advantaged in the Washington print media; those with a narrower issue agenda produce just as many links. As expected, PACs and lobbyists also wield no effect.

The results indicate that the type of interest that an organization represents also affects its prominence on the Web. Again, no evidence suggests that Web publishers are biased toward conservatives or liberals. Organizations representing issue perspectives, however, are significantly more prominent online than professional associations, unions, and identity-group representatives. Controlling for other factors, unions are expected to generate only

20 percent as many links as issue advocates, and identity groups are expected to generate about three-fourths as many. The Web is a medium for deliberation among issue perspectives rather than social groups.

Substantial evidence indicates that the Web empowers specific sectors of advocacy organizations. To see the effects, the Web-links model includes two dichotomous indicators that are related to Web prominence: One differentiates the organizations that represent a libertarian-ideological perspective or a civil-liberties perspective, and the other differentiates organizations that represent technological occupations. Controlling for other factors, organizations that represent a libertarian-ideological perspective or civil liberties perspective are significantly more prominent online; they generate 3.7 times as many links. Organizations representing technologists are also advantaged; they generate 2.6 times as many links. The models suggest that a few types of advocates gain disproportionate prominence online. Nevertheless, in general, the same types of attributes promote media prominence online and offline.

Bringing Back the Supply Side

The results not only provide extensive support for the expectations of Institutionalized Pluralism but also offer nuances for ongoing debates about media bias and the effects of changes in the media. Given the results presented here, scholars should move beyond media-centric explanations of reporters' relative reliance on different political elites. The study of the interaction between the media and political organizations cannot move forward by viewing the process entirely from reporters' or consumers' points of view. The character of the political environment and the distribution of spokespeople offered for different stakeholders affect the content of American journalism. The supply side of expert sourcing explains the main reason some voices are louder than others in public debates in the news media. The pattern of advantaged and disadvantaged public constituencies is reflected in the organizational population as well as the subset of prominent media spokespersons. The attributes that lead organizations to be institutionalized as public representatives and issue advocates likewise matter a great deal to media prominence.

The expectations of Institutionalized Pluralism were mostly confirmed. Structural characteristics of organizations influence their prominence in all types of media. Older and well-staffed organizations are more prominent in Washington media reports, television news broadcasts, and on the Web. One advocacy-group official explained why his large and old organization had become so prominent in news reports: "The media come to trust us over time. They need our point of view. We are easy to find." Organizations with a wider public membership are also more prominent in all types of media, although organizations with local chapters are advantaged only in the mass media. Professional interests suffer a disadvantage in gaining attention in all types of media. Issue agenda breadth is useful for understanding elite and mass media prominence but not for predicting prominence on the Web. As expected, think tanks are more prominent in all types of media, but external lobbyists and PACs wield no effect on media prominence.

Most of the factors that produce prominence in the elite-directed media also produce prominence in the mass media, including size, age, breadth of agenda, and membership. The few exceptions are intuitive. Organizations with local chapters benefit in the mass media but not in the Washington media. Organizations representing consumers are more prominent on television news. Organizations representing either ideological perspective are more prominent in the Washington print media. Yet ideological direction has no independent effect anywhere.

Web publishers act in a similar fashion. Older and well-staffed organizations with more membership as well as think tanks are more prominent online and offline. Breadth of issue agenda, however, is not rewarded online. Consistent with the conventional wisdom that the Web enables fragmentation of media audiences, organizations focused on a single issue area or a small number of issues are just as prominent online as broader groups. As expected, Web publishers also tend to promote organizations that speak on their behalf. Organizations supportive of technologists' interests or civil-libertarian or libertarian perspectives are significantly more prominent online. Web publishers do amplify some interests at the expense of others, but not in the way envisioned by either champions or opponents of new media.

By focusing on the supply side of expert sourcing, the theory of Institutionalized Pluralism has added new insights to traditional debates in media studies. Previous scholarship examined the process of becoming a media spokesperson from the view of reporters. Scholars assumed that media outlets looked for organizations of specific types or organizations representing particular perspectives, rather than simply reinforcing the stature of organizations that have become institutionalized public advocates and policy debate participants. The results here show that the media simply amplify the voices of institutionalized stakeholders. The advocacy system entrenches some organizations as agents of the public in the mediated form of public deliberation that characterizes contemporary democracy.

The public constituencies that are best represented in media political debates are those that have the social capacity and political motivation to mobilize organizations to speak on their behalf. The organizations that succeed in speaking on behalf of those groups are those that become taken-for-granted representatives and stakeholders as a result of their structural characteristics. There is room for some groups to beat the odds, legitimizing themselves by gaining reputations for good work or becoming known as useful sources. The evidence suggests that organizations would do well to build credibility for the role they seek to play, rather than attempt to pay lobbyists or match journalists' biases. Organizations can change their fate at the margins, but these strategic considerations are secondary to the broad patterns identified here.

The results have important implications for Americans' view of the biases in news media political debates. Conservative single-issue perspectives have fewer organized spokespeople in the media than liberal single-issue perspectives because many more large and well-staffed liberal single-issue organizations are present in Washington. The inclusion of advocacy organizations in the elite and mass media mirrors their distribution in Washington. The dominance of corporations and trade associations in Washington may overcome this imbalance and generate a media debate tilted toward the conservative agenda. To the extent that conservatives are disturbed by the prominence of liberal organizations in the media, however, they should look at their own failure to create large single-issue organizations across the issue spectrum, rather than any inherent media bias. The evidence suggests that if more conservative spokespeople for policy issues were active in Washington over an extended period, they would gain attention.

The results should caution scholars away from broad interpretations of previous findings attributing media bias based on interest-group source usage. Groseclose and Milyo (2004), for example, may be correct in finding that media outlets differ in citations of liberal and conservative organizations, but the overall levels of advocate inclusion from each side mirror their organizational population. The baseline used for comparison by Groseclose and Milyo, the relative mentions of organizations in congressional debate, may not indicate whether members of Congress or reporters are enhancing the prominence of some groups at the expense of others. Similarly, Danielian and Page

(1994) may be correct in finding that some types of groups are included less frequently in television-news reports, but the reasons appear to be based on the distribution of Washington organizations as well as their resources and image. Previous case studies of advocacy-group competition in news reports (Terkildsen, Schnell, and Ling 1998; Callaghan and Schnell 2001) may not have sufficiently accounted for the way that institutionalization processes result in regular participation by some advocacy organizations in media debates. Any future attempt to assess media bias based on source usage should account for the important roles of organizational structure as well as the perceptions of expertise and constituency representation. Rich's (2004) analysis of these variables' importance for the relative prominence of think tanks is generally confirmed here and expanded to include a wider population of public advocates.

The clearest lesson to be learned from these results is that media scholars should look beyond the constraints and characteristics of journalists to understand the way that the media present political issues and empower certain voices in the political debate. Given their constraints and norms, journalists tend to amplify the same voices likely to be heard in other forums of policy debate. Researchers can gain knowledge by moving to an analysis of the supply side of expert sourcing. The population of political organizations that seeks to gain media attention and the structure of those organizations wield a substantial effect on the perspectives featured in the media. These factors play an important role in determining the behavior of Washington political reporters, television-news reporters, and Web publishers. The search for ideological bias among reporters may be less important than the analysis of the biases present in the advocacy system and the differential participation of some groups in civil society. The factors governing the participation of advocacy organizations in media political debates are not necessarily specific to the Washington press corps, television news, or the Internet. They are one symptom of the more general problem of the differential mobilization of some interests in American democracy.

6 The Usual Suspects in National Policymaking

Although advocacy organizations try diligently to gain the attention of reporters and the public, the most important audience is policymakers. Advocates are attempting to influence policy outcomes, and that goal requires involvement in the policymaking process. Organizations compete to be heard in multiple policymaking venues at the federal level, including congressional committees, the White House, administrative agencies, and courts. Ideally, these venues provide an open exchange of different public views on policy issues and enable the incorporation of expertise into policymaking. Nevertheless, self-styled policy experts and public advocates are always more numerous than the chairs placed at the policymaking table.

Among the many voices claiming to represent the public in Washington, whose message is heard? Do the same factors influence involvement in congressional hearings, administrative rulemaking, presidential directives, and federal litigation? Scholars have previously viewed these questions as a matter of organizational strategy or "venue shopping." They have studied the way that organizational leaders select venues and lobbying targets, often by asking them directly in surveys and interviews. For example, scholars have learned that nearly all interest groups target Congress, but fewer target the courts (Schlozman and Tierney 1986; Strolovitch 2007). Because these scholars rely on self-reported strategies, they know which tactics leaders view as influential; still, the field has little broad-based knowledge about how the character of an organization affects its involvement in each venue. Perhaps organization leaders overestimate their own agency in making their groups succeed.

Institutionalized Pluralism suggests that only those organizations that become taken-for-granted public constituency advocates and issue position spokespersons will be heavily involved in policymaking. Long-running organizations of large scale with broad issue agendas and formal ties to membership will be the most involved in policymaking in all branches of government. Nonetheless, each venue's characteristics may change its patterns of organizational involvement. In particular, Chapter 5 added a nuance to my theory's central expectations. Venues like Congress and the White House have more control over participation than venues like administrative agencies and courts, which are forced to hear all comers. Because government seeks to hear from many different constituencies, a more diverse cast of organizations will be represented in the two venues with the power to select their participants. These expectations are meant to explain the broad contours of advocacy organization involvement in policymaking. Any strategic decision or chance circumstance may still affect an organization's chance of success, but much of the overall pattern is structurally determined.

Identifying the factors that lead some organizational voices to be heard over others and describing which kinds of public advocates are included in the process together serve as a second route to understanding the general determinants of advocacy group success in the crowded Washington community. Institutionalized Pluralism suggests that the same attributes that produce media prominence will also produce policymaking involvement because organizations' success is determined by whether they are institutionalized as constituency spokespersons and informed position advocates, rather than how their strategies match the specific concerns of each medium or venue. The relative success of different advocacy groups helps to explain why some interests are taken into more consideration in political debate and policymaking.

Venue Selection and Interest Group Strategy

Research on organizational participation in policymaking typically assumes that organizations succeed by making independent strategic decisions about venue selection. Thomas Hansford (2004), for example, argues that organizations select a lobbying target as a critical early decision:

> When an organized interest participates in the policy process, it has to make a series of tactical decisions. This decision process begins with the organized interest choosing the policy venue, or set of venues, in which to focus its lobbying efforts. For example, the interest could opt to lobby Congress, the courts, a federal administrative agency, or some combination of these venues. (172)

Thomas Holyoke (2003) similarly portrays venue selection as an open decision where organizations select both their targets of influence and their level of activity directed toward each target. He finds that these decisions are dependent on organizational coalitions, oppositional mobilization, and policymaker access. Scott Ainsworth (2002) advocates a formal theoretical approach to understanding group strategy in these matters. He contends that, based on its goals and the strategic decisions of its opponents, each organization chooses institutional contexts with rules that benefit it. Mahoney (2008) argues that lobbying should be conceptualized as a seven-stage process, including target selection as well as inside and outside lobbying strategy choices.

Investigations of organizational activity in each venue take a similar strategy-centric approach. Furlong and Kerwin (2005), for example, assert that participation in administrative rulemaking requires a separate causal analysis than the one found in studies of other interest group participation. To construct an alternative model, they rely on survey-respondent opinions regarding the perceived effectiveness of their groups' tactics in administrative policymaking. According to Hansford (2004), analysis of interest-group participation in the courts requires knowledge of whether interest organizations agree with the court's priorities and their policies. Likewise, John Wright (1996) contends that the need for information about policy and its electoral consequences governs a unique set of interactions between members of Congress and interest organizations.

Despite these hypothesized differences across venues, almost everyone involved in Washington politics claims to participate in almost every venue. Schlozman and Tierney (1986), for example, find that the vast majority of interest organizations believe that Congress (97 percent) and executive agencies (93 percent) are important to their activities. Most organizations also believe that the White House is an important target (87 percent), although fewer believe that the courts are an important target (49 percent). Schlozman and Tierney demonstrate that 99 percent of interest organizations attempt to participate in congressional hearings. Furlong and Kerwin (2005) find a slightly lower rate of participation in administrative-agency decisions; 82 percent of interest organizations report participating in the rulemaking process. Most organizations, therefore, attempt to voice their concerns regularly with many types of policymakers.

In each venue, policymaking involvement requires some proactive behavior on the part of advocacy groups and some receptivity from policymakers. These policymakers often have a primary role in encouraging involvement by some groups and erecting barriers to participation by others. The president and members of Congress regularly solicit participation from interest-group leaders and attempt to gain interest-group support for their proposals (Shaiko 1998).

Because almost all organizations seek to participate in policymaking in many venues, asking organizations how and why they choose particular venues and strategies may provide a poor explanation for which groups succeed in becoming actively involved. Because scholars have used this method, the current view focuses on the idea that some organizations choose winning strategies and some choose losing strategies; some select the right targets and the right issue positions, while others choose the wrong side of political debates and the wrong forum. This explanation does not provide predictive power; instead, scholars generally direct attention to successful outcomes and assume successful strategies. More recent scholarship (Mahoney 2008; Baumgartner et al. 2009) evaluates the importance of strategies and resources by comparing the winning and losing sides of policy debates but finds little consistent effect of particular strategies and acknowledges that interest group activity may not be causally related to outcomes.

Most scholarship uses either conventional notions of strategy derived from the discourse of political operatives or rationalist ideas about strategic action derived from game theory. Instead of relying on these notions, I recognize the limits of strategy conveyed by organizational theory. Raymond Miles and Charles Snow (1978, x), for example, argue that organizational strategy is about placement within an existing structure, linking an organization and its purposes with outside organizations. Organizations experience a cycle of focusing on entrepreneurship to new tasks, engineering better ways to achieve goals, and administering existing operations. Most interest-group research on strategy assumes that interest organizations remain in a constant state of engineering; they are able to find new means of achieving their objectives regularly. In settings with highly institutionalized rules, however, organizational theory suggests that this is unlikely. The engineering phase is likely to focus on adaptation to the norms of behavior; in other words, organizations that are not yet institutionalized learn to do the same things others are doing. The most institutionalized organizations are likely to be caught up in administration of their operations, repeatedly implementing the same procedures with only slight adjustments.

Population-ecology approaches in organizational theory, which spotlight competition between organizations, also posit that strategy is not a constant effort to change tactics to achieve goals. According to Michael Hannan and John Freeman (1986, 57), organizational strategy arises from a set of core decisions. After organizations choose their purpose, their structure, and their basic means of achieving success, they have few strategic decisions left to make. Applied to advocacy organizations, this means that few decisions remain after organizations form and decide to influence government on behalf of a constituency. Most remaining decisions are minor, tactical, and unlikely to change an organization's overall level of policymaking involvement.

Each set of political institutions has requirements for organizational access, and each set of policymakers may respond to different types of organizations. This set of facts has led scholars of interest groups to view involvement in policymaking as a two-stage process of "venue selection" on the part of interest organizations and responsiveness on the part of policymakers. Institutionalized Pluralism instead suggests that the benefits of institutionalization should be apparent across the political system. In some sense, these perspectives describe the same process in a different language. Nevertheless, the theory of organizational venue selection and the theory of Institutionalized Pluralism disagree about the amount of agency that organizations and policymakers have in selecting strategies and choosing participants. Institutionalized Pluralism argues that organizational strategy is born of necessity. Most organizations attempt to participate in most venues, and few organizations seek to distance themselves from policymaking venues. After an organization has defined its constituency and its goal of influencing national policy, remaining strategic choices are limited.[1] Successful institutionalization implies that organizations will become stable embodiments of their implied purposes by participating in governance across the board.

Buying Access?

At least one contrary perspective is available to explain how advocacy organizations become regularly involved in policymaking. Some scholars contend that money talks above all else in Washington, enabling some organizations to gain access to members of Congress. Advocacy groups, in this view, gain their access to policymakers simply by buying it. They rely, or the story goes, on campaign contributions from PACs or connections from highly paid K Street lobbyists.

Although the perspective is advanced primarily by popular commentators, some scholarly evidence supports this view. Using one year of testimony by 163 organizations, Kevin Leyden (1995) maintains that ties to PACs and lobbyists increase an organization's level of testimony. Nevertheless, there are substantial problems with applying this analysis to advocacy groups. First, Leyden does not differentiate among different types of interest groups and uses only a small sample of groups beyond corporations and their associations. Second, he omits from his analysis important characteristics of organizations beyond their resources. Third, Leyden uses standard OLS regressions that cannot account for the large number of groups that do not testify at all. No previous analysis offers a compelling explanation for how some groups become regular players testifying substantially more often than other similar groups. Institutionalized Pluralism also makes predictions about organizational involvement in every branch of government, providing a counter to branch-specific explanations of interest group success.

Distributions of Involvement in Policymaking Venues

The evidence is largely consistent with the expectations of Institutionalized Pluralism, rather than any alternative theory. The descriptive information alone helps to clarify the picture of organizational involvement in policymaking. Recall that this book measures policymaking involvement by counting congressional committee testimony appearances as well as mentions in presidential papers, administrative agency rules and decisions, and federal court documents. Table 6.1 reports the proportion of involvement opportunities in each venue accounted for by organizations of different types. It provides distributions across the fifteen-category typology corresponding to the types of constituencies that these groups claim to represent. The distributions indicate that much of advocacy-organization involvement follows from the distribution of organizations with a Washington presence. As expected, however, the distribution of involvement in Congress and with the president more closely mirrors the distribution of organizations than the cast of participants in courts and agencies.

TABLE 6.1. Distributions of policymaking involvement by constituency type.

		Groups	Testimony in Congress	Presidential mentions	Agency rule mentions	Court document mentions
Issue groups	Conservative ideological	1.5%	4.2%	0.8%	0.2%	0.3%
	Liberal ideological	2.1%	2.2%	5.1%	0.5%	2.1%
	Conservative single issue	4.2%	3.4%	3.2%	0.3%	0.6%
	Liberal single issue	17.2%	11.4%	10.7%	4%	12.7%
	Environmental	4.1%	8.3%	3.5%	6.3%	19.5%
	Consumer	1.3%	2.4%	0.8%	2%	2%
	Foreign policy	2.2%	7.6%	4.4%	0.4%	0.8%
	Other issue	5.5%	6.5%	3.8%	2.5%	1.1%
Vocation	Union	4.8%	10.4%	16.9%	29.5%	33.2%
	Professional	33%	24.3%	20.6%	35.2%	17.7%
Identity Groups	Ethnic	6.1%	3.2%	9.7%	1.8%	3.2%
	Religious	3.7%	2%	4.2%	0.8%	2.2%
	Gender	1.7%	1.1%	0.4%	0.1%	0.8%
	Intersectional	4%	1.7%	3.3%	0.3%	0.6%
	Other social group	8.6%	11.2%	12.7%	16.2%	3.2%

NOTE: Table entries report the percentage of total advocacy organizations, congressional testimony appearances, presidential papers mentions, administrative agency rule mentions, and court document mentions accounted for by each category of organizations.

A Herfindhal index, which ranges from 0 to 1, can again be used to measure the concentration of policymaking involvement across types of organizations. The distribution of testimony across fifteen categories reaches a score of .12, as does the distribution of presidential mentions. Both are less concentrated than the distribution of organizations, which has a Herfindhal score of .16. In contrast, the distribution of administrative-agency-rule mentions attains a score of .24, and the distribution of court mentions reaches a score of .20. Involvement in agencies and courts is more concentrated among a few categories of interests than the organizational population or than participation in other venues.

Appearances before congressional committees include a cross-section of the community, at least by organizational type. The main differences are that organizations representing identity groups and professional associations are underrepresented in comparison to their organizational population, whereas unions and issue organizations are slightly overrepresented. Identity groups account for 19 percent of all testimony appearances; representatives of issue perspectives account for 46 percent, and representatives of occupational groups account for the remaining 35 percent. Liberal single-issue groups account for more appearances than conservative single-issue groups, but conservative ideological groups account for a greater share than liberal ideological groups. Organizations like the ACLU testify more often than organizations such as Americans for Tax Reform, but ideological organizations like the American Conservative Union testify more often than general liberal groups such as Americans for Democratic Action. Environmental groups and foreign policy groups are also well represented. An advocacy-organization official explained why committee hearings tend to involve many different sectors of organizations:

> [Congressional committees] look for constituencies that are directly affected. They want a mixed panel. They try to find people to speak for [different] perspectives.

Organizations of all different types are also mentioned in the *Papers of the President*. Representatives of identity groups constitute a greater share (30 percent) of presidential involvement than congressional involvement, and representatives of issue perspectives comprise a smaller share (32 percent). Nevertheless, the proportions, which include mentions in both the Bill Clinton and the George W. Bush administrations, are again largely reflective of the organizational population.[2] Spokespersons for liberal issue perspectives outnumbered those for conservative perspectives, mirroring their organizational population. The main differences are that unions and identity groups are overrepresented, whereas professional groups are underrepresented in comparison to their share of organizations. Among occupational groups, unions account for almost as many mentions (17 percent) as professional associations (21 percent), even though they are a much smaller proportion of the advocacy community.

The most important descriptive finding suggests that the proportions of organizations involved in Congress and with the president roughly mirror the organizational population. This is remarkable given the extremely skewed distributions of policymaking involvement found in Chapter 3. That chapter reported that the distribution of congressional testimony and presidential papers mentions across all organizations is decidedly uneven, with a small number of organizations accounting for a huge proportion of total involvement. Taken together, the skew in the overall distribution and the proportionality in the categorical distribution provide support for the claim that congressional committees and the president seek to involve a diverse group of participants representing different constituencies but rely repeatedly on the same institutionalized organizations in each category to represent each type of group and their policy positions. The implication is that the population of advocates that policymakers sample from is determined by which constituencies have the most political capacity, but only a few organizations representing each constituency type become recognized stakeholders in government.

The distribution of mentions in administrative agency rules and decisions among advocacy organizations is much less representative of the organizational population. Occupational groups account for the vast majority of all mentions. Representatives of other social groups, such as veterans' groups, are also overrepresented in comparison to their organizational population. Representatives of issue perspectives do not constitute a large share. Religious, ethnic, and gender constituencies each comprise tiny proportions of total administrative-agency-rule mentions.

The distribution of mentions in federal court documents is also hardly representative of the organizational population. Occupational groups account for approximately half of all mentions, with unions comprising a larger share than professional associations. Many unions, such as the Service Employees International Union (SEIU), are regularly involved in labor disputes that are resolved in the courts. Identity groups are again underrepresented in every subcategory. Environmental-issue groups are substantially overrepresented in federal court documents, accounting for more than four times their share of the organizational population. Organizations like Environmental Defense sue companies, regulators, and individuals; they also submit amicus briefs in cases in which they are not directly involved. Young (2010) attributes the environmental community's focus on the courts to a conscious decision by organizations founded by lawyers, such as the Natural Resources Defense Council.

Despite differences in the types of organizations involved in each venue, organizations heavily involved in one venue are likely to be involved in policymaking in all branches of government. Involvement with the president and Congress is the closest connection with one another. The correlation between congressional-hearing appearances and presidential-papers mentions is .44. At lower levels, congressional testimony is also correlated with administrative-agency-rule mentions ($r = .28$) and federal-court-document mentions ($r = .27$). Presidential-papers mentions are correlated at lower levels with administrative-agency-rule mentions ($r = .21$) and court-document mentions ($r = .19$). Administrative and court involvement are also correlated ($r = .27$), but they are not as congruent as congressional and presidential involvement.

Predicting Policymaking Involvement

To draw conclusions about the causes of organizational involvement in each venue, one must move to multivariate models. Tables 6.2 and 6.3 present the results of zero-inflated negative binomial regression models to predict testimony before Congress and mentions in presidential papers, administrative-agency rules, and federal-court documents.[3] All of the models include the same organizational characteristics and type variables used to predict media prominence in Chapter 5. Nevertheless, there are two parts for each of these models: One part predicts whether or not organizations will be involved at all in each venue, and the other predicts the amount they will be involved, if they are involved. Each model is designed to predict the total testimony appearances or mentions of each organization in the population from 1995 through 2004.[4]

The results of the model for congressional testimony confirm most of the expectations. Political-staff size is positively and significantly related to both whether or not an organization testifies and the number of testimony appearances. Each additional political representative on an organization's staff increases the expected number of appearances by 18 percent. The age of an organization is also a significant predictor of its level of involvement in congressional testimony, as is the size of its public membership. Think-tank identification is also significant; controlling for other factors, think tanks testify more than four times as often as other advocacy organizations. A broad-issue agenda and connections to local chapters, however, do not increase an organization's involvement in congressional committees. Hiring external lobbyists and establishing an associated PAC are similarly unhelpful. In terms of organization types, professional associations testify a little more than half as often as issue advocates, controlling for other organizational characteristics.

Advocacy organizations do not generate any additional involvement from being nonideological, rather than representing liberal or conservative views. Both liberal and conservative groups were invited frequently, even in a mostly Republican Congress. This may be a result of the structure of interest group

TABLE 6.2. Predicting advocacy organization involvement in Congress and the White House.

	Congressional testimony		Presidential mentions	
	Count	Binary	Count	Binary
Political staff size	.16***	.6***	.05*	.2**
	(.02)	(.16)	(.02)	(.08)
Age of organization	.006***	.005	.003	.014**
	(.002)	(.006)	(.004)	(.005)
Breadth of issue agenda	.02	2.2	.03	.07
	(.01)	(2.1)	(.02)	(.04)
Number of external lobbyists hired	−.02	11.1	−.02	.1
	(.02)	(667)	(.03)	(.1)
Organization has associated PAC	−.07	−.29	−.5	.29
	(.15)	(.75)	(.34)	(.55)
Size of membership (log)	.1***	−.14	.07	.01
	(.03)	(.09)	(.06)	(.08)
Organization has state or local chapters	.03	−.59	.56	−.03
	(.15)	(.41)	(.32)	(.41)
Organization is identified as a think tank	1.45***	17	.17	2.7
	(.34)	(5559)	(.56)	(2.2)

Organizational type					
	Professional association	−.59**	−1.1	−.19	−1.3**
		(.17)	(.61)	(.42)	(.5)
	Union	−.28	18.7	−.48	1.5
		(.25)	(7597)	(.55)	(1.5)
	Identity group representative	−.28	−.76	−.27	.63
		(.16)	(.59)	(.36)	(.47)
	Liberal perspective	−.22	−.62	.7	−.71
		(.17)	(.65)	(.39)	(.41)
	Conservative perspective	.13	−.35	.66	−.84
		(.22)	(.83)	(.55)	(.57)
	Environmental perspective	−.21	14.1	−.26	−.69
		(.21)	(2317)	(.54)	(.65)
	Consumer perspective	.12	18.4	−1.42	−1
		(.34)	(10715)	(1.33)	(1.8)

	Congressional testimony		Presidential mentions	
Constant	.71	.68	.18	1.5
Log likelihood ratio index	.071		.081	
Maximum likelihood R^2	.28		.138	
Zero observations	610		1118	
N	1375		1375	

NOTE: Table entries are zero-inflated negative binomial regression coefficients, with standard errors in parentheses. The binary coefficients correspond to a model predicting whether organizations will testify or be mentioned in presidential papers at least once. The excluded type is organizations representing nonideological issue perspectives. *$p < .05$ **$p < .01$ ***$p < .001$ (two-tailed) participation in legislative politics, which is much less partisan than their participation in elections (Grossmann and Dominguez 2009). One advocacy-organization leader explained the reason he was invited to testify by the majority party even though he opposed their initiative:

> They know what argument we will make. We were the most obvious spokesperson against the proposal. . . . We knew we would be invited. We have a long history. We were not surprised.

In other words, they were invited because they were institutionalized players, the usual suspects even from an issue perspective quite different from the chairman's. As the model suggests, many of the organizations that are regularly involved in congressional testimony are large issue-advocacy organizations representing many different perspectives; the oldest and largest of these organizations are the most involved.

These results are consistent with the findings from my qualitative investigation of three specific congressional hearings in 2006 covering foreign relations, the budget, and services for children.[5] I contacted the majority and minority committee staff for the three committees as well as everyone who testified. For all three hearings, the committee staff and those providing testimony reported that the list of participants was typical of other similar hearings and could have been easily predicted. A chief of staff for one committee stated that it was "fairly obvious" who would participate because they were "all considered major players." The organizations called to testify "have credibility" and "represent a constituency." Another congressional-committee staffer mentioned that the process involved finding the most prominent advocacy group for each constituency:

> We needed someone representing each of the [three groups]. We were in agreement [that] those were the positions that needed to be represented. We had a little debate as to who . . . but we decided the witnesses for these slots . . . It is obvious who the players are on particular issues and who needs to speak and have their voice heard. There are some differences across members and staff . . . but we know the big names. It is a function of age. If they are older and know how to advocate, how DC works, how to present themselves, we talk to them.

Note how these comments match the perspective of Institutionalized Pluralism and would seem foreign to a theory based on exchange or venue selection.

The invited organizations were mostly obvious to everyone because they filled proscribed roles.

Involvement in presidential policymaking is driven by a similar set of factors, but a much greater proportion of the advocacy community is excluded from any involvement. The model to predict mentions in the *Papers of the President* indicates that larger political staff size again significantly increases both the chance that an organization will be involved and its level of involvement. Organizational age is a significant predictor of whether an organization receives at least one mention. Surprisingly, membership and chapters have no effect on presidential-papers mentions. As expected, neither does hiring external lobbyists or founding a PAC to make campaign contributions. Organizational attributes again explain many of the differences in participation across organizational types. Yet being a professional association rather than a nonideological issue group significantly decreases the chance of being mentioned. The president, like policymakers in other venues, is looking for organizations known as the big players. The same process that produces congressional involvement leads to involvement at the White House, but the bar for any level of participation is much higher.

The multivariate analysis in Table 6.3 indicates that many of the same structural attributes increase involvement in administrative rulemaking despite the substantial differences in the most involved types of organizations. Political staff size significantly increases level of involvement, as does organizational age. The results are substantively as well as statistically significant. Each additional in-house political representative increases the expected number of agency-rule mentions by 15 percent. Each decade of experience in Washington likewise increases the expected number of mentions by almost 21 percent. Older and larger advocacy groups are by far the most involved in administrative rulemaking. Hiring external lobbyists, however, does not increase involvement. Unexpectedly, the breadth of an organization's issue agenda and its identification as a think tank also wield no effect. The size of an organization's public membership does have a positive and significant effect on involvement. Having an associated PAC also has a positive effect that just reaches statistical significance.

There are also significant differences in involvement across organizational categories. Controlling for organizational attributes, unions, consumer representatives, and conservative-issue organizations are all significantly more

TABLE 6.3. Predicting advocacy organizations' involvement in agencies and courts.

	Agency rule mentions		Court document mentions	
	Count	Binary	Count	Binary
Political staff size	.14*** (.03)	−.01 (.18)	.12*** (.02)	.49** (.18)
Age of organization	.02*** (.002)	.35 (.18)	.01*** (.003)	.07*** (.02)
Breadth of issue agenda	.0 (.01)	−.18 (.14)	.05** (.02)	.16 (.16)
Number of external lobbyists hired	.06 (.04)	−.08 (.09)	−.07* (.03)	.03 (.08)
Organization has associated PAC	.47* (.22)	−2.7 (2)	−.28 (.21)	1.7 (1.3)
Size of membership (log)	.16*** (.04)	.26 (.27)	.21*** (.04)	−.05 (.09)
Organization has state or local chapters	.26 (.21)	1.6 (2.8)	−.47* (.2)	.46 (.67)
Organization is identified as a think tank	.19 (.55)	31 (11700000)	−1.7** (.8)	−.4 (2)
Organizational type — Professional association	−.64 (.23)	17.1 (642.2)	.31 (.25)	−1 (.5)
Union	1.2*** (.37)	30.4 (7232102)	2.1*** (.4)	2.3 (1.9)
Identity group representative	−.12 (.25)	−2.7* (1.3)	−.42 (.23)	.12 (.48)
Liberal perspective	.95 (.24)	.4 (1)	1.3*** (.2)	.64 (.54)
Conservative perspective	1.3*** (.34)	−1.6 (1.7)	.97** (.33)	.85 (.78)
Environmental perspective	.02 (.31)	1.7 (2)	1.4*** (.33)	.5 (.7)
Consumer perspective	1.4** (.53)	.4 (2.1)	1.2* (.55)	.3 (1)
Constant	1.24	1.25	.81	1.7
Log likelihood ratio index	.065		.072	
Maximum likelihood R^2	.325		.344	
Zero observations	616		648	
N	1375		1375	

NOTE: Table entries are zero-inflated negative binomial regression coefficients, with standard errors in parentheses. The binary coefficients correspond to a model predicting whether or not organizations will be mentioned at least once. The excluded type is organizations representing nonideological issue perspectives. *p .05 **p .01 ***p .001 (two-tailed) involved in administrative rulemaking than non-ideological-issue groups. Identity representatives are significantly less involved. For administrative agencies, therefore, the same organizational attributes associated with institutionalization affect involvement but different types of organizations are most involved.

These results match the qualitative understanding I gained of two administrative rulemaking processes covering environmental policy and privacy in 2006.[6] I contacted the authors of the final rules in the two executive agencies as well as the leaders of advocacy organizations that were referenced in these rules. In both cases, a consensus prevailed that the involved organizations commonly participated in similar rulemaking processes and represented the major players. One agency official who authored a final rule stated that "no one is surprised" at who comments and which comments are referenced because it is "everyone who took an active interest in the issue . . . who understand the impacts and are collective and credible voices." An advocacy-organization official who submitted comments discussed the difficulty they experienced: "It was typical, an excruciating process, time consuming and requiring high expertise. There were so many iterations. [Some of this] goes back fifteen years. [That is why] the other participants are obvious. We know who the players are." Nevertheless, the official noted some differences when compared to Congress: "Congress is more receptive to groups. They understand their role. Administrative agencies are buffered [by the official procedures] . . . but they are sensitized to the public stakeholders." Another advocacy-group official said their participation and the response were "routine." "We have a steady record of work, and we get response." This official described the agency as receptive: "It is in their interest to hear all voices. No one wants to leave somebody out. The agency looks at [the organizations] as its constituents." Note again that there is no exchange visible here and very little evidence of venue selection. Instead, all are routinely carrying out their proscribed roles.

Results for involvement in the federal courts reveal a similar story. Political staff size again significantly increases the chance that organizations will be involved and their level of involvement. Each political employee is expected to increase mentions by approximately 13 percent. Organizational age also significantly affects participation and level of involvement in the courts. Organizations with larger public membership are also more involved. Advocacy organizations often need membership to be given standing by the courts and benefit from representing a category of victims (Young 2010). Broad issue agendas are also helpful in the courts; every additional issue area on an organization's agenda increases expected mentions by more than 5 percent. Unexpectedly, however, hiring more external lobbyists, establishing local chapters, and being a think tank each has significant and negative effects on involvement.

Substantial differences in involvement also exist across organizational types. Compared to non-ideological-issue groups, unions are more involved, as are environmental groups, consumer groups, liberal-issue groups, and conservative-issue groups. The courts seem to promote involvement by organizations having clear perspectives over those gaining legitimacy as nonideological voices.

The results for these four models indicate that many of the same organizational attributes are responsible for increasing the level of advocacy-organization involvement in different policymaking venues. The crucial factors associated with institutionalizing organizations as representatives of political constituencies and position advocates in policy debates performed largely as expected. Organizational age and political staff size, which serve as indicators for a group's longevity and the scale of its Washington presence, were expected to help organizations with institutionalization as both constituency representatives and position advocates; they had particularly consistent positive effects on involvement in policymaking.

To provide a sense of the combined effects of these differences on involvement in all four venues, I estimated the predicted probabilities of generating each count of mentions or appearances for two different types of organizations: a new professional association with one in-house political staff member and a twenty-year-old issue group with ten political staffers. Neither hypothetical group has lobbyists, PACs, chapters, or members. The models predict that the professional association would have only a 20 percent chance of testifying before Congress over the decade and only a 1 percent chance of testifying more than five times. The issue group, in contrast, would have an 80 percent chance of testifying and a 50 percent chance of testifying more than five times. Each group would be unlikely to be mentioned in presidential papers. The issue group, however, would have a 28 percent chance of being mentioned and a 5 percent chance of being mentioned more than five times, whereas the professional association's chance of being included at all would be less than 1 percent. The important effects of institutionalization also combine to produce major differences in agency and court involvement. The professional association would have about a 40 percent chance of being included in administrative agency rules and a 13 percent chance of being mentioned at least five times. The fortunes would be reversed for the issue group; it would have a

60 percent chance of being involved and a 40 percent chance of generating five mentions. For the federal courts, the professional association would almost certainly not be involved, whereas the issue group would likely be included. The chance of participation for the professional group would be less than 2 percent; the chance of participation for the issue group would be approximately 60 percent. Institutionalized organizations are therefore substantially more involved in policymaking across the board. Organizations that are not institutionalized are involved rarely, if at all.

The Mechanisms for Reliance on Institutionalized Organizations

Qualitative evidence also provides support for Institutionalized Pluralism's description of the processes at work. Chapter 5 asked two key questions to determine whether organizational attributes would influence institutionalization: Does the attribute align the organization with its proscribed role in policy deliberation or constituency representation, and does the attribute encourage everyone to view the organization as a stable embodiment of its purpose? Interviewees provided illustrations of the mechanisms involved in each variable's impact that showed that, for the variables identified here, these questions would be answered affirmatively. In making their assessments, the interviewees did not have the history of each organization in mind. They were describing why they rely on institutionalized organizations, rather than evaluating alternative histories that could have brought different organizations to the foreground. The interviews clarified how basic structural characteristics of organizations, such as their longevity and scale, explain most of the variance in involvement.

The president of a prominent advocacy organization, for example, provided an explanation of the effect of age that matches a theory that emphasizes the way that organizations become taken for granted:

If you have history of working on [the] issues, they know what you have to say . . . It's a legitimacy issue, but it's also a time issue, [and it] goes with name recognition. There is certainty about what you are going to say.

A former congressional staffer and official at a prominent advocacy group added that age helps establish organizations as credible spokespeople:

> Having been around longer, being established, gives you credibility, makes you better known . . . It's name identification [but also] associating with an issue, being here for years as a [particular type of] group.

These sentiments demonstrate that advocacy-group success is not about the provision of new information to policymakers or any direct exchange of resources. In fact, policymakers prize groups that they already know and can gauge the words they are likely to say. This would be difficult to explain with a theory based on exchange. The policymakers are receiving nothing that they have not heard before. Institutionalization is associated with credibility, recognized knowledge, ease of placement into a social position, and a taken-for-granted role in the process.

Interviewees also explained the reason why a large internal staff of political representatives helps advocacy organizations become institutionalized, but lobbyists do not. One congressional-committee staffer compared the benefits of internal staff to hired lobbyists:

> I'd rather talk to someone who knows the issue . . . I don't care that you hired someone from K Street who called to set up a meeting . . . If you come talk to me about an issue, you have to have some depth. I think external lobbyists sometimes don't have that.

The chief-of-staff for the majority side of a congressional committee agreed that internal staffers have more credibility with policymakers:

> [If organizations have internal staff rather than lobbyists], they look less like hired guns or paid advocates. They have more credibility . . . I can think of a couple of hearings where we identified experts but held back [on inviting them to testify] because they were a lobbyist.

From policymakers' point-of-view, not all "boots on the ground" are equally credible. Compare the explanations for this phenomenon. If this process is about buying access, lobbyists should do the trick. If it is instead about building credibility for playing a proscribed democratic role, they would not. Organizations must become the site of expertise and representation; they cannot outsource these key functions to lobbying firms.

The models also indicate that formal ties to a public constituency help organizations become more involved in most venues. A chief of staff for a congressional committee explains the reason why:

> If they represent a constituency, we do give more weight to [their] testimony ... If they are large, their support will be more important. They are established.

Organizations need to demonstrate constituency support, therefore, but weak indications such as staff and membership size suffice to signal their representative roles. One advocacy-organization leader compared his prominent group to three similar groups with fewer members:

> We are perceived differently. We are a mainstream group, and we carry more weight. We get listened to a bit more. We have respect. We are more representative. We represent many constituents throughout the political spectrum.

Another group official told me that his group actively promotes its membership numbers:

> We tell them our number of members, show our field work, and reflect what we are hearing from the public ... it give us credibility ... we can be a third-party validator.

A large membership provides an indication that an organization is a credible constituency representative. Building a membership is not merely a fund-raising tactic designed for organizational maintenance or an army of loyalists designed for electoral threats. Instead, it is a simple signal of representational credibility.

According to policymakers, issue expertise and position taking also play important roles in advocacy group success. Institutionalized Pluralism's claim that some advocacy groups are institutionalized into the role of informed position advocates also matched qualitative assessments of the role of the variables considered here. One congressional committee staffer said that think-tank identification and issue-agenda size, for example, jointly establish formal expertise in the minds of policymakers:

> Think tanks are broader ... they do not have specific narrow policy goals. They have credibility ... they are a bank of policy experts.

As expected, no perceived trade-off occurs between having expertise and a particular perspective. A think-tank leader stated that policymakers respect their expertise but know the policy view they seek to advance:

> They believe our numbers are accurate. We have a reputation for solid research ... They are aware of our point of view, but they respect our analytical work and use our numbers.

Finally, interviewees helped explain why establishing a PAC to make campaign contributions did not produce a greater level of involvement among advocacy groups. As one congressional chief of staff stated, "[Whether an organization has a PAC] doesn't come up. No one bothers to look it up." Another committee staffer echoed these same sentiments: "I usually don't even know about stuff like [PACs]. It usually doesn't even come into my thinking."

It is possible that these interviewees presented self-serving views, biasing their statements in a way that avoided admitting direct resource exchanges. Because the quotations are consistent with the empirical evidence, however, readers should not immediately suspect their intentions. In these interviews, many committee staff did not seem to know which organizations had PACs and lobbyists, but they certainly knew which organizations had large internal staffs and had been in Washington for extended periods.

The similarity of effects across institutions and groups is striking given the dissimilarity of the formal processes involved in participation in each venue. Congressional staff and agency administrators, for example, described a wide range of processes that lead to advocacy group inclusion. Some congressional committees have the majority party committee staffers select all of the witnesses, with the exception of one witness selected by the minority staff. Others split the witness selection evenly between majority and minority staff. Other committees agree on a joint list of witnesses. One committee even had an application process for testimony. The formality of how committees develop their lists of potential participants also varies considerably. Some committees maintain long written lists of experts; others create new lists hurriedly as issues arise. Still others never create a full list of potential witnesses for any hearing; they simply call their first choices and locate additional witnesses only if their first choices are unavailable. Similarly, administrators do not respond to comments in the same fashion across agencies or across individuals. In some cases, they reference only those organizations in the rules that have spoken directly with them about their comments; in others, they cite almost the entire list of advocacy groups who submit comments. Still other administrators divide respondents into categories based on their constituency and name only the lead organization in each category.

Despite this wide variation, many of the same institutionalized organizations make the cut in each venue and are consistently more involved across the board. Several interviewees commented that no matter the formal process, everyone seems to reach collective agreement on the list of major players. An advocacy-group leader explained that the same groups are always involved in rulemaking: "It is usually obvious who is going to weigh in. The key stakeholders weigh in. We know who they are going in." An administrative agency official said that they respond to all of the categories of advocacy groups that they hear from regularly:

> We see certain people over and over again . . . but there are a wide variety of commenters: consumers, teachers, librarians . . . [responding to all of them] rounds out the picture with other perspectives.

A congressional-committee staffer said that their committee selects the same list of participants, whether they construct it internally or consult outsiders:

> We find people, we canvass. It is not a very long list. We look for expertise and experience . . . We consult with some outside groups, but we all know the [same] universe [of groups].

An advocacy-group official stated that only organizations viewed as major players are typically invited, even if other groups might fill a niche:

> To be invited to testify, you have to be a primary stakeholder. There may be a slot associated with your interest, but you have to be one of the primary organizations. They almost never call anyone but the primary lobbying organizations.

Policymakers share opinions about whose comments must be heeded and those who must be appeased; the same actors keep arising. One advocacy-group official explained why the four largest organizations in their issue area, including his own organization, are repeatedly invited:

> We don't have to push ourselves to go testify. They invite the people. They know what they will say . . . Only a handful of groups are considered. They are the most obvious.

A congressional-committee staffer quoted by Leyden (1995, 434) explains how the process of witness selection is likely to lead to the same group of participants whether it is led by Congress or by interest group leaders:

> There are two ways people get to testify. They are either asked to testify or they ask to testify. The people who are asked (by us) to testify are the major players in a particular issues. The people who ask to testify are not always the major play-

ers . . . for months or years before the issue comes up you have gone in to talk with the congressmen and the committee staff people—before the hearing—so they know what your position is. You have to establish relations beforehand.

In other words, a group is either initially recognized as a usual suspect, or it works to make itself into one.

Although the distribution of participation across venues can be quite different, institutionalized organizations find a way to abide by any formal process and regularly find a seat at the table. They are the usual suspects because their structural features help them fill their proscribed roles. Yet the mechanisms identified here could also provide an opening for policymakers to change their impressions of organizations as these attributes change. The mechanisms do not explain the over-time institutionalization process of each organization. For that, scholars and policymakers would need to closely observe how reputations develop. Many of the comments provided in interviews may not even sound like full explanations for policymaker behavior. Part of the point made by Institutionalized Pluralism is that many decisions about involving advocacy organizations are made off the cuff and without a full analysis of strengths and weaknesses of each option. This produces considerable reliance on shortcuts. Observers may be hoping that political actors consider the pros and cons of each group systematically and understand their histories, but this is unlikely. Instead, policymakers rely on basic signals about organizations that allow them to make comments like "they have credibility" and "they're a known player" without fully processing how they arrived at these judgments.

Assessing Institutionalized Pluralism

The theory of Institutionalized Pluralism offers a predictive framework for understanding the way that advocacy organizations become actively involved in Washington policymaking. Institutionalized Pluralism performed well when contrasted with other theories, especially the resource-based theory of buying access offered by Leyden (1995). Resources used to hire lobbyists or to contribute campaign donations are not the chief sources of advocacy-group success. In every model, the number of lobbyists that an organization hires was insignificantly or negatively related to its policymaking involvement. According to the models for each venue, establishing a PAC increases involvement only in agency rulemaking; it has no effect on involvement in other venues.

Alternative models comparing the amount of contributions given by organizations over the decade also reveal almost no effects of PAC contributions.

Institutionalized Pluralism's analysis of the limits to organizational strategy and the differences across policymaking venues also fared well in the empirical analysis. Many of the same organizational attributes promote high levels of involvement in most or all venues. Differences in statistically significant effects across the models did not add up to any consistent patterns of attributes that helped organizations in some cases but not in others. There was no indication that resources spent on lobbyists or PACs could overcome the structural disadvantages of small, young, narrowly focused, or professional groups in any venue. There were some differences based on organization types across venues, but they were not susceptible to easy categorization. For example, think tanks were more involved in Congress but less involved in the courts, the opposite conclusion one might expect from the theory that institutions without electoral incentives are more likely to prize information provision (Mahoney 2008, 4). Matching previous studies (Furlong and Kerwin 2005; Strolovitch 2007), however, identity-based and issue-based groups were less involved in agencies and courts than professional associations.

As expected, however, the distribution of organizational involvement in congressional committees and in presidential announcements was broadly representative of the advocacy-organization population in Washington. The distribution of involvement in administrative agencies and federal courts was less reflective of the population. As a result of their lack of control over participation, agencies and courts enable more participation by the types of organizations that are direct economic stakeholders. It is worth remembering that lawmakers have invented tools to promote wide public participation in agencies and courts, such as the public notice-and-comment procedures required by the Administrative Procedures Act and the inclusion of *amicus curiae* briefs in court procedures. In designing these procedures, however, lawmakers have unwittingly made these venues receivers of advocacy, rather than seekers of advocacy. When given the chance to build the community of participants in their venue, policymakers tend to rely on a representative cast. When made to hear all comers, policymakers do not have such a choice. The result may be policymaking forums less responsive to a broad range of interests and views, ironically made possible by the very institutions designed to increase public responsiveness.

Important limits apply to the current scholarly approach to advocacy group involvement in policymaking venues, which emphasizes the tactical decisions of organizational leaders. An organization cannot choose its way to high levels of involvement in any venue without becoming an established representative and an entrenched advocate. Within these macrolevel patterns, interest groups still have some agency in determining their fate; particular contingencies may help explain why some organizations outperform others with similar characteristics. Scholars may be able to learn from case studies of these outliers. Yet, just as electoral candidates face different likelihoods of victory based on experience and partisanship, the basic circumstances that organizations face are determined by their structure: their scale, longevity, scope, and ties to public supporters and issue expertise.

The results presented here offer a new starting point for research on advocacy-organization involvement in policymaking. The baseline models identify many of the most important factors promoting involvement in each venue. The same organizational attributes but different organizational categories predict high levels of participation in each venue. The results provide little support for a theory of organizational success that relies only on resource mobilization or venue selection strategy. According to these data, resources used to build a larger Washington presence are well spent, but not all expenditures produce policymaking involvement, especially those directed toward hiring lobbyists and establishing PACs. When it comes to policy influence, Baumgartner et al. (2009) also find that it is difficult to draw a direct line from more interest group resources to being on the winning side of a policy debate; they find that resource advantages can help organizations achieve short-term policy change, especially for those who want no policy change rather than new government action, but many structural factors like executive-branch support are far more influential.

This study's findings add that the policymaking involvement of an advocacy organization is largely dependent on its structural attributes and external image. Instead of asking interest groups about every tactical decision and helping to confirm the assumption that each of these decisions makes a difference, one can examine the factors that influence an organization's involvement in policymaking. The results indicate that levels of advocacy group involvement vary considerably and are mostly a consequence of structural features of organizations.

Some organizations have aligned their structure with presumed roles as informed advocates of policy positions and representatives of public constituencies, largely following from the length of their tenure, their scale, their membership ties, and their reputation of issue expertise. This does not leave much room for strategic action in any particular case, but it does indicate that extended organizational development by less-mobilized constituencies would likely make a difference. Resourceful organizations tied to their constituencies could legitimate themselves over a long period of political advocacy. Organizational success requires articulating a representative purpose in line with democratic expectations and creating a structure that signals the way that a group advances their purpose.

The evidence suggests that weak signals can suffice to position advocacy groups as representatives of public constituencies and informed position advocates. The scholarly fascination with the role of resources in this process has directed attention to some important factors in determining how advocacy groups succeed. Yet scholars have been too quick to assume that resources are effective as a result of quid pro quo exchanges and self-interested strategic interaction. Resources help advocacy organizations reach exalted public positions and dignified social roles in the collective imagination; their assumed roles grant them access to public decision making. These roles, however, are premised on a deeply held conception of democratic practice, not on direct material or information exchanges. Americans' unrealistic norms that leaders heed all perspectives and listen to all constituencies in national political debates provide social roles to be filled. Some entities must speak for the many different viewpoints and represent the variety of different stakeholders. The infusion of the democratic values of public representation and political expertise into the advocacy community enables particular organizations to fill these social roles.

The day-to-day role of advocacy groups in policymaking may only tenuously advance democratic values. Nevertheless, the normative expectations of democratic decision making influence the patterns of cooperation between government and outside interests and provide an opening for the regular participation of advocacy organizations in American governance. Elected policymakers, at least, appear to hear from a representative cast of the advocacy community, even as they empower the same usual suspects to substitute repeatedly for public perspectives and constituencies. In all venues, spokespeople for public interests and ideas are treated as recognized and important stakeholders in political conflict. The implied role they fill in democratic politics provides a platform for their regular involvement in public decision making.

Conclusion

Listening to Everyone

Organized advocates of public interests and ideas now capture the attention of policymakers, media elites, and citizens in almost every policy area. Many advocacy organizations have become political institutions in their own right, becoming taken for granted as permanent political actors with legitimate roles in public life. Some social groups have generated a level of organized advocacy that provides them with a source of political power to be used as a potential veto over public policy change. The deep-rooted roles played by advocacy organizations in American politics offer insights into the contemporary political process and the inherent challenges of democratic governance. Understanding the advocacy system requires re-evaluating received wisdom about how public groups engage in collective action, how different views are heard in political debate, and how the public is represented in policymaking.

Research on the factors that govern advocacy-organization success and public-group representation is important for building knowledge about one set of political actors and one mode of public participation. This work does not cover the entire interest group community or all modes of public representation and policy debate. Advocacy-organization research, however, can provide a broader view of crucial empirical debates about policymaking in each branch of government, political debate in each kind of news medium, and the political capacity of public groups. Providing a macrolevel analysis of who is represented by advocacy organizations and whose voice is heard among them helps answer central questions about the connection between theories of democracy and governance and their execution in American political institutions.

This book's parallel analysis of the advocacy system as a community of organizations and as sectors of public-group representatives shows that the foundations of contemporary interest-group research should be subjected to more scrutiny. In contrast to the expectations of collective action theory, the primary lens through which scholars investigate public-group mobilization, hundreds of different social groups and political perspectives generate organized advocates to speak on their behalf. No major category of interests or ideas is excluded, but public groups have widely differing levels of organized representation. The assumptions of prior interest-group research regarding organizational behavior and strategy fare no better. Many organizations have pursued similar strategies and tactics, but only a limited community has become the stable, acknowledged participants in national politics. The distribution of resources, as well as prominence and involvement, across the advocacy community is uneven and skewed, with some advocacy groups making their way into the governing process but most remaining largely unknown and uninvolved.

This book introduced and provided evidence for two theories to explain the vast differences in levels of organized representation for each public constituency and in degrees of prominence and involvement for each organization. Using traditional group theory and contemporary theories of public political behavior, Behavioral Pluralism explains why some public groups generate the most organized advocacy. Augmenting traditional group theory with contemporary institutional theories of organization, Institutionalized Pluralism explains why some organizations become major players in media debates and policymaking. In line with pluralist ideas, many different social groups and political perspectives generate interest organizations that participate in governance as the assumed representatives of public constituencies. Given the role of civic and political engagement in individual political behavior, however, constituencies having the capacity, attention, and motivation to participate in public life develop substantially greater levels of organized representation. In particular, the average levels of political efficacy and civic membership within American social groups and single-issue constituencies are related to the extent to which they develop organized representation to speak on their behalf. Constituencies that vote at higher rates are also better represented by advocacy organizations, whether they are large or small. The advocates for these constituencies succeed only by becoming institutionalized as constituency representatives and as position-takers in policy debates. As a result, only the oldest, largest, and broadest of these organizations succeed in Washington. The results show that the age, political staff size, and agenda breadth of advocacy organizations help determine their level of prominence in the media and involvement in policymaking. Ties to public membership and identification as a think tank are also influential factors in organizational success, but ties to PACs and lobbyists have little effect.

The basic underlying processes of interest mobilization and aggregation are uniform across the political system. Few organized leaders appear to succeed independently of their constituency and their basic organizational characteristics. The targets of political advocacy are also largely immaterial to success in Washington. The same attributes help organizations become institutionalized players in all parts of American politics. Print, television, and online media, including outlets directed at both public and elite audiences, empower similar types of advocates. Congressional committees, the president, administrative agencies, and federal courts all involve institutionalized advocates in the policymaking process as well. No matter the venue or outlet, organized advocates succeed by aligning their structure and attributes with the democratic purposes of public representation and policy deliberation. No matter the type of constituency, public groups need to be made up of civically and politically engaged citizens to develop extensive organized representation to fill this role.

The Implications for American Governance

Policymakers and media elites are responding to democratic expectations that suggest bringing everyone into the process and hearing all views. Advocacy organizations seek to voice important public concerns and perspectives. Constituents also participate in organizations to advance their interests and ideas in competition with others they consider less important. The universal democratic demand to be listened to, to have one's voice heard in governance, comes to fruition in the advocacy community. The vaguely stated norms of listening to everyone and incorporating all perspectives reach their empirical potential in the relationship between government and the advocacy community. Political elites walk through the motions of heeding alternative public voices and ideas. Organizations go through the motions of presenting constituency voices and ideas, often framed in terms of the public interest. Nevertheless, the advocacy community empowers some public groups more than others. American government and media likewise empower some spokespeople over others. Although the advocacy system is built on a foundation of legitimate democratic expectations, it functions in practice as a reflection of the relative political capacity of societal groups and the relative organizational capacity of group leaders in Washington.

The tendency of all branches of government and the media to empower organized representatives to speak on behalf of public constituencies also makes it nearly impossible to isolate the relative independent power of each American political institution. Scholars cannot assume that elected officials, media outlets, and policymaking venues are sovereign actors with independent agency. In asking whose voices are heard in the political process, analysts must pay attention to claims to speak on behalf of constituencies and to the competition among political factions in all political arenas. Certain public groups, including Jews, lawyers, and gun owners, may gain advantage in every system designed to incorporate public advocates.

Analyses of the role of the public in governance also cannot assume that individuals participate as a unified public voice or in isolation. Groups with shared interests or ideas are foundational units in political competition. The attempted incorporation of competing interests and ideas into political institutions and public policy involves the aggregation of these groups' views. The advocacy system is one important reflection of factional competition, but the same processes underlie elections and party competition. American governance, in large part, is a product of factional competition. Scholars should expect groups advantaged in organized mobilization to be advantaged in political competition across the board.

Nonetheless, there are important differences in the scope and relative balance of factional competition within each institution. The distribution of policymaking involvement in each branch of government may serve as proxies for the extent to which policymaking in each venue takes into account a range of views as well as proxies for the types of interests advanced in each arena. Courts and administrative agencies appear to empower a less representative cast of the advocacy community than Congress and the president. Congressional committees, in particular, rely on a diversity of organized advocates to testify. Courts and agencies instead empower particular categories of interests. If certain types of organizations are more successful in some venues than others, the explanation may lie in the rules of the game in each governing arena.

Different mediums of public debate and expression may similarly empower different public groups to participate. Analyzing the factors that influence organizational participation in each type of news media provides a new lens through which to view debates over media bias and the changing technological landscape. The results indicate that no major type of news media systematically favors conservative or liberal advocacy. Nevertheless, the mass television-news media are more likely to empower groups with local and consumer ties, whereas the elite-directed print media are more likely to highlight the views of ideological groups on both sides. The rise of Web publishing as a new medium does not portend a new era in which different styles of political organizing become dominant in political debate; on the contrary, it is a medium that advantages the same institutionalized organizations that are prominent elsewhere, with the exception of a few particular interests of Web publishers.

The American political system offers multiple opportunities for participation by the organized claimants of constituency representation. Each branch of that system appears to be subject to some universal processes that legitimize certain participants as well as some distinct elements that distinguish policymaking and debate in each competitive arena. To understand what Schattschneider called the "mobilization of bias" in the American political system, scholars must examine both the generic processes of institutionalization that allow organizations to stand in for wider constituencies and the particular factors influencing success in each venue.

The Implications for Public Representation

The findings also offer a new perspective on public representation in the political process. Previous studies of public representation by elected officials generally relied on assessments of whether the views of legislators reflected the views of their electorates. Attention to the structure of the advocacy community offers new insights about the relative mobilization of different interests that are absent from these studies. Advocacy organizations play important roles in voicing public concerns and attending to public groups' interests. Rather than represent public opinion as a whole, the advocacy community disproportionately represents the public groups with the most political capacity.

Many citizens may believe that their interests are more effectively represented by a section of the advocacy community than by their elected officials. Nevertheless, the advocacy community as a whole cannot be said to be representative of the public in its entirety. Many of the same public groups are more active in both elections and interest-group politics, but electoral advantages are conditioned by the size of the group's voting bloc. Elections thus provide a potent source of power for larger groups over smaller ones; the advocacy system provides no such advantage. The public is represented in the advocacy system as a series of distinct stakeholders, small and large.

Despite the advocacy community's role in public representation, it is not easy for citizens to hold their advocacy organization leaders accountable. Individuals can withhold resources, but an organization may still gain credit for claiming to represent their interests in Washington. Constituents can found competing organizations, but it is difficult to challenge the lead of institutionalized actors. As a result, exchange-based theories provide an unrealistic backdrop for normative evaluations of interest groups. Constituents amassing resources to hire leaders to speak on their behalf are not objectionable, but organizations that gain the status of representing entire ethnic groups or single-issue constituencies by being the largest and the longest-running actors are worthy of scrutiny.

We can draw some insights about the possibility of reform in the advocacy system from the sociological literature on deinstitutionalization. New actors can reduce the influence of institutionalized organizations by undermining faith in their normative underpinnings or disassociating their behavior from their claimed social roles (Lawrence and Suddaby 2006). When it comes to the advocacy community, however, most actors seek only to undermine the claims of their political opponents, rather than to discount the idea that any organizations can stand in for public constituencies and perspectives. Most organizations seeking to become alternatives to the advocacy system have copied the strategies of others and become part of the community, using its normative foundations on their own behalf.

Many of the rules established to allow group leaders to have a voice in government decision-making, such as open-hearing requirements, public-liaison offices, administrative procedures, and *amicus curiae* opportunities, are justified by the goals of involving the public in governance and providing public forums for policy deliberation. Because most of the public is disinterested or inattentive to everyday policymaking, however, these forums rarely involve a broad cross section of the American public. Instead, they empower advocacy organizations to play the role of representing public groups and issue perspectives. These organizations compete not only with other advocacy groups but also with traditional stakeholders who have a direct role in administering or complying with public policy, such as government units and corporations. Thus, institutions designed to empower public participation may have created a system of weak stakeholder governance, whereby constituencies without direct interests are assumed to be represented by organizations that gain some semblance of constituency support. General perspectives are believed to be advanced by organizations with some claim to speak as informed advocates of policy positions.

Many of these advocacy organizations are rightly viewed as important sources of countervailing power against corporations or governmental units in the policymaking process. A large part of the source of their power, however, is the myth that they fulfill underlying democratic roles. As policymakers and stakeholders have come to take the role of advocacy groups for granted, advocates have become another primary source of public representation in policymaking, almost as renowned for their public advocacy as elected officials. The mechanisms behind this representative role are less straightforward than those provided by elections or delegated powers but no less important. In asking whether public views weave their way into political institutions and policy outcomes, scholars must consider the unique role of the advocacy community in public representation, not merely the extent to which government action coincides with public opinion.

The Implications for Interest Intermediation

Advocacy organizations are obvious candidates for study as intermediaries between political elites and the public, along with traditional institutions like political parties. Nevertheless, advocacy organizations serve as placeholders for various constituencies and policy perspectives, not just as claimants of public support. In an important sense, advocacy groups are more reflective of the social and ideological diversity of the American public than political parties. Whereas advocacy organizations regularly pursue the interests of many ethnic, religious, social, and occupational groups in national politics, no political parties fulfill this role. Whereas advocacy organizations represent many different issue publics and ideological views, the two-party system cannot reflect the same diversity of issue viewpoints and salience within the public.

Because they are intermediaries, advocacy organizations also lack much independent agency. They are constrained by their capacity to mobilize constituents and provide issue perspectives for policy debates in government institutions. Yet they are rarely required to confirm that their constituents share their views. Even the limited accountability mechanisms offered by political-party primaries, where citizens can vote against party favorites, have few equivalents in advocacy-group behavior. In addition, public advocates are forced to compete with corporations and other institutions as stakeholders in policy debates. They are often treated as comparable participants in policymaking even though advocacy groups have a unique role in intermediation. Although the involvement of advocacy groups in policymaking relies on democratic theories justifying interest intermediation, the facts on the ground are not easy to reconcile with any normative theory of governance by public representatives.

Whether or not the position of advocacy organizations is justified, it nevertheless gives organizations power to influence the perceptions of government among their constituents and the image by which their constituents are remembered by policymakers. When political elites discuss the feelings of the "black community" or the "evangelical community," for example, they are often presenting the perspectives of their organized leaders. These effects on perceptions can also run in reverse. Many people learn about the actions of government from the organized leadership for their social group or political perspective (Mansbridge 1992). Advocates have incentives to claim that they are facing great obstacles. As intermediaries, advocacy groups present only partial views of their constituents to policymakers and only partial views of the political system to their constituents.[1] The results may include a shrinking sense of responsiveness on the part of citizens, many of whom are constantly told that their perspectives are not adequately included in policymaking, as well as a caricatured view of public cleavages on the part of policymakers, who assume that advocacy-group conflicts equate to public divides.

Building Interest-Group Theory

The research presented here is designed to extend the agenda of interest group scholarship. Given the substantial impact of advocacy organizations on the American political system, the role and behavior of advocates deserves future attention from scholars. The investigations presented here should give pause to continuing in the same scholarly direction. Interest groups were once treated as central features of any empirical political theory because interest mobilization and aggregation are key aspects of democracy. The theoretical weight attached to interest-group studies waned because scholars were diverted, not because of any change in their empirical role or importance. If anything, the expansion of the interest group community in Washington in the last fifty years, especially among public advocates, should have increased attention to theories of the governmental process based on interest groups.

The diversion was not accidental. It was, in large part, a product of the most important intellectual movement in political science in the past few decades, namely, the rise of rational choice theory. The attraction of mathematically tractable theories of decision making based on plausible assumptions has been quite strong. Unfortunately, the base assumptions were incorrect and led to conclusions that were accepted even though they were disconfirmed. In interest-group theory, the resulting trajectory of empirical work resulted in an obsession with the way that membership groups generate support without selective material incentives. It also stimulated a theory of interest-group influence that focused on direct exchanges of resources and information between policymakers and interest groups.

If the totality of evidence against rational choice theory from psychological experiments and studies of mass behavior and political institutions have not convinced scholars to abandon this trajectory, it is quite unlikely that results from studies such as this one will have any effect on this intellectual agenda. Nevertheless, the evidence confirms that people mobilize in groups to pursue many different kinds of collective goals. Policymakers also respond to these groups even if they are not offered anything in direct exchange. Reporters also reach out to similar actors absent any resource exchange or electoral incentive. Some kind of rational choice model may be able to explain these results post hoc, but the findings suggest that the rationality premise is a poor guide to understanding organized political advocacy. If scholars have a choice between starting from the premise that people act in their rational self-interest or from the premise that people share interests and ideas with others promoting joint action, they should select the latter.

These criticisms are not original. The new emphasis that this book brings to the debate is that rational choice theory was put forward as a reason to reject the dominant theoretical perspectives of an earlier era, especially group theory. In effect, Olson's argument against Truman suggests that group theory was inadequate because groups of the kind envisioned would not rationally form and engage in politics. When those groups actually formed, scholars sought to modify the new rational choice framework rather than resuscitate the old one. The rise of rational-choice perspectives in interest-group theory was problematic not only because it failed to explain the phenomenon at hand but also because it dislodged a productive and useful framework for understanding the governmental process.

Olson's analysis of the history of American interest organizations may still be valuable, but not as a critique of Truman's group theory. Olson's discovery that some advocacy groups were founded as offshoots of private enterprises or organizations with mandatory membership may help to explain why particular organizations were founded earlier and became the dominant group associated with a particular constituency. Tracing the development of AARP and observing the fact that selling insurance played an important role, however, are quite different from analyzing whether the elderly were likely to produce an advocacy organization to speak on their behalf. There are many contingencies that may explain how AARP became prominent relative to other organizations, but there is no realistic counterfactual under which older Americans would have no organization speaking on their behalf. The rise of Social Security and Medicare likely motivated this constituency, providing an additional basis for organizational mobilization and support. The roles to defend these programs and to represent the elderly, however, were available for an organization to fill. The organizational development was also inseparable from the development of political capacity by the constituency itself. Despite being forgotten, Truman's emphasis on public groups was a useful starting point for understanding organized advocacy.

Group theories of politics definitely need to be extended and modified. Fortunately, scholarship on individual political participation has continued to provide relevant insights for Truman's unfinished project of determining which types of public groups mobilize most extensively. Research on civic participation offers additional factors relevant to both local and national political mobilization. Similarly, theories of organizational institutionalization within sociology offer useful tools to understand how interest organizations become permanent parts of American governance.

Aggregated to the group level in Behavioral Pluralism, theories of individual political behavior and local civic engagement offer the best potential to advance scholarly understanding of the interest mobilization process. Political constituencies vary widely in their levels of political attentiveness and efficacy, as well as civic and political participation; these differences correspond to their levels of organized representation, no matter the type of public group or political perspective under consideration. Research on the development of organized representation for public groups over an extended period could help connect these findings to traditional understandings of the way that organizations develop and survive.

Additional work on advocacy organizations in political institutions can use the baseline models associated with the theory of Institutionalized Pluralism as a starting point. Organizations that have been in Washington for many years, have developed a large internal political staff and public membership, and have created an expansive issue agenda become the most prominent in news media reports and the most involved in policymaking venues. Advocacy organizations relying instead on lobbyists and PACs do not succeed in Washington. These models of institutionalization need to be extended, but relying on assumptions of resource exchange will be less helpful than thinking about the way that organizations develop the taken-for-granted status of public representatives and issue-position advocates. Future studies of policymaking in particular venues or of public debate in particular forums can modify the baseline models presented here but should not lose sight of the importance of the basic structural features and the assumed roles of advocacy organizations. Studies of strategy and tactics can refine the circumstances under which group leaders can change their likely fate, but they cannot ignore structural features any more than studies of candidate strategy can ignore electoral context.

Toward a Macropolitics of Interest Groups

Scholars want to understand "who governs." This will require a more complicated theoretical model and empirical analysis. Scholars cannot yet claim to fully understand the dynamic interactive processes among public constituencies, organized representatives, and political elites, but this analysis offers hope for such a research agenda. Using data sets that combine mass survey data on different social groups with data on the activities of their organized representatives offers a path toward knowledge about political mobilization and influence as well as a method of testing common ideas about those groups most advantaged in systems of representation. Scholars of Congress (Sulkin 2005; Bishin 2009) have built macropolitical theories that analyze legislative representation, noting that political elites respond to their public constituencies. In contrast, the interest group subfield has yet to integrate mass behavior.

Scholars must think about macrolevel political processes involving interest groups, rather than analyzing organizational behavior from the organization's point of view. To gain ground on the perennial question of who is represented, research must link public affiliations and mass behavior to competition within government institutions.[2] Organizations that represent public constituencies, for example, not only raise resources from them; they also gain legitimacy based on the presumption of support. Organizations that advocate policy positions are not merely finding a niche in order to survive in Washington; they are becoming recognized stakeholders in policy debates. Scholars should not separate studies of interest-group mobilization and interest-group influence because the process of mobilization is related to the capacity for influence.

The most recent comprehensive study of lobbying (Baumgartner et al. 2009) takes a macrolevel view of interest group influence, but it takes the population of major interest group players as a given, rather than investigating why some constituencies mobilize more than others or why some organizations become much more involved than others. The authors report that the population of major players is relatively constant (3) but find important dynamics underlying the competition among these major interest groups, emphasizing the status quo bias of the policymaking system and the limited effect of resource advantages in achieving policy change. In contrast, this book has investigated how and why the community of major players is limited and which public groups are represented in this community, but it has stopped short of explaining who wins and loses policy debates among well-represented groups. In part, this is simply a methodological limitation. Interest groups are but a slice of the policymaking system, and it may be dangerous to look at who wins and loses only from their perspective. Baumgartner et al. (233), for example, find that ties to government officials help interest groups defend the status quo; yet this may be a reflection of the irrelevance of interest groups to which side wins and loses, rather than a sign that some groups lobby more effectively. To successfully analyze influence, interest-group scholars will have to consider the multitude of factors that influence policy change, even those that have little to do with groups.

In addressing interest mobilization, a macrolevel perspective would emphasize the common patterns across groups and contexts, rather than assuming that groups are each engaged in unique tactics and political movements.

Because all constituency groups and their leaders face similar opportunities and constraints, the generic dynamics of organized representation, rather than the particular choices of leaders or constituency-group members, explain much of their differential mobilization and influence. Scholars of particular social groups or policy areas have much to add to the story of how interests mobilize, but the groups of interest to them may not mobilize through an entirely distinct process or on the basis of unique foundations.[3]

Scholarship on business involvement in government could also benefit from a macrolevel perspective. This book has emphasized that corporations and their associations mobilize through a different process than advocacy organizations. Businesses are not credited for representing public constituencies in policy debates. Nevertheless, they may receive credit for representing areas of the economy. In other words, both the economy and society may be represented by organized advocates; business lobbyists may receive credit for representing the economy. This perspective suggests that general characteristics of industries, such as the proportion of economic activity that they represent, would be related to the prominence and involvement of their Washington policy offices. If this conjecture were correct, corporate political activity would constitute taken-for-granted economic representation. Whether or not business political activity can be subsumed under a future theory of economic representation, one can gain an important set of insights from applying a macrolevel perspective connecting organizations to the economic sector they seek to advance.

Interest groups cannot be thought of as independent political agents because they are intimately tied to their targets of influence and to their constituencies, whether they are public groups or economic sectors. Interest-group research is particularly vulnerable to failure under the traditional political science division between "institutions" and "behavior." Interest groups, after all, represent an aggregation of public behavior and a set of actors in political institutions. Separating these two research agendas does not make these two roles empirically disconnected, but it does lead scholars to consider them separately. This division has led to a path whereby scholars modify collective action theory to understand mobilization and then modify exchange theory to understand influence. The division in research has hidden the intermediary role of interest groups from view.

The problem of how political factions mobilize and become part of the governing process has implications for research throughout social science.

Nevertheless, scholars in fields like ethnic politics, environmental policy, and political economy will come to see interest group theory as a useful tool only if interest-group scholars connect their research to the concerns of each field. By returning to broad questions of who is represented and whose voice is heard, interest-group scholars can serve an important role in the broader project to merge scholarly investigations of public political behavior and political institutions. In the process, scholars may notice that institutional development is dependent on the outcomes of political competition among public factions. Scholars may come to believe that individual political participation can be understood only in the context of group affiliations and the behavior of organized representatives. Both the development of political institutions and the behavior of the American public are likely to be dependent on the process of interest intermediation. Still, the advocacy community is not the only system reliant on the principles of public representation and policy deliberation; elections and legislative politics also rely on these democratic objectives. Wherever these values form the background of political practices, scholars should look for the role of public representation in providing political elites with legitimacy.

Democratic Theory and the Empirical Problem of Factions

A research program designed to study the mobilization and representation of public groups can inform perennial debates about the way that democracy does and should function. As Madison recognized in *Federalist 10,* the "problem of factions" is fundamental to democracy's justifications and its operations. The causes of faction are "sown in the nature of man." Its effects are seen in the "necessary and ordinary operations of the government." Despite many empirical and normative theories of the differential influence of some groups over others, scholars have not fully described the types of political factions that benefit most in the American political system, much less compared the results to any coherent democratic theory of whose interests should be incorporated into policy outcomes. Madison, like others, defined factions in opposition to an imagined aggregate public interest. This book has shown, however, that the contemporary debate over what constitutes the public interest is just as divided by factions, constituencies based on issue positions or ideology, that organize like social groups.

The empirical problem of factions is not merely an outdated concern of traditional democratic theory but also a continuing roadblock for each of the newest attempts to create alternative foundations for democracy via communitarian, deliberative, and associational models (Kane 2002; Stokes 2002). Normative theory scholars cannot easily circumnavigate the problem of factions by proposing alternatives. Communitarian approaches, for example, envision common agreement on the public interest via a reassessment of long-running shared values. Yet different groups rely on alternative conceptions of values to mobilize politically; political views and issue perspectives are represented just like interests in the advocacy system. In addition, basic social interests and values stemming from shared occupations, ethnicities, and religions tend to stimulate organized representation for a subset of the population, rather than the community as a whole.

Another set of normative theories, deliberative approaches, advocates in-person discussion of political issues to reach collective consensus. On a national level, their approach is also unlikely to be practicable. Political discussion occurs in the news media, with people advocating positions as known spokespeople for each major side or stakeholder. Citizens generally communicate about politics with others who share their goals or interests precisely because they believe that other groups have agreed on different goals or interests. That does not leave much room for national deliberation.

A third set of normative theories, associational approaches, also fails to offer a solution to the problem of factions. This set of approaches relies on extending the use of voluntary organizations and communities to eclipse the role of government. This model does feature the more realistic premise that groups have distinct values and interests that promote cooperation among like-minded communities. Nevertheless, it assumes that this cooperation can occur outside the political competition surrounding government action. Contemporary advocacy organizations representing hundreds of public groups, however, seek to influence the actions of the state. It is both unworkable and morally suspect to expect groups not to pursue government action if their values and interests compel them to do so. Truman's emphasis on the inevitable gravitation of social associations toward government comports more with the history and purpose of many voluntary groups.

Associational, deliberative, and communitarian perspectives each offer a potential vision for political change. Yet each of these political theories is merely another shared set of ideas that may promote collective action among a subset of the population. If a public subpopulation mobilizes around any of these shared visions, it will have to compete against constituencies associated with all other political perspectives and interests to reach its goals. The effort to subsume all political activity under one umbrella perspective about how politics should be practiced is doomed to fail. As they move toward even ideal-typical implementation, political theories contend with the problem of factions. People have different ideas and interests, and they cooperate in order to compete with other groups over collective decision making. No coherent political theory has emerged to propose an alternative formulation of politics that takes into account this fundamental aspect of democracy. Madison's problem of factions is still the best statement of these difficulties. If the constitutional system he helped design is unable to control the effects of faction, no coherent alternative system may be available.

Most normative critiques of democratic decision making, including recent concerns about civic engagement, civil society, and special-interest politics, are new variations on two fundamental uncertainties of democratic government: whether and how the ideas and interests of public groups can be represented by leaders and whether and how the conflicting ideas and interests of the community can be incorporated into national political outcomes. The two chief worries of commentators bemoaning the decline of civic and community life are that contemporary styles of social organization empower political elites over the populace and that these styles of organization are conflictual rather than consensual. These anxieties are just repetitions of the original concerns about political factions. People inevitably associate themselves with distinct political leaderships and pursue partial interests or ideas. If social organization has evolved beyond traditional civic life, it only reflects the fact that public perspectives and interests are more national and political than they have been in the past.

This book's empirical results do not undermine the importance of the major concerns of advocates of civic engagement, but they make them concerns about democratic governance in general rather than about modern social and political organizing. It is not clear whether self-appointed leaderships for broad public groups or perspectives can be justified; yet, wherever there are widely shared points of view, they will be represented by the few on behalf of the many. It is also not self-evident that different political views and interests can be combined in any fair and balanced method; integrating interests to form agreeable solutions is a fundamental democratic challenge.

Concerns about the functioning of democratic government have promoted a rise in interest in the concepts of civil society and state–society relations. The premise of these ideas suggests that government by elites working in their own interests can be tempered by the inclusion of actors from society who will have societal interests in mind. Nevertheless, society has multiple and competing interests, and any civil society is likely to be a reflection of the relative strength of the multiple constituencies associated with those interests. Any civil society will also empower some people to speak on behalf of others, creating a new class of political elites that have legitimacy based on that presumed role. If these new intermediary actors inherently have their own collective interest, no one claiming to represent the public interest can overcome this imbalance between leaders and followers. Newly mobilized "public interest" groups also have a constituency with only a partial view of societal goals and interests.

Civil society and civic engagement are commonly thought to be alternatives to the dreaded "special interests." In a sense, social organization designed to represent public interests and ideas is distinct from the political activities of corporations and governmental units, justifying this opposition. Yet each set of public interests and ideas will be only partial, and each set of leaders will be only tenuously connected to the constituencies that they claim to represent. This partiality does not occur because of any fundamental fault of these leaders or their ideas but arises from the basic nature of the problem of factions. People disagree and are stimulated to be involved in politics to advance their agendas over those of others. Advocacy organizations, as the current instantiations of American civil society, owe their prominence and involvement in governance to the public principles or subpopulation interests that they claim to advance. They endure the same opportunities and difficulties in organizing to influence collective decision making that all other political factions face.

The role of empirical knowledge in understanding contemporary American civil society and its potential alternatives is to illustrate that which seems inherent in any system of collective representation and to identify the processes at work that may benefit some groups or organizations over others. Factional mobilization of all shapes and sizes has produced an advocacy system in Washington that includes a great diversity of interests and ideas but promotes them at radically different levels in the national conversation and the policy-making process. The differences in social and political characteristics among public groups produce an advocacy system that represents some groups more than it does others. The rituals practiced by political elites going through the motions of bringing everyone into the process empower some leaders to speak on behalf of these public groups and make some organizations into institutions with staying power in American governance. Organized advocates and policymakers do not ignore the broad expectation that democracy requires listening to everyone. Because it is impossible to meet in practice, Americans have collectively institutionalized an advocacy system that largely substitutes for public representation and policy deliberation.[4] The potential of the advocacy system and its limits not only provide lessons for the practicalities of organizing and governing but also signal the depth of the foundational dilemmas of the democratic experiment.

Appendix

Data Sources and Methods

Despite an abundance of previous hypotheses about the way that advocacy organizations succeed and which public groups generate organized representation, no large-scale effort has been launched to investigate which factors lead to higher levels of success for organizations or higher levels of representation for public groups. Whereas many studies of organizational opinion and behavior have been conducted on large populations, most studies of organizational involvement in policymaking or public group representation have been conducted via case studies (Baumgartner and Leech 1998). Thus, no data sets were available for testing the hypotheses of Institutionalized Pluralism or Behavioral Pluralism. I therefore use original data on a broad population of advocacy organizations and their constituencies, including new data that I collected on organizational attributes, prominence, and policymaking involvement. I combine these new data with survey data on the characteristics of constituencies and an original content analysis of organizational websites.

The Organizational Population

I investigate the characteristics of more than 1,600 advocacy organizations speaking on behalf of social groups or public-issue perspectives in national politics. The population includes all organizations with a presence in the Washington area that aspire to represent a section of the public broader than their own institution, staff, and membership. I combine the study of the organized representation of ethnic, religious, demographic, and occupational groups with the study of the organized representation of particular ideological or issue perspectives.

I use the population of Washington advocacy organizations to ensure complete representation of all types of advocacy groups and every combination of organizational attributes. The population is not intended to be a sample of all interest organizations. Companies, governments, and their associations represent a large portion of the interest-group community, but theory and previous research indicate that they are likely to be subject to different opportunities and constraints in their efforts to become successful. Because most studies of advocacy groups include only a small portion of the population, such as religious representatives, the results of this analysis are already generalized to a much larger community of organizations than extant research. The results cannot be generalized, however, to help understand the activities of business; if corporations operate differently and succeed via a contrasting process, a distinctive theory and analysis will be necessary to understand their behavior; if they operate similarly and succeed via a similar process, this analysis will need to be conducted on a larger population of organizations to draw that conclusion.

Some debate remains about where to draw the line between advocacy organizations and other interest groups. Some scholars believe that professional associations and unions constitute a separate category that is a gray area between corporations and advocacy organizations. Nevertheless, they are included in this population because they seek to represent broad occupational categories rather than specific institutions. The analysis notes where the attributes of these organizations differ from those of other groups.

To identify advocacy organizations, I relied on reference sources and organizational websites. I used the *Washington Representatives* directory and checked for additional organizations in the *Encyclopedia of Associations, The Capital Source,* the *Government Affairs Yellow Book, Public Interest Profiles,* and the *Washington Information Directory.* With two research assistants, I confirmed that all organizations in the population seek to represent social groups or issue perspectives in national politics.

We catalogued every public constituency claimed by these organizations, using reference-text descriptions and organizational websites. Rather than attempt to assess whether organizational leaders properly represent their claimed constituencies, I took the representative claims of the interest organizations at face value. If an advocacy organization claims to speak on behalf of a social group, I considered the organization that group's representative. If an advocacy organization maintains that it speaks on behalf of a particular ideological or issue perspective, I considered the organization a representative of the public group of supporters for that political perspective. If an organization asserts that it represents multiple types of public groups, I coded them as representatives of more than one constituency. In a reliability check on these categorizations, a research assistant reached the same list of claimed constituencies as me for more than 90 percent of the organizations. Table A.1 lists all of the social groups with organized representation in Washington that we located. Table A.2 lists all of the issue perspectives with organized representation that we located.

We also categorized these organizations into 210 sectors corresponding to the constituencies they seek to represent. We created sectors only when more than one organization claimed to represent the same constituency. Many organizations are included in more than one sector. In a reliability analysis, our categorizations into these sectors were again consistent for more than 90 percent of the organizations. When available, we compared our categorizations with those used by scholars of particular advocacy-group sectors (Hertzke 1988; Hofrenning 1995; Berry 1999; Shaiko 1999; Hays 2001). Our categorizations were also consistent with those used by these scholars for more than 90 percent of organizations.

TABLE A.1. Social groups with organized representation in Washington.

Constituency type	Social Groups Represented (466)
Ethnic groups (41)	Afghan Americans, African Americans, Alaskan native, American Indians, Arab Americans, Armenian Americans, Asian Americans, British Americans, Cameroonian Americans, Caribbean Americans, Cherokees, Chinese Americans, Cuban Americans, Czech Americans, European immigrants, Filipino Americans, French Americans, general minority, German Americans, Greek Americans, Hispanics, Indian Americans, Irish Americans, Italian Americans, Japanese Americans, Kashmiri Americans, Korean Americans, Kurdish, Kuwaiti Americans, Latin Americans, Latinos, Latvian American, Lebanese Americans, Mexican Americans, Navajos, Polish Americans, Puerto Ricans, Russian Americans, Southeast Asian Americans, Taiwanese Americans, Turkish Americans
Religious groups (26)	Agnostics, atheists, Bahai, Baptists, Catholics, Christians, Church of Christ, Church of the Bretheren, Episcopalians, Ethical Society, Evangelicals, general religious, Jews, liberal Christians, the Lubavitch movement, mainline Protestants, Muslims, Presbyterians, Quakers, Reform Jews, Scientologists, secular, Seventh-Day Adventists, social gospel, Unitarian Universalists, United Methodists

TABLE A.1. (continued)

Constituency type	Social Groups Represented (466)
Occupations (255)	Abortion providers, accountants, actuaries, administrative judges, admissions counselors, aerospace doctors, aging researchers, agricultural aviators, air traffic controllers, allergists, anesthesiologists, anthropologists, appraisers, arbitrators, archeologists, architects, art teachers, artists, association executives, astronomers, audiologists, auditors, authors, automotive engineers, bakers, bank directors, biochemists, biological scientists, biology teachers, biophysicists, biotechnologists, bishops, bond lawyers, bricklayers, broadcast employees, builders, building managers, building trades, business executives, business proprietors, cardiologists, carpenters, cataract surgeons, cell biologists, chemical engineers, chemists, chest physicians, chiropractors, child psychiatrists, civil engineers, collection attorneys, college registrars, commercial realtors, communication trades, communications lawyers, compliance professionals, composers, consumer affairs professionals, cooperative farmers, corn growers, corporate directors, corporate lawyers, corporate professionals, corrections officers, cotton growers, court reporters, criminal defense lawyers, criminal investigators, dairy farmers, decorators, dental researchers, dentists, dermatologists, dieticians, diplomats, district attorneys, doctors, economists, educational consultants, elected officials, electrical engineers, electrical workers, emergency managers, emergency room doctors, engineering educators, engineers, entertainers, entrepreneurs, environmental managers, farmers, financial professionals, fire chiefs, fire fighters, fishermen, flight attendants, food workers, foresters, fundraisers, gastroenterologists, geneticists, geographers, geologists, gerontologists, government accountants, government employees, government lawyers, government managers, government professionals, gynecologists, health educators, health lawyers, health scientists, health trades, hematologists, hospice caregivers, hotel workers, humanities researchers, immigration lawyers, immunologists, information technologists, information trades, insulators, insurance agents, intellectual property rights lawyers, intelligence officers, interior designers, international lawyers, ironworkers, journalists, judges, landscape architects, language and area studies researchers, lawyers, librarians, linguists, lobbyists, longshoremen, managers, manufacturing workers, marketing professionals, marriage therapists, maternal doctors, math teachers, mathematicians, mechanical engineers, medical professors, microbiologists, midwives, military teachers, milk farmers, mine workers, mineralogists, music therapists, musicians, natural resource trades, naval engineers, nephrologists, neurological surgeons, newspaper editors, nonprofit sector workers, nuclear cardiologists, nurse anesthetists, nurses, nutritionists, obstetricians, occupational therapists, oceanographers, office employees, ophthalmologists, opticians, optometrists, orthopedic surgeons, osteopathic surgeons, otolaryngologists, painters, paper workers, pathologists, pediatricians, pension professionals, pharmacists, physical scientists, physician assistants, physicists, physics teachers, physiologists, pilots, planners, plant biologists, plastic surgeons, plumbers, podiatric doctors, police chiefs, police officers, policy analysts, postal supervisors, postal workers, postmasters, principals, private educators, professors, psychiatric nurses, psychologists, public health professionals, public relations

professionals, radiologists, railroad engineers, railroad workers, real estate agents, real estate brokers, recording artists, resource economists, restaurant workers, roofers, school administrators, school psychologists, science teachers, scientists, seafarers, secretaries, service workers, sheet metal workers, sheriffs, social scientists, social studies teachers, social workers, sociologists, speech therapists, sports lawyers, statisticians, steelworkers, taxi drivers, teachers, technical educators, technical trades, therapists, toxicologists, traditional crafts, trainers, translators, transplant surgeons, transportation engineers, transportation trades, travel agents, treasurers, trial lawyers, truckers, university attorneys, urologists, veterinarians, women's health researchers

Other social groups (79)	AIDS sufferers, Air Force veterans, aircraft owners, Americans living abroad, aneurysm sufferers, anxiety disorder sufferers, Army veterans, automobile drivers, bikers, blind, boat owners, brain injury sufferers, breast cancer sufferers, cancer sufferers, children with learning disabilities, college students, consumers, dancers, deaf, digestive disease sufferers, disabled, disaster victims, elderly, epilepsy sufferers, families with adopted children, fitness oriented, gays, gifted children, graduate students, gun owners, heart disease sufferers, high school students, hikers, homeowners, immigrants, investors, kidney disease sufferers, law school students, lesbians, leukemia sufferers, liver disease sufferers, lung disease sufferers, Marine veterans, medal-winning veterans, medical school students, men, mentally ill, military families, motorcyclists, national guard members, Navy veterans, parents, ovarian cancer sufferers, Parkinson's sufferers, poor, P.O.W. families, prostate cancer sufferers, railroad passengers, retarded, retired, runners, rural residents, sleeping disorder sufferers, smokers, space enthusiasts, sportsmen, stockholders, sufferers of diseases, trauma sufferers, unemployed, union members, urban residents, vegetarians, veterans, Vietnam veterans, welfare recipients, westerners, women
Intersectional groups (64)	African Jews, African American accountants, African American bankers, African American business owners, African American dentists, African American doctors, African American engineers, African American government employees, African American meeting planners, African American police officers, African-American state legislators, African American teachers, African American union members, African American women, African Americans in energy, American Indian teachers, Asian American business owners, blind students, blind veterans, Catholic doctors, Catholic veterans, Catholic women, Christian lawyers, Christian men, Christian women, conservative women, Democratic college students, disabled business owners, disabled veterans, elderly African Americans, elderly women, Filipino veterans, gay and lesbian Republicans, Hispanic corporate executives, Hispanic doctors, Hispanic journalists, Hispanic lawyers, Hispanic nurses, Hispanic police officers, homeless veterans, Indian Republicans, Jewish Democrats, Jewish holocaust survivors, Jewish immigrants, Jewish veterans, Jewish women, military chaplains, minority contractors, pastoral counselors, professional women, Puerto Rican women, Republican college students, Republican Jews, Russian Jews, student journalists, university women, women athletes, women business owners, women doctors, women entertainers, women legislators, women lobbyists, women policy analysts, women scientists

TABLE A.2. Issue perspectives with organized representation in Washington.

Constituency type	Issue perspectives represented (146)
Ideological perspectives (9)	Conservative, economic conservative, economic liberal, liberal, libertarian, moderate Democrat, moderate Republican, social conservative, social liberal
Liberal issue perspectives (56)	Alternative energy, alternative medicine, animal rights, anti–child labor, anti–death penalty, antinuclear, antipesticides, antipoverty, anti–religious right, anti–youth marketing, arts funding, bird conservation, broadcasting rights, campaign finance reform, civil libertarian, civil rights, clean air, clean water, climate change, conservation, cooperative housing, criminal-justice reform, Democratic Party affiliated, domestic violence control, drug policy reform, education expansion, electricity price control, energy conservation, energy regulation, environmentalist, feminist, financial regulation, forest preservation, health care quality, health coverage expansion, homeless rights, horse protection, immigrant rights, insurance reform, labor rights, marijuana legalization, marine conservation, media reform, national park conservation, population control, prochoice, progressive taxation, public housing expansion, public power, refugee rights, right to die, river conservation, senior housing, stem cell research, technology regulation, trail creation, wetlands preservation, wildlife refuge protection
Conservative issue perspectives (28)	Anti–affirmative action, antienvironmentalist, antieuthanasia, anti–gay marriage, anti–government waste, anti-immigration, antitaxation, antiunion, charter schools, deficit reduction, domestic security, educational standards, English only, entitlement reform, estate tax reform, federalist, flat tax, gun rights, land rights, local control, proenergy, pro-life, property rights protection, Republican Party affiliated, right-to-work, school choice, strict constructionist courts, tort reform
Foreign policy issue perspectives (28)	African democratization, African wildlife preservation, aid to Africa, America-first foreign policy, antihunger, antilandmine, antimalaria, arms control, export promotion, free trade, general foreign policy, human rights, international child welfare, international economic competitiveness, international religious liberty, Latin American human rights, liberal internationalist, Middle East peace, neoconservatives, pacifists, pro–United Nations, pro–foreign aid, pro–international development, support for Israel, trade protectionists, vaccine availability, world government
Other issue perspectives (25)	antialcohol, anti–child abuse, anticrime, antidrug, antismoking, auto safety, child welfare, children's health, dispute settlement, electoral reform, ethics promotion, general economic, general education, general health care, good government, historical heritage, local support, reading promotion, recreation/parks supporters, regional support, technology expansion, transparency, veteran welfare, wildlife management, women's health

Constituency Characteristics

The project also requires identifying the public constituency associated with each sector of organizations. Unfortunately, no previous public-opinion survey has specifically attempted to measure group-level attributes of a large number of political constituencies. As the best available option, I use the cumulative General Social Survey (GSS) to identify members of a public constituency and to measure their demographics and their levels of engagement and participation, as well as their opinions and beliefs. This introduces several sources of potential measurement error in these data, which I attempt to minimize. The methodological difficulties of this analysis make it impossible to move beyond descriptive analysis of constituency characteristics with great confidence. Nevertheless, the solutions that I introduce provide the best analysis to date of the differences in representation of public groups in American national politics.

I use cumulative GSS data from 1972 through 2004 to isolate constituency members among the 45,803 respondents to the survey. To identify ethnic, religious, ideological, and demographic constituencies in survey data, I use respondent self-reports. To identify occupational constituencies, I use my coding of the *International Standard Occupational Codes* used by the GSS. To identify single-issue constituencies, I use strong supporters of the sector's issue position when the GSS contained relevant questions. For some organizational sectors, I had to construct scales of multiple questions to identify the relevant group of supporters.

I identify members of a public group using a response or set of responses to survey questions in the cumulative GSS file. Table A.3 describes the variables that I use to isolate each constituency. These variables are also used to determine constituency size, which is measured as the proportion of all respondents to the same set of surveys who fall into each category. The "Constituency" column contains the name of a constituency that I included in the analysis. The "GSS variables" column indicates which variable names I used in the cumulative GSS file. The "Response categories" column records the responses that classified respondents as a member of the constituency. If I used more than one variable, I include the responses for both variables separated by the conjunctions "and" or "or." The use of "and" signifies that both sets of answers are necessary, whereas the use of "or" indicates that either set of answers is sufficient. For occupational categories, I report the set of responses associated with the 1988 occupational code; the categories used from the 1968 occupational code are substantially similar. The final column lists the number of respondents in the category from all years of the cumulative surveys.

For each constituency, I recorded data on the group's population size and its mean socioeconomic status and mean levels of attention to the news media, internal political efficacy, belief in government responsiveness to ordinary citizens, confidence in government, and membership in civic organizations. I recorded its rates of local meeting attendance, voting turnout, financial contributions, and government-official contacting. I also recorded the level of ideological cohesion within each group and the extremity of the group's policy opinions on the environment, health, education, welfare, and the military.

Because I could not identify all constituencies in all years of the survey, I do not have a large number of respondents for all constituencies. In addition, the respondents associated with each group are not distributed equally over the same years of the survey. To eliminate many of the problems associated with compiling information from surveys administered in various years, I record the attributes of constituencies by using the difference between the mean within a constituency and the mean among all respondents to the same set of surveys. Using an analysis of a subset of thirty constituencies for which more data were available, I confirmed that this process provides accurate measures of how constituencies differ from the general public and from other constituencies.

TABLE A.3. Variables used to isolate public constituencies.

Constituency	GSS variables	Response categories	Total n
Conservative	Polviews	6, 7	6,596
Economic conservative	Eqwlth	7	2,974
Social conservative	Prayer, abany	2 and 2	5,281
Moderate Republican	Partyid, polviews	5, 6 and 4	3,171
Liberal	Polviews	1, 2	5,280
Economic liberal	Eqwlth	1	4,256
Social liberal	Prayer, abany	1 and 1	2,584
Moderate Democrat	Partyid, polviews	0, 1 and 4	5,727
Consumer	Lessreg	4, 5	569
Liberal internationalist	Usintl, usun	1 and 1	9,838
Neoconservatives	Amownway	1	306
Foreign aid supporters	Nataid	1	1,487
National security	Natarms	1	6,299
Israel foreign policy	Israel	0	1,773
Export promotion	Nafta2, nafta2a	1, 1 or 2	534
Environmental	Natenvir	1	16,492
Population control	Popgrwth	1	196
Civil libertarian	Spkath, spkrac, spkcom, spkmil, pornlaw	1 and 1 and 1 and 1 and 2, 3	4,153

Constituency	GSS variables	Response categories	Total n
Drug policy reform	Grass	1	6,593
Pro-Choice	Abnomore, abpoor, absingle, abany	1 and 1 and 1 and 1	8,607
Feminist	Sex, fehome, fework, fepol	2 and 2 and 1 and 2	6,059
Animal rights	Antests	5	258
Civil rights/affirmative action	Natrace, natracey; racpush	1, 2 and 1, 2 and 4	3,360
Criminal justice reform	Courts, courtsy	1, 1 or 1, 1	1,979
Favor gun control	Gunlaw, owngun	1 and 2	13,783
Oppose death penalty	Cappun	2	10,047
Progressive taxation	Progtax	1	337
Health coverage expansion	Helpsick	1	6,319
Education expansion	Nateduc	1	17,385
Housing expansion	Aidhouse	1	476
Labor rights	Unprog, unionsok	4 and 1, 2	320
Media regulation	Polviews, conpress	1, 2 and 3	890
Energy regulation	Ownpower	2	1,012
Financial regulation	Ownbanks	2	828
Antipoverty/poor	Helppoor	1	3,732
Social Security protection	Natsoc	1	16,228
Arts funding	Sparts, natarts	1, 2 and 1	741
Pro-life	Abnomore, abpoor, absingle, abany	2 and 2 and 2 and 2	11,227
Guns/2nd Amendment	Gunlaw, owngun	2 and 1	4,112
Anti–affirmative action	Affrmact	4	4,738
Conservative women	Sex, fehome, fework	2 and 1 and 2	1,359
Immigration control	Letin, letin1	5 or 5	1,736
English only	English, bilinged, engvote	1 and 4 and 1	1,737
Domestic security	Demrghts	2	373
Legal strict constructionist	Conjudge, courts	3 and 2	3,753
Right to work/Antiunion	Unprog, unionsok	1, 4 or 5	359
Educational standards	Coneduc, polviews	3 and 6, 7	909
Media watch (conservative)	Polviews, conpress	6, 7 and 3	1,876
Entitlement reform	Natsoc	3	1,794
Tax cuts	Progtax	3, 4, 5	712
Antienvironmentalist	Busdecid	1	358
Deficit/spending control	Cutgovt	1	1,258
Antismoking	Nosmoke	1, 2	304
Antidrugs	Grass; natdrug	2 and 1	8,095
Child welfare	Aidkids, sppoorkd	1 and 1	335
Anticrime	Courts(y), cappun	2 and 1	23,597
Recreation supporters	Natpark	1	9,630
Space support	Natspac	1	3,237
African American	Race	2	5,660
Hispanic/Latino	Ethnic	17, 22, 25, 38	2,131
Mexican	Ethnic	17	1,120
Puerto Rican	Ethnic	22	378
Asian American	Ethnic	5, 20, 40	429
Chinese	Ethnic	5	163
Japanese	Ethnic	16	103
Indian (Asian)	Ethnic	31	141
Arab American	Ethnic	37	72
American Indian	Ethnic	30	1,583
Italian	Ethnic	15	2,068
Greek	Ethnic	12	154

TABLE A.3. (continued)

Constituency	GSS variables	Response categories	Total n
Irish	Ethnic	14	4,427
Russian	Ethnic	23	585
General minority	Race	2, 3	8,030
Evangelical Christian	Fund, relig	1 and 1	14,262
Mainline Protestant	Denom	10–50 (not 14, 32)	17,058
Baptist	Denom	10–18	9,547
Catholic	Relig	2	11,416
Muslim	Relig	9	54
Social gospel	Fund, relig	1 and 3	5,853
Jewish	Relig	3	973
Secular	Relig	4	4,292
Gay and lesbian	Sex, sexsex	(1 and 1) or (2 and 3) or (1–2 and 2)	479
Veterans	Vetyears	1–4	3,348
Military families	Vetfamnw	1	144
Elderly/Retired	Age	–65	8,049
College students	Wrkstat	6	1,391
Immigrants	Born	2	2,898
Urban residents	Xnorcsiz	1	8,040
Rural Residents	Xnorcsiz	9, 10	6,448
Homeowners	Dwelown	1	11,912
Drivers	Carprivt, cardealr	1 or 1	530
AIDS sufferers	Aidswho	1–4	135
Mentally ill	Relmhsp1-3, hlth2, mntlcare	1 or 1 or 1	390
Fitness oriented	Actsport, dosports	1 or 1	1,104
Outdoor Sportsmen	Hunt	1, 2, 3	5,226
Women	Sex	2	26,074
Union members	Union	1	3,772
Small business proprietors	Wrkslf	1	5,037
Corporate professionals	Isco88	1210–1240, 2110–2139, 2411–2419, 3421–3429	3,496
Financial professionals	Isco88	1231, 2411, 3411	971
Government employees	Wrkgovt	1	1,877
Government professionals	Isco88	1120, 3441–3449	601
Law enforcement	Isco88	A3450, 5162	224
Postal workers	Isco88	4142	251
Fire fighters	Isco88	5161	96
Service workers	Isco88	5100–5152, 9110–9162	6,433
Manufacturing workers	Industry, indus80	8121–8290, 9320–9322	2,977
Building trades	Isco88	2141, 2148, 7121–7143	
Traditional crafts	Isco88	7211–7442	3,113
Communication trades	Isco88	7244, 3132	283
Transportation trades	Isco88	3140–3145, 8310–8324, 8340, 9331–9333	1,463
Information trades	Isco88	2131–2139, 2431–2432, 4121–4141	2,116
Health trades	Isco88	2229–2230, 3133, 3211–3232	2,179

Constituency	GSS variables	Response categories	Total n
Natural resource trades	isco88	6141–6154, 7111–7113, 8111–8113	164
Office workers	Isco88	3431–3439, 4111–4223	6,234
Public health professionals	Isco88	3151–3152, 3223	48
Lawyers	Isco88	2421–2422	265
Farmers	Isco88	6111–6133	591
Artists	Isco88	2451–2454	294
Entertainers	Isco88	2452–2455, 3470–3475, 5210	424
Pilots	Isco88	3143	54
Doctors	Isco88	2221	134
Nurses	Isco88	2230	903
Dentists	Isco88	222	27
Therapists	Isco88	2445–2446, 3460, 3226	608
Pharmacists	Isco88	2224	44
Engineers	Isco88	2142–2147	468
Bankers	Isco88	A3411, 3421	191
Information technologists	Isco88	2131–2139, 3121–3123	499
Insurance agents	Isco88	3412	246
Real estate professionals	Isco88	3413	251
Journalists	Isco88	2451	146
Teachers	Isco88	2320–2359	1,901
Scientists/researchers	Isco88	2310	838
Physical scientists	Isco88	2110–2114	98
Biological scientists	Isco88	2211–2213	72
Social scientists	Isco88	2441–2446	352
Professional women	Sex, isco88	2 and professional	2,006

Table A.4 describes the variables from the cumulative GSS file that I use to measure the characteristics of each public constituency. The "Coding" column includes information about how I measured each attribute. The "Years included" column references the years of the survey in which the GSS asked the relevant questions. The final column lists the number of total respondents to these questions.

Organizational Attributes and Activities

I also collected information about the attributes and activities of each organization. I collected data on all of the attributes thought to be relevant to an organization's prominence in the media or involvement in policymaking. To assess longevity, I used data on the age of the organization as reported on organizational websites or descriptions in reference texts. To assess the scale of

TABLE A.4. Variables used to measure aggregate characteristics of public constituencies.

Characteristic	GSS variables	Coding	Years included	Total n
Socioeconomic status	Sei	Mean	All	23,232
Media attentiveness	News	Mean	All	28,190
Internal efficacy	Polleff3, poleff11	Mean on combined scale	1985, 1996	3,369
Government responsiveness	Anomia7	Percentage	1973–1994	19,083
Confidence in government	Confed, conlegis	Mean on combined scale	All	30,524
Civic membership	Memnum	Mean	1972–1994, 2004	20,438
Attending meeting/ rally	Polrally, attrally(1)	Percentage	1987, 2004	2,939
Interpersonal Trust	trust	Percentage	All	29,147
Voting rate	Vote68–vote00	Percentage who voted in latest election	All	43,068
Financial contributions to candidate or cause	Gavepol, polfunds(1)	Percentage	1987, 2004	2,940
Contact public official	Othlobby, cntctgov(1)	Percentage	1987, 2004	2,942
Ideological cohesion	Polviews	Variance	All	37,137
Opinion extremity	Natenvir, natheal, nateduc, natfare, natarms	$\Sigma \mid$ (group mean $-$ total mean) $\mid$	All	26,815

their Washington operations, I used the number of internal political representatives on their Washington staff as reported in *Washington Representatives*. This measure omits staff dedicated to other pursuits, such as administration and membership maintenance; it reflects the organization's political presence in Washington. To assess an organization's formal ties to a public constituency, I relied on membership size and the existence of local chapters. I used the number of individual members reported on organizational websites or in reference texts. I also recorded whether an organization has associated local or state chapters. To assess the scope of an organization's policy agenda, I used the number of policy issues on which it lobbies, as recorded in *Washington Representatives*. To assess whether an organization has formal links to policy expertise, I record whether it is identified as a think tank in Rich's (2004) interview-based study. To test the importance of variables thought to be important by other scholars, I use the number of external lobbyists an organization has hired, and I record whether it has an associated PAC, as reported in *Washington Representatives*. When these variables were unavailable from the sources listed, I supplemented the information with data from scholarly studies of specific interest group sectors (Hertzke 1988; Hofrenning 1995; Berry 1999; Shaiko 1999; Hays 2001) and Washington media reports. The analysis includes complete information about 1,454 organizations in the population. Removing organizations in which I use supplemental data sources has no substantive effect on results. By removing organizational age and membership information from all models, I can analyze almost the entire population of organizations. The results of the models without these two variables are substantially similar to those presented here.

With the help of a research assistant, I also conducted a content analysis of organizational websites. That research assistant visited the home pages of all organizations along with one other page that appeared to be the most likely to call for direct action among supporters. She recorded the average number of requests for visitor action on their Web pages. She also assessed whether or not the site requested that visitors call Congress, attend a protest, and attend an in-person meeting as well as whether it mentioned any specific legislation or executive-agency decisions. These data were collected between February and May of 2005 from all organizations in the population having websites. I content analyzed a sample of one hundred of these websites and agreed with more than 90 percent of her coding decisions.

To assess each organization's level of activity in Washington, I collected data on the number of times each organization was mentioned from 1995 through 2004 in three daily calendars of Washington political events, namely, the *Federal News Service Daybook,* the *Federal Document Clearing House Political Transcripts,* and *The Washington Daybook.* For all searches, one research assistant and I content analyzed thirty results to ensure that the references are related to the correct organization. In a test of separate analyses of organizational mentions, we agreed more than 95 percent of the time.

Prominence and Involvement

To measure the prominence of each organization, I use three types of media. First, I use data on the number of advocacy-organization mentions from 1995 through 2004 in the Washington print media directed at political elites. The sources of these mentions are *Roll Call, The Hill, National Journal, Congress*

Daily, The Hotline, Congressional Quarterly, and *The Washington Post* as re-corded in the *LexisNexis* news index. The Washington political media allow political elites to share information among themselves and report on the important activities of the Washington political community. Second, I use an indicator of organizational prominence in the mass media. I count the number of times that each organization was mentioned in national and local television-news broadcasts from 1995 through 2004 using the *Video Monitoring Services of America* index. The index includes transcripts of all network- and cable-news broadcasts as well as summaries of local-news broadcasts in major markets. Berry (1999) uses mentions in *Congressional Quarterly* as well as mentions in television news as a measure of interest-organization success. Salisbury (1984) and Holyoke (2003) also use media mentions to assess the activity levels of interest groups. Third, I use an indicator of each organization's prominence in new media. I count the number of links provided by other Web publishers to each organization's website on the World Wide Web. I use the Google index of backward links. It includes links from all websites in the search engine's database; Google uses this index to rank the pages that it returns in response to user searches.[1]

To analyze organizational involvement in policymaking venues, I use one measure for each venue, namely, congressional committee hearings, presidential announcements, administrative-agency rulemaking, and federal-court proceedings. To assess involvement in congressional policymaking, I use the number of times that each organization participated in committee hearings. The measure stems from a search for organizational names in the sections describing those who gave testimony from 1995 through 2004 in the database of *Federal Document Clearing House Congressional Testimony* maintained by *Congressional Quarterly*. Congressional-hearing testimony was the best available measure of involvement in Congress. It is not a comprehensive measure of all participation in Congress, but validation checks confirmed that the advocacy organizations testifying regularly are the organizations that are most generally involved in congressional policymaking.[2]

To assess involvement in presidential policymaking, I use a search for organizational names in the *Papers of the Presidents* from 1995 through 2004. This database is consulted by scholars of the presidency to assess each president's attention to various issues and the president's participation in policymaking. Although the process of presidential policymaking is often obscure, the president and the offices surrounding him make critical decisions of importance to advocacy organizations and involve them in discussions. The presidential papers include much of their correspondence and the president's publicly expressed attention to the groups.

To assess organizational involvement in administrative-agency rule-making, I search for organizational names from 1995 through 2004 in the database maintained by *LexisNexis* that contains the Final Rules and Administrative Decisions issued by more than one hundred executive branch decision-making bodies. Administrators typically refer directly to an organization in final rules when they are quoting or responding to its submission.

To assess organizational involvement in federal-court proceedings, I search for organizational names from 1995 through 2004 in the database maintained by *LexisNexis* containing case law and legal documents from the Supreme Court, all federal district courts and courts of appeal, as well as several specialty federal courts. Being mentioned frequently requires participation and active attention from the courts; organizations having their briefs cited by judges, for example, receive more mentions.

A content analysis of a subset of the mentions of each organization confirmed the reliability of the measures. We searched for organizations using multiple forms of the organizational names when necessary. We assessed thirty mentions of each organizational name to ensure that the references were connected to the correct organization. When mentions of the organization's name did not refer to the organization in question, we estimated the number of correct organizational mentions from a sample of fifty. When appropriate, we refined the search to isolate mentions of the organization. In a reliability analysis, a research assistant and I agreed on the number of mentions for more than 90 percent of organizations. Two research assistants also separately collected information about the prominence and involvement of one hundred organizations; the results were highly correlated.

The Design and Analysis

The units of analysis in Part I of the book are sectors of organizations associated with public constituencies. To assess the representation of each constituency, I aggregate this organizational data for each sector. I record the number of organizations in each sector, the number of political staff representing each constituency, the number of times that the Washington political media mention an organization in each sector, and the number of times that someone

from an organization in each sector testifies before congressional committees. Some organizations are included in multiple sectors, and some sectors
are subsets of others.

In Part II of the book, I move to the individual organization as the unit
of analysis. The investigation includes descriptive data on the distribution of
resources, activities, attributes, prominence, and involvement across organizations. I also include multivariate models of organizational prominence
in three mediums and policymaking involvement in four venues. To assess
which organizational attributes influence prominence and involvement, I
present one model for each type of medium and each venue. To account for
differences across types of organizations, the models include organizational
attributes as well as dichotomous variables representing the categories of professional associations, unions, and identity groups, as well as organizations
representing liberal-, conservative-, environmental-, and consumer-issue perspectives. The excluded category in these regressions is the representatives of
nonideological issue perspectives not labeled liberal or conservative.

Because all seven dependent variables in the multivariate analysis are
integer counts, I use maximum-likelihood count models to estimate the effects of each variable. To select among count models, Long and Freese (2001)
recommend using tests of overdispersion to determine whether Poisson or
Negative Binomial count models should be used and likelihood ratio tests to
determine whether or not the zero-inflated versions of these models should
be used. Using these tests, I determined that negative binomial regressions
are most appropriate for measures of media prominence, and zero-inflated
negative binomial models are most appropriate for predicting involvement
in each venue. These procedures are also the most sensible theoretically because media prominence is a general measure of notoriety whereas different factors may influence whether organizations are involved at all in each
policymaking venue and the amount of their involvement. The results of the
zero-inflated models include two coefficients for each independent variable;
the binary coefficients correspond to the model predicting whether organizations will receive a count of at least one, and the other coefficients correspond
to the model predicting the number of times that an organization will testify
or receive mention. The procedure is similar to using a logit model to predict
whether organizations will be involved at all in each venue and then using a
count model to predict the number of times those who are engaged will be
involved (Long and Freese 2001). Conventional reporting of zero-inflated re-

gressions includes binary coefficients that correspond with models to predict whether cases will receive a count of 0. I do not follow this convention because it makes positive values indicate lower levels of involvement. In the models reported here, positive coefficients indicate greater levels of involvement.

Because some institutional theory envisions a bright line between institutionalized organizations and others, some readers may question statistical tests that imply probabilistic causality and use continuous variables to measure attributes related to institutionalization. Nevertheless, the institutionalization process examined here does not rely on a dichotomous distinction. Organizations may be in the midst of becoming institutionalized, and their attributes may reflect this intermediary stage. Organizations may also be institutionalized only as constituency representatives or only as policy debate position advocates. In addition, only some reporters or policymakers may recognize organizations as fulfilling these roles. In any of these circumstances, their attributes will reflect an intermediary level of institutionalization.

Generic problems with cross-sectional data collection and analysis may also pose concerns for some readers. Institutionalization implies an over-time process. Organizations are likely to become more involved in policymaking as they become institutionalized; the inclusion of organizational longevity in these models accounts for this process. Although there is a possibility of some feedback effects from policymaking involvement to organizational characteristics, this concern is not a serious one for this analysis. Congressional-committee hearing appearances and mentions in policymaking documents, for example, are unlikely to affect an organization's structure and purpose directly or strongly. These models meet the standards of conventional cross-sectional models in social science.

The Interview Materials

The broad quantitative study offers the best tests of Institutionalized Pluralism. Nevertheless, the theory implies mechanisms that involve mental processes; these mechanisms may be better observed with qualitative data. Although it would be impossible to observe the minds of policymakers or organizational leaders or to ask all of them about their perceptions, interviews can provide illustrative examples of the mental processes at work. The quotations referenced in this study are derived from twenty anonymous interviews with congressional-committee staff, administrative-agency officials, and advocacy-organization spokespeople. I conducted these thirty-minute in-person or telephone interviews in the Washington area in June 2006. They cannot be said to constitute a random sample of any population. I did not have a previous personal or working relationship with any of the interviewees, and I have no reason to believe that they are unrepresentative of the wider community of relevant individuals involved in national policymaking. Anonymity was requested by these interviewees and ensured openness. Interviews can provide information to assess the plausibility of the mechanisms implied by the theory and to complement the quantitative analysis.

Notes

Introduction

1. This number is based on my own count of advocacy organizations, explained in Chapter 2.

2. This organization was formerly known as the National Association for the Advancement of Colored People but is now known only as the NAACP.

3. By public groups, I mean any group of citizens that serves as a constituency for an interest group in Washington, such as African Americans, Jews, gun owners, lawyers, and environmentalists. In Chapter 1, I identify all interest groups that seek to represent social groups or public-interest perspectives in national politics and catalog every public group that they claim to represent.

4. By *advocacy organizations,* I mean any organization that seeks to represent public groups or issue perspectives in Washington. I include organizations that are sometimes called "citizens' groups" or "public-interest groups," as well as ethnic and religious organizations and occupational associations. I include both membership and nonmembership organizations. In Chapter 1, I further define this population of organizations. In Chapter 3, I review several measures of their prominence in the news media and their involvement in policy-making venues.

5. This report is taken from Dan Balz and Jose Antonio Vargas, "Bloggers Give Clinton a Mixed Reception," *The Washington Post,* August 5, 2007.

6. I review the relationship between interest group research and these fundamental questions in a previous article (Grossmann 2006a). Some text throughout the book, especially the descriptions of interest group literature, are taken from that article.

7. To show that these groups have more representation, I identify advocacy organizations in Washington who claim to represent each constituency, including

religious groups like Catholics and Jews, and count the number of political staff and lobbyists that represent each group. I explain the results of this analysis in Chapter 2.

8. This organization was formerly the American Association of Retired Persons, but its official name is now AARP.

9. My usage of this term differs from Kernell (1997), who uses "Institutionalized Pluralism" as a moniker for the relationship between presidents and party coalitions.

10. This theory, which I call Behavioral Pluralism, draws on important theories built by other scholars that I review in Chapter 2, especially works by Truman (1951), Almond and Verba (1963), Schlozman and Tierney (1986), Walker (1991), Verba et al. (1995), Baumgartner and Leech (1998), Berry (1999), and Strolovitch (2007).

11. This theory, called Institutionalized Pluralism, draws on important ideas from the organizational theory of institutions (Meyer and Rowan 1977; Friedland and Alford 1991; DiMaggio 1997) and findings from interest group research (Schlozman and Tierney 1986; Walker 1991; Wright 1996; Berry 1999; Heaney 2004), which I review in Chapter 4.

12. The theory of interest representation proposed here does not idealize the American state or pretend that every group is equally equipped to pursue policy influence. Instead, the group basis of politics is an analytic starting point; it describes politics as the process of fractured interest aggregation through organized attempts to influence government.

Chapter 1

1. Dean Mathiowetz (2008) argues that all attempts to observe interests ascribe qualities to the people analyzed. In this analysis, I draw from the subjective views of organized leaders in Washington. I do not imply that these leaders, often self-appointed and unelected, have reached proper conceptions of their constituency.

2. A presence includes a political office, political unit, or hired political representation in the Washington region, including suburban Virginia and Maryland.

3. I do not attempt to assess how well the interests of each constituency are expressed by its organized advocates. I take the representative claims of the interest organizations at face value.

4. Although it is always somewhat problematic to define the scope of the units included in an analysis, researchers have to draw the line somewhere. Walker (1991), for example, chose to include only membership organizations but voiced concern with the decision.

5. The advocacy organizations included in my analysis have a range of tax statuses, including 501(c)3, 501(c)4, 501(c)5, 501(c)6, 501(c)7, 501(c)8, 501(c)19, and 501(c)23. These categorizations are not always intuitive; they separate veterans' organizations and farmers' organizations into their own categories but include religious, educational, charitable, scientific, and animal-cruelty organizations within the same designation.

6. Most "think thanks" represent a public political perspective, and most advocacy groups regularly produce research. According to Schlozman and Tierney (1986), 92 percent of interest organizations produce research and present it to policymakers. The line between the two is driven by reputation and relative focus. Some "nonprofit private institutions," such as church groups, also make a clear claim to social group representation.

7. Empirical work on business political activity has largely relied on business-specific factors to analyze relative levels of mobilization (Salaman and Siegfried 1977; Grier, Munger, and Roberts 1994; Hansen and Mitchell 2000). Combining studies of businesses and advocacy organizations may lead to incorrect conclusions about the relative mobilization of each sector (Hart 2004).

8. I note differences among unions, professional associations, and other advocacy groups throughout the book.

9. Only a small proportion of small business owners were mobilized into advocacy organizations. A men's association and a group opposing chain stores engaged in a long conflict to become the voice of the constituency (Young 2010). Today, organizations claiming to represent entrepreneurs and the self-employed enlarge this sector.

10. If an organization's website was not listed in reference text descriptions, we searched for the organization's site using Google, and we called the office.

11. This statement is available at www.fapa.org/main/about_fapa.htm and was retrieved on February 28, 2010.

12. This statement is available at www.athiest.org/about and was retrieved on February 28, 2010.

13. This statement is available at www.afponline.org/pub/gr/advocacy.html and was retrieved on February 28, 2010.

14. This statement is available at www.annanurse.org and was retrieved on February 28, 2010.

15. Some scholars (Strolovitch 2007) refer to "intersectional" groups as only those with overlapping disadvantaged identities, such as poor ethnic minorities. I include any organizations that claim to represent constituencies that share more than one identity, including both disadvantaged and advantaged groups. For examples, black doctors are a constituency at the intersection of an advantaged group and a disadvantaged group.

16. Most of these organizations present themselves as "public interest groups." I categorize them based on the particular ideological or single-issue perspective they claim to advance.

17. I generally follow Erikson, MacKuen, and Stimson (2002) in categorizing liberal issue perspectives as those seeking to advance the size or role of government in programs or regulation and conservative issue perspectives as those seeking to contract the size or role of government. Some noneconomic groups like abortion opponents, however, have obvious ideological affiliations that do not match this division; in these cases, we followed the common ideological associations. When a question arose, I categorized a perspective as nonideological.

18. This statement is available at www.fairus.org/site/PageNavigator/about/ and was retrieved on February 28, 2010.

19. This statement is available at www.equineadvocates.org/aboutus/whoweare .html and was retrieved on February 28, 2010.

20. I collected membership and chapter information for more than 90 percent of advocacy organizations by relying on reference texts and organizational websites.

21. Information about the collection of all indicators is available in the appendix.

22. We lost this basic framework as the "community power" debates over pluralism and elitism locked scholars into bitter disputes (Polsby 1963). Truman's theories were linked with those in the pluralist camp as it became unfashionable to advocate pluralist ideas. Theories of politics premised on interest group conflict, however, remained popular until Olson's (1965) book.

23. Salisbury claims to find only mixed support for these hypotheses. Nevertheless, they seem consistent with my evidence.

24. I confirmed this comparison with both Google Scholar and the Social Science Citation Index.

25. For organizations that do mobilize members, selective benefits are the least important category stimulating membership (McFarland 2004; Gray and Lowery 1996).

Chapter 2

1. These findings reflect my own analysis, reported later in this chapter.

2. Schlozman and Tierney (1986), for example, compare the size of the population in such broad economic roles as "managerial/administrative" and working "at home" with the size of organizational sectors that they view as associated with these roles.

3. This measure includes staff members working on political issues or lobbying policymakers. I generally use the organizational listing in *Washington Representatives*.

4. In previously published material, I reported results with these data for environmental groups (Grossmann 2006b) and ethnic groups (Grossmann 2007). Several descriptions of data and research method are repeated here, matching the wording used in previous publications.

5. I track the mentions of any organization in each sector in the sections describing those who gave testimony from the database of *Federal Document Clearing House Congressional Testimony* maintained by Congressional Quarterly.

6. I focus on advocacy organizations because their activities offer an important view of the process of public interest mobilization, not because they are the only critical actors in political competition. The aggregation of public groups into party coalitions also involves mobilization of some groups more than others. The relative mobilization of corporations, industries, and governments is also important for political outcomes.

7. These analyses use a smaller population size because the associated survey question was asked in fewer years on the cumulative GSS.

Chapter 3

1. I collected data from reference texts, organizational websites, scholarly studies, and Washington media reports.

2. I discuss the procedures for this content analysis along with the coding and collection of each indicator in the appendix.

3. These broad categories are different from the specific sectors of constituency representatives that I reported earlier. Information about the content analysis that led to this categorization is available in the appendix.

4. PAC-contribution data by industry, topic, and year are available from the Center for Responsive Politics at www.opensecrets.org/pacs/sector.php?txt=Q01&cycle=2010 and were retrieved on December 13, 2010.

5. The daily Washington event calendars are the *Federal News Service Daybook,* the *Federal Document Clearing House Political Transcripts,* and *The Washington Daybook.*

6. For a news report on the panel, see Ashish Kumar, "Pakistan Flooding Stirs U.S. Fears," *The Washington Times,* August 25, 2010.

7. A video of the panel is available online at www.heritage.org/Events/2010/10/Polar-Bear and was retrieved on December 13, 2010.

8. A video of the discussion is available online at www.americanprogress.org/events/2010/10/irandebate.html and was retrieved on December 13, 2010.

9. Some notions of access are much more expansive, referring to both regular working relationships and general favoritism (Hansen 1991). In my analysis, interest groups could be quite involved without being favored by policymakers. Hansen (1991), for example, looks not only at whether organizations testify but also at how their testimony is received in back-and-forth exchanges with members of Congress. Involvement would be a step prior to this evaluation.

10. The appendix contains information about the collection and reliability of these indicators.

11. Schlozman and Tierney (1986), Walker (1991), and Strolovitch (2007) each collected measures of the involvement of different sectors of interest groups in different government venues. Their measures were based on self-reports of organizational involvement rather than on publicly observable participation in policymaking.

12. I report information about the collection and reliability of these indicators in the appendix.

13. Bennett Roth, "Union Brass Making No Overtures to the GOP," *Roll Call,* November 17, 2010.

Chapter 4

1. Hansen (1991) finds that policymakers provide expansive access to interest groups that are known to represent constituencies. He argues that they respond strictly to electoral incentives, abandoning interest groups when they no longer represent constituent views. His findings, however, are also consistent with the view that

policymakers do not listen to interest groups that lack the legitimacy associated with public representation. I find that many institutionalized advocacy organizations lack much electoral threat but are still known for their representation.

2. This report is available at www.npr.org/templates/story/story.php?storyId =120069183 and was retrieved on December 5, 2010.

3. Anonymous, "A Closer Look at Retiree Advocacy Groups," *Kiplinger's Retirement Report,* July 1, 2004.

4. Nicholas Confessore, "Bush's Secret Stash," *Washington Monthly,* May 1, 2004.

5. These statistics originate in Senate lobbying office and Federal Election Commission reports and are reported online by the Center for Responsive Politics at www .opensecrets.org/. They were retrieved on December 6, 2010.

6. Anonymous, "Still the Biggest Bruiser? The AARP," *The Economist,* February 5, 2005.

7. Sheryl Gay Stolberg, "An 800-Pound Gorilla Changes Partners over Medicare," *The New York Times,* November 23, 2003.

8. Jeffrey H. Birnbaum, "AARP Leads with Wallet in Fight over Social Security," *The Washington Post,* March 30, 2005.

Chapter 5

1. These reports are taken from Alexander Bolton, "Reid Reassures the Left Lieberman Is on Board," *The Hill,* November 3, 2009, and Jeffrey Young, "House Healthcare Clamor: Business and Drug Groups Blast Bill; Doctors are Uneasy," *The Hill,* October 30, 2009.

2. These reports are taken from Jim Snyder and Silla Brush, "Abortion Resurfaces as Hot Topic on Capitol Hill," *The Hill,* December 1, 2009.

3. This report is taken from Molly K. Hooper, "Gallegly Backs Effort to End 'Barbaric' Cruelty," *The Hill,* September 30, 2009.

4. This report is taken from Thalia Assuras, "PL346: A Look at the G.I. Bill," *CBS Sunday Morning* [CBS News Transcripts], June 22, 2009.

5. I use these models because the dependent variables are integer counts whereby the distributions do not meet the assumptions of Ordinary Least Squares (OLS) regressions. Statistical tests discussed in the appendix confirm that negative binomial count models are the most accurate for predicting media prominence.

6. In these data, most advocacy organizations are mentioned when a representative of that organization is appearing on television or being quoted or paraphrased by a reporter in a print news story. Some advocacy group mentions do not fall into these categories, however, including a few in which the group is being criticized. Nevertheless, these kinds of mentions account for less than 5 percent of cases. Media mentions are therefore an imperfect measure, but one that largely reflects the organizations used as sources by reporters.

7. These models also include separate categories for environmental and consumer organizations.

Chapter 6

1. Institutionalized Pluralism may be broadly consistent with the view that lobbying is a subsidy to policymakers (Hall and Deardorff 2006), but I emphasize the symbolic gains of government institutions rather than the additional staffing resources provided to individual legislators.

2. I collected and aggregated data over the entire ten-year period. As a result, it was impossible to test for differences between organizational mentions in the two administrations. I did collect year-by-year data for a sample of thirty organizations, however, and concluded that the same organizations were involved in both administrations.

3. I use zero-inflated models because the dependent variables are integer counts in which the distributions include a large number of zeros. Statistical tests discussed in the appendix confirm the improved accuracy of these models in comparison to others. The zero-inflated model specification is similar to using a logit together with a count model (Long and Freese 2001) and is most appropriate when different factors may influence whether organizations are involved at all and their amount of involvement. Even though conventional reporting of zero-inflated regressions includes binary coefficients that correspond with models to predict whether cases will receive a count of 0, the models reported here are reversed: Positive coefficients indicate greater levels of involvement.

4. The models are, of course, imperfect representations of the underlying causal processes. Some potential excluded variables, including the experiences and relationships of the staff at each organization, may be important. There are also potential endogeneity problems, because policymaking involvement in previous periods may affect the growth or survival of organizations. Over-time data are needed to pose additional tests for the mechanisms implied by the theory. Nevertheless, these models represent the closest attempts at causal inference yet to be pursued in this research area. They meet the standards of conventional cross-sectional models in social science, such as those used in published work on committee testimony (Leyden 1995; Berry 1999; Rich 2004). The problems associated with them are no more severe than consistent problems in social science, such as those in the analysis of public voting behavior.

5. I chose three hearings that included advocacy organizations as witnesses and had immediately preceded my time in Washington. I do not report the organizational affiliations of my interviewees because I promised anonymity.

6. I chose two final rules that referenced a small number of advocacy organizations as witnesses and had immediately preceded my time in Washington.

Conclusion

1. As Mathiowetz (2008) argues, researchers can present only partial views of these constituencies and their interests. Even though images of group interests are inherently problematic as representations of individuals and their ideas, one should observe that these images play a role in contemporary politics because they are taken for granted by many participants.

2. Most research on the way that political behavior affects competition within government institutions focuses on the impact of election results and public opinion, rather than interest-group mobilization and influence. Erikson et al. (2002), for example, construct a macropolitical model of the relationship between policy outcomes and aggregate partisanship and political ideology in the electorate. Policy-feedback research (Mettler 2005) focuses on this relationship from the other direction, how government policy creates new political behavior. Scholars have yet to develop similar macropolitical models in interest-group research.

3. In other work (Grossmann 2007), I have shown that organizations representing ethnic groups are not distinct from other advocacy organizations. The sectors representing African Americans and Asian Americans, for example, exhibit patterns of behavior and political involvement that more closely resemble different nonethnic interest-group sectors rather than each other. Like ethnic interests, each interest group category may be more productively analyzed in relationship to all other advocacy sectors, rather than as a community responsive to similar circumstances.

4. If interest organizations could be eliminated from governance or made irrelevant, alternative political systems relying on elections or party power could still be justified by relying on democratic norms of public representation and policy deliberation. It is difficult to imagine an electoral or party system that could satisfactorily represent all of America's interests, however, without opening many potential roles for interest groups.

Appendix

1. We visited all of the websites and conducted all of the searches between March and June of 2005. Not all organizations had accessible websites. The models of Web prominence contain approximately one hundred fewer organizations than the other models.

2. The number of times an organization testified, for example, is significantly and strongly correlated with the number of times that it was mentioned by any participant in hearings ($r = .75$) and the number of times that it was mentioned in congressional floor debate over the same decade ($r = .69$). Measures of organization's prominence in congressional hearings and floor debate are derived from *Lexis-Nexis* searches of the Congressional Record from 1995 through 2004.

References

Ainsworth, Scott H. 2002. *Analyzing Interest Groups: Group Influence on People and Policies.* New York: W. W. Norton.

Almond, Gabriel A., and Sidney Verba. 1963. *The Civic Culture: Political Attitudes and Democracy in Five Nations.* Princeton, NJ: Princeton University Press.

Alterman, Eric. 2004. *What Liberal Media? The Truth about Bias and the News.* New York: Basic Books.

Anderson, Brian, and Burdett A. Loomis. 1998. "Taking Organization Seriously: The Structure of Interest Group Influence." In *Interest Group Politics,* 5th ed., edited by Allan J. Cigler and Burdett Loomis, 83–95. Washington, DC: C.Q. Press.

Anderson, David M. 2002. "Cautious Optimism about Online Politics and Citizenship." In *The Civic Web: Online Politics and Democratic Values,* edited by David. M. Anderson and Michael Cornfield, 19–34. New York: Rowman & Littlefield Publishers.

Andrews, Kenneth T., and Bob Edwards. 2004. "Advocacy Organizations in the U.S. Political Process." *Annual Review of Sociology* 30 (1): 479–506.

Arnold, Douglas. 1992. *The Logic of Congressional Action.* New Haven, CT: Yale University Press.

Axelrod, Robert, and D. Scott Bennett. 1993. "A Landscape Theory of Aggregation." *British Journal of Political Science* 23 (2): 211–233.

Baron, David. 2006. "Persistent Media Bias." *Journal of Public Economics* 90 (1): 1–36.

Bartels, Larry. 2008. *Unequal Democracy: The Political Economy of the New Gilded Age.* Princeton, NJ: Princeton University Press.

Baumgartner, Frank R., Jeffrey M. Berry, Marie Hojnacki, David C. Kimball, and Beth L. Leech. 2009. *Lobbying and Policy Change: Who Wins, Who Loses, and Why.* Chicago: University of Chicago Press.

Baumgartner, Frank R., and Bryan D. Jones. 1993. *Agendas and Instability in American Politics*. Chicago: University of Chicago Press.

Baumgartner, Frank R., and Beth L. Leech. 1998. *Basic Interests: The Importance of Groups in Politics and Political Science*. Princeton, NJ: Princeton University Press.

Bentley, Arthur F. 1935. *The Process of Government: A Study of Social Pressures*. Evanston, IL: The Principia Press.

Berry, Jeffrey. M. 1989. *The Interest Group Society*, 5th ed. New York: HarperCollins Publishers.

Berry, Jeffrey M. 1999. *The New Liberalism: The Rising Power of Citizen Groups*. Washington, DC: Brookings Institution Press.

Birnbaum, Jeffrey. H., and Alan Murray. 1987. *Showdown at Gucci Gulch: Lawmakers, Lobbyists, and the Unlikely Triumph of Tax Reform*. New York: Vintage Books.

Bishin, Benjamin. 2009. *Tyranny of the Minority: The Subconstituency Politics Theory of Representation*. Philadelphia: Temple University Press.

Borsook, Paulina. 2000. *Cyberselfish: A Critical Romp through the Terribly Libertarian Culture of High Tech*. London: Little, Brown and Company.

Brint, Steven, and Charles S. Levy. 1999. "Professions and Civic Engagement: Trends in Rhetoric and Practice, 1975–1995." In *Civic Engagement in American Democracy*, edited by Morris P. Fiorina and Theda Skocpol. Washington, DC: Brookings Institution Press.

Browne, William P. 1990. "Organized Interests and their Issue Niches: A Search for Pluralism in a Policy Domain." *Journal of Politics* 52 (2): 477–506.

Burstein, Paul. 2007. "Jewish Educational and Economic Success in the United States: A Search for Explanations." *Sociological Perspectives* 50 (2): 209–228.

Burstein, Paul, and April Linton. 2002. "The Impact of Political Parties, Interest Groups, and Social Movement Organizations on Public Policy: Some Recent Evidence and Theoretical Concerns." *Social Forces* 81 (2): 380–408.

Callaghan, Karen, and Frauke Schnell. 2001. "Assessing the Democratic Debate: How the News Media Frame Elite Policy Discourse." *Political Communication* 18 (2): 183–212.

Campbell, Andrea Louise. 2003. *How Policies Make Citizens: Senior Political Activism and the American Welfare State*. Princeton, NJ: Princeton University Press.

The Capital Source. 2004. Washington: National Journal Group.

Clemens, Elisabeth S. 1997. *The People's Lobby: Organizational Innovation and the Rise of Interest Group Politics in the United States, 1890–1925*. Chicago: University of Chicago Press.

Cigler, Allan J. 1991. "Interest Groups: A Subfield in Search of an Identity." In *Political Science: Looking to the Future: American Institutions*, edited by William J. Crotty, 99–135. Evanston, IL: Northwestern University Press.

Converse, Philip. 1964. "The Nature of Belief Systems in Mass Publics." In *Ideology and Discontent*, edited by David Apter, 206–261. New York: Free Press.

Corrigan, Matthew. 2000. "The Transformation of Going Public: President Clinton, the First Lady, and Health Care Reform." *Political Communication* 17 (2): 149-168.

Dahl, Robert A. 1961. *Who Governs? Democracy and Power in an American City.* New Haven, CT: Yale University Press.

Dahl, Robert A. 1963. *A Preface to Democratic Theory.* Chicago: University of Chicago Press.

D'Alessio, Dave, and Mike Allen. 2000. "Media Bias in Presidential Elections: A Meta-Analysis." *Journal of Communication* 50 (4): 133–156.

Danielian, Lucig H., and Benjamin I. Page. 1994. "The Heavenly Chorus: Interest Group Voices on TV News." *American Journal of Political Science* 38 (4): 1056–1078.

Davis, Richard, ed. 1999. *The Web of Politics: The Internet's Impact on the American Political System.* Oxford, UK: Oxford University Press.

De Tocqueville, Alexis. 1835–1840. *Democracy in America.* London: Saunders and Otley.

Delli Carpini, Michael X., and Scott Keeter. 1997. *What Americans Know about Politics and Why It Matters.* New Haven, CT: Yale University Press.

DiMaggio, Paul. 1997. "Culture and Cognition." *Annual Review of Sociology* 23 (1): 263–287.

Domhoff, G. William. 1967. *Who Rules America?* Englewood Cliffs, NJ: Prentice-Hall.

Downs, Anthony. 1957. *An Economic Theory of Democracy.* New York: Harper and Row.

Encyclopedia of Associations. 2004. New York: Gale Group.

Erikson, Robert S., Michael B. MacKuen, and James A. Stimson. 2002. *The Macro Polity.* Cambridge, UK: Cambridge University Press.

Fernandez, Roberto M., and Roger V. Gould. 1994. "A Dilemma of State Power: Brokerage and Influence in the National Health Policy Domain." *American Journal of Sociology* 99 (6): 1455–1491.

Fiorina, Morris P. 1999. "Extreme Voices: A Dark Side of Civic Engagement." In *Civic Engagement in American Democracy,* edited by Morris P. Fiorina and Theda Skocpol. Washington, DC: Brookings Institution Press.

Foxman, Abraham. 2007. *The Deadliest Lies: The Israel Lobby and the Myth of Jewish Control.* New York: Palgrave Macmillan.

Friedland, Roger, and Robert A. Alford. 1991. "Bringing Society Back In: Symbols, Practices, and Institutional Contradictions." In *The New Institutionalism in Organizational Analysis,* edited by Walter W. Powell and Paul J. DiMaggio, 232–263. Chicago: University of Chicago Press.

Furlong, Scott R., and Cornelius M. Kerwin. 2005. "Interest Group Participation in Rule Making: A Decade of Change." *Journal of Public Administration Research and Theory* 15 (3): 353–370.

Gans, Herbert J. 1979. *Deciding What's News.* New York: Vintage Books.

Goldberg, Bernard. 2003. *Bias: A CBS Insider Exposes How the Media Distorts the News.* New York: HarperCollins.

Goss, Kristin A. 2006. *Disarmed: The Missing Movement for Gun Control in America.* Princeton, NJ: Princeton University Press.

Government Affairs Yellow Book: Who's Who in Government Affairs. 2004. Washington, DC: Leadership Directories.

Graber, Dorris A. 2002. *Mass Media and American Politics,* 6th ed. Washington, DC: C. Q. Press.

Gray, Virginia, and David Lowery. 1996. *The Population Ecology of Interest Representation: Lobbying Communities in the American States.* Ann Arbor: University of Michigan Press.

Gray, Virginia, and David Lowery. 2004. "A Neopluralist Perspective on Research on Organized Interests." *Political Research Quarterly* 57 (1): 163–175.

Greenberg, Stanley B. 2004. *The Two Americas: Our Current Political Deadlock and How to Break It.* New York: Thomas Dunne Books.

Grier, Kevin B., Michael C. Munger, and Brian E. Roberts. 1994. "The Determinants of Industry Political Activity, 1978–1986." *American Political Science Review* 88 (4): 911–926.

Groseclose, Tim, and Jeffrey Milyo. 2004. A Measure of Media Bias. *Quarterly Journal of Economics* 120 (4): 1191–1237.

Grossmann, Matt. 2006a. "The Organization of Factions: Interest Mobilization and the Group Theory of Politics." *Public Organization Review* 6 (2): 107–124.

Grossmann, Matt. 2006b. "Research Note: Environmental Advocacy in Washington." *Environmental Politics* 15 (4): 628–638.

Grossmann, Matt. 2007. "Just Another Interest Group? Organized Ethnic Representation in American Politics." *National Political Science Review* 11 (1): 291–307.

Grossmann, Matt, and Casey B. K. Dominguez. 2009. "Party Coalitions and Interest Group Networks." *American Politics Research* 37 (5): 767–800.

Hacker, Jacob S., and Paul Pierson. 2006. *Off Center: The Republican Revolution and the Erosion of American Democracy.* New Haven, CT: Yale University Press.

Hacker, Jacob S., and Paul Pierson. 2010. *Winner-Take-All Politics: How Washington Made the Rich Richer—and Turned Its Back on the Middle Class.* New York: Simon & Schuster.

Hall, Richard L., and Alan V. Deardorff. 2006. "Lobbying as Legislative Subsidy." *American Political Science Review* 100 (1): 69–84.

Hall, Richard L., and Frank W. Wayman. 1990. "Buying Time: Moneyed Interests and the Mobilization of Bias in Congressional Committees." *American Political Science Review* 84 (3): 797–820.

Hannan, Michael T., and John H. Freeman. 1986. "Where Do Organizational Forms Come From?" *Sociological Forum* 1 (1): 50–72.

Hansen, John Mark. 1991. *Gaining Access: Congress and the Farm Lobby, 1919–1981.* Chicago: University of Chicago Press.

Hansen, Wendy L., and Neil J. Mitchell. 2000. "Disaggregating and Explaining Corporate Political Activity: Domestic and Foreign Corporations in National Politics." *American Political Science Review* 94(4): 891–903.

Hansford, Thomas G. 2004. "Lobbying Strategies, Venue Selection, and Organized Interest Involvement at the U.S. Supreme Court." *American Politics Research* 32(2): 170–197.

Hart, David M. 2004. "Business Is Not an Interest Group: On Companies in American National Politics." *Annual Review of Political Science* 7(1): 47–67.

Hays, R. Allen. 2001. *Who Speaks for the Poor? National Interest Groups and Social Policy.* New York: Routledge.

Heaney, Michael T. 2004. "Outside the Issue Niche: The Multidimensionality of Interest Group Identity." *American Politics Research* 32 (6): 611–651.

Heinz, John P., Edward O. Laumann, Robert L. Nelson, and Robert H. Salisbury. 1993. *The Hollow Core: Private Interests in National Policy Making.* Cambridge, MA: Harvard University Press.

Hertzke, Allen D. 1988. *Representing God in Washington: The Role of Religious Lobbies in the American Polity.* Knoxville: University of Tennessee Press.

Hess, Stephen. 1989. *The Washington Reporters.* Washington, DC: Brookings Institution.

Hofrenning, Daniel. 1995. *In Washington but Not of It: The Prophetic Politics of Religious Lobbyists.* Philadelphia: Temple University Press.

Hojnacki, Marie. 1997. "Interest Groups' Decisions to Join Alliances or Work Alone." *American Journal of Political Science* 41 (1): 61–87.

Holyoke, Thomas T. 2003. "Choosing Battlegrounds: Interest Group Lobbying across Multiple Venues." *Political Research Quarterly* 56 (3): 325–336.

Huckfeldt, Robert. 2007. "Information, Persuasion, and Political Communication Networks." In *The Oxford Handbook of Political Behavior,* edited by Russell J. Dalton and Hans Dieter Klingemann. Oxford, UK: Oxford University Press.

James, Michael Rabinder. 2004. *Deliberative Democracy and the Plural Polity.* Lawrence: University Press of Kansas.

Kagan, Robert A. 2001. *Adversarial Legalism: The American Way of Law.* Cambridge, MA: Harvard University Press.

Kane, John. 2002. Democracy and Group Rights. In *Democratic Theory Today,* edited by April Carter and Geoffrey Stokes. Cambridge, UK: Polity Press.

Kernell, Samuel. 1997. *Going Public: New Strategies of Presidential Leadership,* 3d ed. Washington, DC: Congressional Quarterly Press.

Kerwin, Cornelius M. 2003. *Rulemaking: How Government Agencies Write Law and Make Policy,* 3rd ed. Washington, DC: Congressional Quarterly Press.

Key, V. O. 1964. *Politics, Parties, and Pressure Groups,* 5th ed. New York: Crowell.

Krosnick, Jon A. 1990. "Government Policy and Citizen Passion: A Study of Issue Publics in Contemporary America." *Political Behavior* 12 (1): 59–92.

Lasswell, Harold. 1958. *Politics: Who Gets What, When, How.* New York: World Publishing.

Laumann, Edward O., and David Knoke. 1987. *The Organizational State: Social Choice in National Policy Domains.* Madison: University of Wisconsin Press.

Lawrence, Thomas B., and Roy Suddaby. 2006. "Institutions and Institutional Work." In *The SAGE Handbook of Organization Studies,* 2nd ed., edited by S. Clegg, C. Hardy, T. B. Lawrence, and W. R. Nord, 215–254. London: Sage Publications.

Leyden, Kevin M. 1995. "Interest Group Resources and Testimony at Congressional Hearings." *Legislative Studies Quarterly* 20 (3): 431–439.

Long, J. Scott, and Jeremy Freese. 2001. *Regression Models for Categorical Dependent Variables Using Stata.* College Station, TX: Stata Press.

Lowery, David, and Virginia Gray. 2004. "Bias in the Heavenly Chorus: Interests in Society and Before Government." *Journal of Theoretical Politics,* 16 (1): 5–30.

Mahoney, Christine. 2008. *Brussels Versus the Beltway: Advocacy in the United States and the European Union.* Washington, DC: Georgetown University Press.

Mansbridge, Jane. 1992. "A Deliberative Theory of Interest Representation." In *The Politics of Interests: Interest Groups Transformed,* edited by Mark P. Petracca. Boulder, CO: Westview Press.

Martin, Isaac William. 2008. *The Permanent Tax Revolt: How the Property Tax Transformed American Politics.* Stanford, CA: Stanford University Press.

Mathiowetz, Dean. 2008. "Interest Is a Verb: Arthur Bentley and the Language of Interest." *Political Research Quarterly* 61 (4): 622–635.

Mayhew, David R. 1974. *Congress: The Electoral Connection.* New Haven, CT: Yale University Press.

McCarty, Nolan, Keith T. Poole, and Howard Rosenthal. 2008. *Polarized America: The Dance of Ideology and Unequal Riches.* Cambridge, MA: MIT Press.

McFarland, Andrew S. 1987. "Interest Groups and Theories of Power in America." *British Journal of Political Science* 17 (2): 129–147.

McFarland, Andrew S. 2004. *Neopluralism: The Evolution of Political Process Theory.* Lawrence: University of Kansas Press.

Mearsheimer, John, and Stephen Walt. 2007. *The Israel Lobby and U.S. Foreign Policy.* New York: Farrar, Straus and Giroux.

Melnick, R. Shep. 1994. *Between the Lines: Interpreting Welfare Rights.* Washington, DC: The Brookings Institution.

Melzer, Scott. 2009. *Gun Crusaders: The NRA's Culture War.* New York: New York University Press.

Mettler, Suzanne. 2005. *Soldiers to Citizens: The G.I. Bill and the Making of the Greatest Generation.* Oxford, UK: Oxford University Press.

Meyer, John W., and Brian Rowan. 1977. "Institutional Organizations: Formal Structure as Myth and Ceremony." *American Journal of Sociology* 83 (2): 340–363.

Miles, Raymond E., and Charles C. Snow. 1978. *Organizational Strategy, Structure, and Process.* New York: McGraw-Hill.

Miller, Kristina C. 2007. "The View from the Hill: Legislative Perceptions of Constituents." *Legislative Studies Quarterly* 33 (4): 597–628.

Miller, Mark C. 1995. *The High Priests of American Politics: The Role of Lawyers in American Political Institutions.* Knoxville: University of Tennessee Press.

Miller, Warren E., and J. Merrill Shanks. 1996. *The New American Voter.* Cambridge, MA: Harvard University Press.

Mills, C. Wright. 1956. *The Power Elite.* Oxford, UK: Oxford University Press.

Morris, Charles R. 1996. *The AARP: America's Most Powerful Lobby and the Clash of Generations.* New York: Times Books.

National Trade and Professional Associations of the United States. 2004. Washington, DC: Columbia Books.

Olson, Mancur. 1965. *The Logic of Collective Action: Public Goods and the Theory of Groups.* Cambridge, MA: Harvard University Press.

Patashnik, Eric. 2003. "After the Public Interest Prevails: The Political Sustainability of Policy Reform." *Governance* 16 (2): 203–234.

Patterson, Bradley H. 2000. *The White House Staff: Inside the West Wing and Beyond.* Washington, DC: Brookings Institution Press.

Polsby, Nelson W. 1963. *Community Power and Political Theory.* New Haven, CT: Yale University Press.

Post, Robert C., and Nancy L. Rosenblum. 2002. "Introduction." In *Civil Society and Government,* edited by Robert C. Post and Nancy L. Rosenblum. Princeton, NJ: Princeton University Press.

Public Interest Profiles. 2004. Washington: Congressional Quarterly.

Putnam, Robert D. 2000. *Bowling Alone: The Collapse and Revival of American Community.* New York: Simon & Schuster.

Rich, Andrew. 2004. *Think Tanks, Public Policy, and the Politics of Expertise.* Cambridge, UK: Cambridge University Press.

Rorty, Richard. 1989. *Contingency, Irony, and Solidarity.* Cambridge, UK: Cambridge University Press.

Rudolph, Thomas J, Amy Gangl, and Dan Stevens. 2000. "The Effects of Efficacy and Emotions on Campaign Involvement." *Journal of Politics* 62 (4): 1189–1197.

Sahr, Robert. 1993. "Credentialing the Experts: The Climate of Opinion and Journalist Selection of Sources in Domestic and Foreign Policy." In *Media and Public Policy,* edited by Robert Spitzer, 153–170. Westport, CT: Praeger.

Salaman, Lester M., and John J. Siegfried. 1977. "Economic Power and Political Influence: The Impact of Industry Structure on Public Policy." *American Political Science Review* 71 (3): 1026–1043.

Salisbury, Robert H. 1984. "Interest Representation: The Dominance of Institutions." *American Political Science Review* 78 (1): 64–76.

Salisbury, Robert H. 1992. *Interests and Institutions: Substance and Structure in American Politics.* Pittsburgh: University of Pittsburgh Press.

Schattschneider, Elmer. E. 1960. *The Semisovereign People: A Realist's View of Democracy in America.* New York: Holt, Rinehart and Winston.

Scheingold, Stuart A. 2004. *The Politics of Rights: Lawyers, Public Policy, and Political Change.* Ann Arbor: University of Michigan Press.

Schlozman, Kay Lehman, and John T. Tierney. 1986. *Organized Interests and American Democracy.* New York: Harper & Row.

Schwartz, Stephen. 2006. *Is It Good for the Jews? The Crisis of America's Israel Lobby.* New York: Doubleday.

Sears, David O., and Jack Citrin. 1982. *Tax Revolt: Something for Nothing in California.* Cambridge, MA: Harvard University Press.

Selznick, Philip. 1957. *Leadership in Administration: A Sociological Interpretation.* Evanston, IL: Row & Peterson.

Shaiko, Ronald G. 1998. "Reverse Lobbying: Interest Group Mobilization from the White House and the Hill." In *Interest Group Politics,* 5th ed., edited by Allan J. Cigler and Burdett. Loomis, 255–281. Washington, DC: The Congressional Quarterly Press.

Shaiko, Ronald G. 1999. *Voices and Echoes for the Environment.* New York: Columbia University Press.

Skocpol, Theda. 2003. *Diminished Democracy: From Membership to Management in American Civic Life.* Norman: University of Oklahoma Press.

Skrentny, John D. 2002. *The Minority Rights Revolution.* Cambridge, MA: Harvard University Press.

Smith, Richard A. 1984. "Advocacy, Interpretation, and Influence in the U.S. Congress." *American Political Science Review* 78 (1): 44–63.

Smith, Richard A. 1995. "Interest Group Influence in the U.S. Congress." *Legislative Studies Quarterly* 20 (1): 89–139.

Smith, Jackie, John D. McCarthy, Clark McPhail, and Boguslaw Augustyn. 2001. "From Protest to Agenda Building: Description Bias in Media Coverage of Protest Events in Washington, DC." *Social Forces* 79 (4): 1397–1423.

Spitzer, Robert J. 2004. *The Politics of Gun Control,* 3rd ed. Washington, DC: CQ Press.

Staggenborg, Suzanne. 1994. *The Pro-Choice Movement: Organization and Activism in the Abortion Conflict.* Oxford, UK: Oxford University Press.

Stokes, Goeffrey. 2002. "Democracy and Citizenship." In *Democratic Theory Today,* edited by April Carter and Geoffrey Stokes. Cambridge, UK: Polity Press.

Streb, Matthew J., and Brian Frederick. 2008. "The Myth of a Distinct Catholic Vote." In *Catholics and Politics: The Dynamic Tension between Faith and Power,* edited by Kristin E. Heyer, Mark J. Rozell, and Michael A. Genovese. Washington, DC: Georgetown University Press.

Strolovitch, Dara Z. 2007. *Affirmative Advocacy: Race, Class, and Gender in Interest Group Politics.* Chicago: University of Chicago Press.

Sulkin, Tracy. 2005. *Issue Politics in Congress.* Cambridge, UK: Cambridge University Press.

Tenner, Ed. 2005. "Engineers and Political Power." *Technology Review,* April, 72.

Terkildsen, Nayda, and Frauke Schnell. 1997. "Issue Frames, the Media and Public Opinion: An Analysis of the Women's Movement." *Political Research Quarterly* 50 (4): 877–899.

Terkildsen, Nayda, Frauke Schnell, and Cristina Ling. 1998. "Interest Groups, the Media and Policy Debate Formation." *Political Communication* 15 (1): 45–61.

Truman, David B. 1951. *The Governmental Process: Political Interests and Public Opinion.* New York: Knopf.

Tuchman, Gaye. 1978. *Making News: A Study in the Construction of Reality.* New York: The Free Press.

Uhlaner, Carole J., Bruce E. Cain, and D. Roderick Kiewiet. 1989. "Political Participation of Ethnic Minorities in the 1980s." *Political Behavior* 11 (3): 195–231.

Van Atta, Dale. 1998. *Trust Betrayed: Inside the AARP*. Washington, DC: Regnery Publishing.

Verba, Sidney, Kay Lehman Schlozman, and Henry Brady. 1995. *Voice and Equality: Civic Voluntarism in American Politics*. Cambridge, MA: Harvard University Press.

Walker, Jack L. 1991. *Mobilizing Interest Groups in America: Patrons, Professions, and Social Movements*. Ann Arbor: University of Michigan Press.

Washington Information Directory. 2004. Washington: CQ Press.

Washington Representatives. 2004. New York: Columbia Books.

Weaver, David H., and G. Cleveland Wilhoit. 1991. *The American Journalist: A Portrait of U.S. News*. Bloomington: Indiana University Press.

Wilson, Harry L. 2007. *Guns, Gun Control, and Elections: The Politics and Policy of Firearms*. Lanham, MD: Rowman & Littefield Publishers.

Wilson, James Q. 1995. *Political Organizations*. Princeton, NJ: Princeton University Press.

Winters, Michael Sean. 2008. *Left at the Altar: How the Democrats Lost the Catholics and How the Catholics Can Save the Democrats*. New York: Basic Books.

Wright, John R. 1996. *Interest Groups and Congress: Lobbying, Contributions, and Influence*. Boston, MA: Allyn and Bacon.

Young, McGee. 2010. *Developing Interests: Organizational Change and the Politics of Advocacy*. Lawrence: University of Kansas Press.

Zaller, John R. 1992. *The Nature and Origin of Mass Opinion*. Cambridge, UK: Cambridge University Press.

Index

CPSIA information can be obtained
at www.ICGtesting.com
Printed in the USA
LVHW08s0057090718
583122LV00001B/80/P